COUNSELING AND DEVELOPMENT SERIES
ALLEN IVEY, Editor

CONSTRUCTIVIST THINKING IN
COUNSELING PRACTICE, RESEARCH, AND TRAINING
Thomas L. Sexton & Barbara L. Griffin, Editors

RESEARCH AS PRAXIS
Lessons from Programmatic
Research in Therapeutic Psychology
Lisa Tsoi Hoshmand & Jack Martin, Editors

THE CONSTRUCTION
AND UNDERSTANDING OF
PSYCHOTHERAPEUTIC CHANGE
Conversations, Memories, and Theories
Jack Martin

Constructivist Thinking in Counseling Practice, Research, and Training

EDITED BY

Thomas L. Sexton
Barbara L. Griffin

FOREWORD BY OSCAR F. GONÇALVES

TEACHERS
COLLEGE
PRESS

Teachers College, Columbia University
New York and London

Published by Teachers College Press, 1234 Amsterdam Avenue, New York, NY 10027

Library of Congress Cataloging-in-Publication Data

Constructivist thinking in counseling practice, research, and training
  / edited by Thomas L. Sexton, Barbara L. Griffin ; foreword by Oscar
  F. Gonçalves.
        p.   cm. — (Counseling and development series ; 3)
    Includes bibliographical references and index.
    ISBN 0-8077-3610-4 (cloth : alk. paper). — ISBN 0-8077-3609-0
(pbk. : alk. paper)
      1. Counseling. 2. Constructivism (Psychology) 3. Counselors —
Training of. I. Sexton, Thomas L., 1953–   . II. Griffin,
Barbara L. III. Series.
  BF637.C6C564 1997
  158′.3 — dc21   96-51969

ISBN 0-8077-3609-0 (paper)
ISBN 0-8077-3610-4 (cloth)

Printed on acid-free paper
Manufactured in the United States of America

04 03 02 01 00 99 98 97   8 7 6 5 4 3 2 1

To our children:
Jennifer, Matthew, Michael, and Tamela Denise

We are seeing in our lifetimes the collapse of the objectivist worldview that dominated the modern era, the worldview that gave people faith in the absolute and permanent rightness of certain beliefs and values. The worldview emerging in its place is constructivist. If we operate from this worldview we see all information and all stories as human creations that fit, more or less well, with our experience and within a universe that remains beyond us and always mysterious. . . . Learning about such things, continually reexamining beliefs about beliefs, becomes the most important learning task of all the others needed for survival in our time.

   —Walter T. Anderson, *Reality Isn't What It Used to Be*

Contents

Constructivism and the Deconstruction of Clinical Practice

There is an old Chasidic story of a humble man who, in search of God's enlightenment and without knowing the appropriate prayers, cried out to God while reciting the alphabet, "Since I don't know the prayers I am sending you the alphabet so that you can make the prayers out of the letters I am sending." There is no record of what God did, but if She is indeed the supreme constructivist of the universe, She would certainly have helped this creature with the construction of his prayers through her own discourse.

Constructivists believe that in the counseling or therapeutic situation we are confronted with a task similar to that faced by God in this Chasidic story — helping our clients with the construction of knowledge by the expansion of their alphabet into more flexible, viable, and complex acts of telling (language, conversations, and narratives).

For the past two decades, constructivism has captured the interest of those who understand the individual as an "active agent seeking order and meaning in social contexts where his or her uniquely personal experiences are challenged to continue developing" (Mahoney, 1996, p. 5). As a result of this interest, Mahoney (1996) has recently pointed out, the number of "constructivist" words has nearly doubled during the last 20 years in the psychological literature. This vocabulary increase reflects an equivalent burgeoning of constructivist perspectives, connected only by the idea of continuous, active, and multiple possibilities for existing and knowing (Gonçalves, 1995a).

These postmodern times are characterized by an accelerating movement through life that creates a context for a multivocal, multicultural, and multiphrenic society. The individual is faced with the task of living multiple lives with alternative selves, within the space of what used to be considered a single life. Helping the individual to continue developing creatively with this multiplicity is a common object of constructivist practice.

Given the pluralistic nature of constructivism, a single scholastic conception would be a contradiction in terms. It is interesting to note that constructivism has been growing in influence across several schools of counseling and psychotherapy, including cognitive (e.g., Mahoney, 1995); experiential (e.g., Greenberg & Pascual-Leone, 1995); and family systems (e.g., White & Epston, 1990). As a result of the diversity of its conceptual roots, we are faced with multiple constructivist approaches to counseling and psychotherapy that could generically, as pointed out by Neimeyer (1995), also be organized in different metaphors: therapy or counseling as personal science (Kelly, 1955; Neimeyer & Neimeyer, 1987); therapy as selfhood development (Guidano, 1991; Ivey, 1986; Mahoney, 1991); therapy as narrative development (Gonçalves, 1995b); and therapy as conversational elaboration (Efran, Lukens, & Lukens, 1990).

Sexton and Griffin face the major challenge of representing in a single volume this diversity of constructivist approaches and identifying how these diverse notions converge in a set of common proposals for counseling practice, research, and training. Counseling psychology was born out of a need to create an alternative model to the traditional clinical practice. Unfortunately, for several decades the modernist and positivist philosophies have threatened counseling psychology with extinction. I see Sexton and Griffin's book as an important part of a movement that will take us back to our original commitment to cultural, developmental, and societal issues, thus bringing new breadth to counseling as well as new scope to all clinical practices.

Within the diversity and richness of the contributions that Sexton and Griffin have put together, I can easily identify what I believe are the core assumptions of a postmodernist version of constructivism, emphasizing the centrality of language, conversations, and narrative in knowing. Let me briefly go through some of these assumptions.

EXISTENCE AS KNOWLEDGE

The constructivist approaches represented here are consistent in their emphasis on the inseparability of existence and knowledge. As we have been reminded by evolutionary biology, all living beings know and change their knowledge in the course of existence. Unicellular beings know their environment without the need for assuming the existence of any representational system; to live is to know. This primacy of an experiential knowing is in firm opposition to all essentialist and apriorist models of cognition, which seek to establish the primacy of essences over existence.

This experiential view of knowing has two correlative implications. First is the proactive nature of human beings. Equating existence with knowledge implies a conception of individuals as intentional, motoric, and proactive beings. That is, by existing, human beings are always in the process of creating new and alternative realities. To exist is to create and to create is to know. In this way, the work of counseling is approached not as a sort of technical intervention to adjust minds, but rather as a supportive process to help overcome any blocking in this creative process of existing.

Second, equating existence with knowledge brings the body to a new position of centrality—*not* the body as a location for new psychological essences, as was the dream of phrenology, but a body in process and movement. Whatever we do involves us totally with our body and this cannot be separated from our knowing. Our mind is intrinsically embodied, in the sense that we do not *have* a knowledge more than we *are* a knowledge.

KNOWLEDGE AS HERMENEUTICS

Let me turn now to the second assumption—the assumption that all knowledge (and by implication, all existence) is hermeneutic. Constructivism, in substituting the retroactive sensorial models of knowing by proactive motoric ones, switches the emphasis to an individual constructing knowledge through a process of active encoding. In fact, the symbolic construction of reality corresponds to a process of meaning–generation operating through the imposing of hermeneutic processes. What characterizes psychological phenomena is precisely this process of active construction of meanings and the process by which these meanings come to be the psychological world of the individual. In this sense, to understand human behavior is above all to understand the interpretative systems used by the individuals to construct and expand the meaning of their experiences.

Writing of the centrality of meaning brings me back to the issue of hermeneutics—the discipline concerned with the interpretation of the narrative. Here, hermeneutics assumes a completely different meaning from the one that inspired its tradition for centuries. Hermeneutics was the searching for general and final meanings capable of offering, within its limits, clarifications for the meaning of existence itself. Initially used in the interpretation of sacred literature and later on of legal writings, by the turn of the century hermeneutics was finally applied to the interpretation of individual discourse by psychoanalysis. In all these cases, hermeneutics has attempted interpretation based on a set of predefined and essentialist assumptions. In psychoanalysis, a hermeneutic coding system (metapsychology) was used to bring meaning to clients' experience.

By contrast, within the constructivist approach, the hermeneutic role is fundamentally a liberating one. It is our hermeneutic nature that allows us to creatively liberate our knowledge for multiple constructions of meaning. There are no definite or final meanings just as there are no other essences. Our knowledge is hermeneutic in the sense that it allows multiple interpretations. The multiplicity of existence in its infinite forms implies the possibility of multiple meanings and therefore an infinitely complex unfolding of knowledge.

I am arguing against the existence of any foundational and authoritative epistemology as the illuminating source of knowledge, and for the existence of a hermeneutic that allows multiple and creative knowing in a multivocal, multilinguist, multicultural, multiphrenic, and kaleidoscopic reality.

HERMENEUTICS AS NARRATIVE DISCOURSE

I have argued, so far, that knowledge is inseparable from existence and that both are organized in the individual in a hermeneutic process of meaning construction. It is now important to clarify the hermeneutic process. Here we face two major hypotheses. For the defenders of logical positivism, hermeneutics is synonymous with a universal and abstract logic originating within a formalized system of cognitive operations with a set of fundamental and invariant processes. Mainstream psychology has enthusiastically embraced this concept of a mathematical formulation of thought that could legitimate a closer connection with the so-called hard sciences. This is the main theme for the first cognitive revolution. The computer metaphor grows out of this attempt to establish a digital hermeneutic; and current evolutions of the metaphor as represented by the connectionist and neoconnectionist approaches (moving from linear to parallel and distributed process) are further refinements in this attempt to map out a universal and formal logic of meaning.

This digital and abstract hermeneutic, however, begins to fail once we apply it to the process by which actual human beings construct meanings out of their existence. Individuals behave in a different manner from the one that would be dictated by the inspection of logical alternatives.

The construction of meanings outside a logical hermeneutic is not synonymous with an individual's operating in an irrational way, however. Quite the contrary: the ability to construct multiple reasons and meanings at any moment of an experience is rendered possible by the multiple and creative nature of human language and discourse. It is in language that meaning is constructed. Increasingly, psychology is recognizing that language and discourse are both the means and the ends of meaning and knowing. Contrary to mainstream tradition, language and discourse should be approached directly, head-on, and not simply as indicators of a preexisting internal or external reality.

A hermeneutic of language, the alternative I am suggesting, cannot be seen as resulting exclusively from the words taken as the single elements of abstract symbolization. If this were the case, the words would turn into the new quarks of a discursive psychology and we would regress to some of the essentialist perspectives that have dominated psycholinguistics. The hermeneutic and meaning nature of language results, above all, from the process by which words are combined with one another in the establishment of a narrative plot or matrix. It is within this narrative matrix that the individual proactively and creatively constructs a reality of meanings. We are talking here of a narrative in action, a narrative that exists only in the process of telling (Gergen & Kaye, 1992), a narrative as a speech act (Harré & Gillet, 1994).

Narrative is a fundamental aspect of human knowing. It is narrative that links us in interpretative and multipotential ways to an experience. We think in the same way we live — through narratives. Narrative is a process of experiencing the complexity of our space and time. Contrary to logic, which grants primacy to the abstract, narrative condenses meaning in a language of particulars, the language of existence. There is therefore no need to refer to essences dissociated from the individual's experiential matrix; in remaining close to existence, narrative is liberating. For the human species, narrative and being are inseparable; from this tight association results the infinite creativity of human knowledge.

NARRATIVE DISCOURSE AS CULTURE

It is important to clarify that — similar to words and other aspects of existence — narrative is not located in an isolated individual, originating and closing itself in a system of exclusive autopoiesis. Narrative, by its existential and hermeneutic nature, is intertwined within a network of relationships. Contrary to some recent accounts in schema theory, narratives are not here seen as essential elements stored in the more passive or active archives of short- or long-term memory. Narratives exist only in an interpersonal discursive world and as such are absolutely inseparable from their cultural locations. All narrative, as all knowledge, is interpersonal and contextual: people in conversation.

It is now widely recognized that knowledge can be meaningful only when located in a given time and place and therefore in the narrative interpersonal context surrounding it. Narratives are therefore systems of signification that operate in a dialogical context and are located in the space of interindividuality. That is, they are neither within nor outside the individual; they are a continuous flux between individuals. Narratives bring meaning to existence by making the experiences communal. In the human being, constructing meaning is a process of making common, of sharing and exchanging. Narratives form the patterns that unify or connect individuals within and between themselves, offering the possibility for individuals to know more about themselves by exploring the boundaries between themselves and others.

In this evolving process, the individual experiences simultaneously a process of differentiation and communality, as two sides of the same coin. As differentiation grows it increases the communality and solidarity of the discursive construction. The final anthropogenic objective of all the narrative differentiation is to render the experience communal.

Ultimately, it is the conception of an individual self as the central element of human experience that is being challenged. As stated before, the self is in process — a self that can be defined only by the possibilities of transcending itself in a process of continuous movement. Individuals are defined by their movement in the cultural space. The deconstruction of a single self as a final and stable essence of identity is probably one of the great challenges facing current psychological theory and practice. The challenge to transcend the self is particularly threatening for psychotherapy, which was born and developed with the idea of a distinctive self, and has as its clinical objective this very project: to know thyself.

These four assumptions, explicit or implicit in the following chapters, are major challenges for the deconstruction of counseling and clinical practices. For decades, counselors and therapists — across most of the therapeutic orientations — have been working under a central metaphor: as the doctors of the individual interior. That is, our clients have been characterized as well-identified, autonomous, and isolated individuals facing various kinds of inner issues. The objective of counseling within this metaphor is a quick cure of an individual inner issue with the counselor as the doctor/fixer. I believe that the major task for psychology and psychotherapy in the next century is to understand how the objective of clinical practice can move from the individual as entity to the narrative interspace between individuals — the proximal zone for psychological development: to treat the narratives of our practice not as revelations of individual traumas, but as cultural tellings that can by means of a conversational process evolve into a new order of coherence and complexity.

To return to the Chasidic story with which I began, Sexton and Griffin did well their job of helping the impressive list of contributors in this volume construct creative meanings out of our common alphabet. The following chapters are comprehensive, challenging, and stimulating, and will help us all think about our practices, research and training in new, more inclusive and viable ways. I believe that the reader will be inspired.

OSCAR F. GONÇALVES

REFERENCES

Efran, J. S., Lukens, M. D., & Lukens, R. J. (1990). *Language, structure and change.* New York: Norton.

Gergen, K. J., & Kaye, J. (1992). Beyond the narrative in the negotiation of therapeutic meaning. In S. McNamee & K. Gergen (Eds.), *Therapy as social construction* (pp. 166–185). London: Sage.

Gonçalves, O. F. (1995a). Hermeneutics, constructivism, and the cognitive-behavioral therapies: From the object to the project. In R. Neimeyer & M. J. Mahoney (Eds.), *Constructivism in psychotherapy* (pp. 195–230). Washington, DC: American Psychological Association.

Gonçalves, O. F. (1995b). Cognitive narrative psychotherapy: The hermeneutic construction of alternative meanings. In M. J. Mahoney (Ed.), *Cognitive and constructivist psychotherapies* (pp. 139–162). New York: Springer.

Greenberg, L., & Pascual-Leone, J. (1995). A dialectical constructivist approach to experiential change. In R. Neimeyer & M. J. Mahoney (Eds.), *Constructivism in psychotherapy* (pp. 169–194). Washington, DC: American Psychological Association.

Guidano, V. F. (1991). *The self in process.* New York: Guilford Press.

Harré, R., & Gillet, G. (1994). *The discursive mind.* London: Sage.

Ivey, A. E. (1986). *Developmental therapy.* San Francisco: Jossey-Bass.

Kelly, G. A. (1955). *The psychology of personal constructs.* New York: Norton.

Mahoney, M. J. (1991). *Human change processes.* New York: Basic Books.

Mahoney, M. J. (Ed.). (1995). *Cognitive and constructive psychotherapies.* New York: Springer.

Mahoney, M. J. (1996). Constructivism and the study of complex self-organization. *Constructive Change, 1,* 3–8.

Neimeyer. R. A. (1995). Constructivist psychotherapies: Features, foundations, and future directions. In R. Neimeyer & M. J. Mahoney (Eds.), *Constructivism in psychotherapy* (pp. 11–38). Washington, DC: American Psychological Association.

Neimeyer, R. A., & Neimeyer, G. J. (1987). *Personal construct therapy casebook.* New York: Springer.

White, M., & Epston, D. (1990). *Narrative means to therapeutic ends.* New York: Norton.

Preface

Professional knowledge develops in evolutionary ways. As knowledge grows, so do questions. Questions lead to the discovery of exceptions, which breed *new* ways of thinking that provide increasingly viable maps of the territory. We have come to the constructivist way of thinking in much the same evolutionary manner. In our work as counselors, educators, and researchers we repeatedly experienced the limitations of the modernistic assumptions that form the foundation of counseling knowledge and practice. To us as practitioners, the worlds of our clients were always richer and more complex than the descriptions rendered from applying any of our current theories. Even though we were both trained in the techniques and assumptions of the scientific method, we have been increasingly concerned with the ecological validity of research that is singularly defined as a logical positivist process. As educators we struggle with the immense responsibility of preparing new members of the profession and the challenge of facilitating their development in such a way that they will be both flexible and effective in a rapidly changing world. Through these activities we have become increasingly convinced that it is the core assumptions that form the foundation of these professional endeavors that is limiting.

This volume is an important step along our path of attempting to make sense of the changing world of counseling practice, research, and training. We also think it represents an important new direction for the professions involved in the application of psychological science. In 1993, a group of us gathered at the annual meeting of the Association of Counselor Educators and Supervisors and began a dialogue about constructivism. We spent most of three days together debating, learning, and questioning what to us was something very new: social constructionism. We know now that these *new* ideas are in fact quite old; however, to us they were an exciting and refreshing perspective from which to pull together many of the concerns and questions we had developed through our professional lives. The core of that group has stayed together, added others along the way, and continued to dialogue. The results of this collaboration can be found in the following chapters.

CONSTRUCTIVIST THINKING IN COUNSELING PRACTICE, RESEARCH, AND TRAINING addresses the application of a postmodern perspective to counseling and psychology. In these pages each of the authors engages readers in a dialogue about deconstructing the very fundamental assumptions of the psychological professions *and* the constructivist alternative.

This book is based on three assumptions. First, we chose *constructivism* to represent the approaches contained within these pages. Constructivism is a broad philosophical arena with historical roots in various disciplines (see Chapters 1 and 2 for a more complete discussion). We see constructivism as a term that represents the many specific theoretical and therapeutic variations currently being developed in this area. We chose to treat these variations in a broad and inclusive way and to leave the fine philosophical distinctions for other forums.

Our second assumption has to do with the intended audience of this book. Our focus is on the variety of professions that are involved in *psychological science*. Psychologists, counselors, and social workers all engage, to one degree or another, in the practice of therapeutic change, systematic research, and/or professional training. We are interested in addressing the core assumptions that are shared by the various psychological professions.

Our third assumption is that activities of these professionals extend well beyond the therapeutic activities of individual, group, and family counseling. Psychological science also encompasses systematic inquiry into the behaviors of clients and principles of practice that might effectively promote therapeutic change. Furthermore, it involves the education, training, and supervision of those who aspire to enter these professions. Our journey into postmodern thought has led us to believe that the constructivist paradigm may provide a useful frame for understanding each of these areas of professional activity.

The volume is organized in five parts. Part I provides the *theoretical basis* for the chapters that follow. In Chapter 1, Sexton discusses the developing questions about psychological science as a modern enterprise and places the constructivist thinking within a context of evolving eras of human believing. In Chapter 2, Hayes and Oppenheim make the case that while there are different variations of constructivism, each shares a common core of assumptions that is constructivist thinking. The final three chapters of this section place the theoretical issues of Chapters 1 and 2 into the *context* of current professional practice. Chapter 3 takes a constructivist lens to the cultural context in which practice, research, and education exist. Wentworth and Wentworth propose a dialectical link between the socially constructed structures of culture and our personal and professional mind-selves. Gender, both a biological reality and complex social construction, is the focus of Chapter 4. Terry Guyer and Rowell deconstruct traditional feminist theory and propose a constructivist rebuilding in which the concept of equality as sameness is replaced with the idea of equality in time and space. Chapter 5 (Rigazio-DiGilio) proposes a constructivist model for understanding the developmental evolution of clients and counselors.

Parts II through IV apply these theoretical principles to the activities typically engaged in by counselors, psychologists, and social workers. Part II reflects the integration of constructivist thinking into the core elements of counseling practice. Gordon and Efran (Chapter 6) illustrate how constructivist thinking can provide a common perspective from which to view successful behavior change processes and argue that language is at the center of the change process. Steenbarger and Pels (Chapter 7), Peavy (Chapter 8), and Forster (Chapter 9) apply these common principles to counseling practice in multicultural, vocational, and educational contexts (respectively).

Part III applies constructivist principles to the methods of counseling research. Nelson and Poulin (Chapter 10) detail a postmodern perspective for systematic inquiry in which systematic qualitative methods may be most helpful. Daniels and White (Chapter 11) apply these principles to the complex task of defining and measuring therapeutic change.

Part IV details the developments in professional training and supervision that have accompanied a constructivist shift in thinking. Neufeldt (Chapter 12) takes a constructivist look at supervision, one of the primary ways in which student counselors learn and develop a therapeutic repertoire. In Chapter 13, Lovell and McAuliffe look at the process of counselor training, while Winslade, Monk, and Drewery (Chapter 14) discuss their narrative-based counselor training program in New Zealand.

In Part V, we pull these constructivist strands together and look ahead at the broad issues of implementing a new paradigm. In the final chapter (Chapter 15) we consider the political and paradoxical implications of adopting this paradigm. Constructivism is based on the premise that there are multiple realities. While providing a new perspective, constructivism acknowledges that it only represents a *different* lens from which to view counseling and psychology.

We are indebted to many individuals who have contributed to this work in either direct or indirect ways. It was Jay Carey and Ernest Washington at the University of Massachusetts who organized the social constructivist think tank from which this collaboration originated. Along the way our clients and students have provided us with a forum for questioning, discussing, and thinking about our assumptions of practice, research, and training. It was in these conversations that many of these ideas took shape. Brian Ellerbeck and Carol Collins of Teachers College Press provided the support and guidance necessary to make the project a reality. Sarah Biondello and Lyn Grossman served as development and production editors, providing an invaluable eye to detail. Michelle Weibel was exceptionally patient and helpful in typing and editing. Finally, as Series Editor, Allen Ivey was instrumental in giving us the opportunity to write the book.

PART I

The Constructivist Paradigm

CHAPTER 1

Constructivist Thinking Within the History of Ideas: The Challenge of a New Paradigm

Thomas L. Sexton

Like the other behavioral sciences, counseling and psychology wholeheartedly embraced the dominate assumptions of the scientific method. Today, modernistic assumptions form the foundation of these professions. It is increasingly apparent, however, that research and theory based on modernistic assumptions may not be the most viable way to understand the personal and professional worlds in which we live (Gergen, 1994). Consider a number of examples. We are apparently unable to find the fundamental principles of behavior change (Mahoney, 1991), the common elements of successful counseling and psychotherapy (Bergin & Garfield, 1994), or the most useful match between client and theory (Orlinsky & Howard, 1986). Furthermore, we have yet to determine what characteristics and skills constitute an effective counselor (Christenson & Jacobson, 1993), or which interpersonal factors constitute an effective counseling relationship (Gelso & Carter, 1985; Sexton & Whiston, 1994). Practitioners do not seem influenced by counseling research because of its seeming irrelevance to the reality of clinical practice (Howard, 1986). In addition, there are increasing calls from disenchanted consumers questioning the relevance and applicability of our theoretical models to various social, ethnic, and gender groups (Enns & Hackett, 1993).

As these and other concerns grow, it appears that there is a quiet revolution under way that has the potential to dramatically change the face of counseling practice, supervision, and training. It is an increasing disenchantment with the validity of our epistemological and ontological assumptions of the scientific method that fueled this revolution (Gergen, 1982, 1994; Hoffman, 1990; Kuhn, 1970; Taylor, 1971; von Foerster, 1984; von Glasersfeld, 1984). This growing revolution is being carried out as part of an era characterized by a *postmodern* critique that has focused attention on the fundamental

3

epistemological foundations of professional knowledge and practice of all the behavioral sciences (Gergen, 1985; Howard & Conway, 1986; Wittgenstein, 1969).

The purpose of this volume is to apply a *constructivist* lens to the varied activities of psychologists, counselors, and social workers. At the center of all of these activities is a set of assumptions, both individual and professional, that guide our varied actions. The purpose of this chapter is to apply the constructivist models that have grown from this epistemological revolution into a perspective relevant for counseling practice, research, supervision, and training and thus to provide a *context* for the chapters that follow.

Like the modernist phase, the emerging constructivist era of thinking is but one phase in the ongoing history of human ideas. It, like previous eras, forms a context in which professional knowledge develops and methods of practice evolve (Bartley, 1984; Gergen, 1994; Houts, 1989; Kuhn, 1977). These eras of human believing are the first subject of this chapter. Many of the theoretical and research dilemmas with which psychological science is struggling may be more epistemological than technical. Thus, the limitations of the prevailing modern approach to knowledge and the postmodern challenge to these prevailing beliefs are the second topic of consideration. Third, the alternative postmodern perspective in general, and constructivism in particular, is discussed. Constructivism offers a unique and potentially valuable alternative paradigm for psychological practice, research, and training (Mahoney, 1991). The final section offers suggestions regarding the application of a constructivist paradigm across the spectrum of counseling and psychology that serves as an outline for the remainder of the volume.

THE CHANGING NATURE OF HUMAN BELIEF SYSTEMS

It is easy to assume that the manner in which any one of us views reality is founded on facts that are stable and enduring. However, from a historical perspective, we have experienced a number of *distinct* periods of prevailing human belief systems that have evolved through time (Popper, 1972a; Popper & Eccles, 1977).

Each of these periods of human thinking embraced a dominate view of reality (ontology), a model for how one develops knowledge within that view of reality (epistemology), and a set of accepted practices based on those assumptions. These epistemological and ontological assumptions socialize those living in a specific time and form the basis for how individuals understand themselves and how they make sense of the events occurring in the world. These basic assumptions support certain ways of understanding, knowing, and behaving (they are logical within the prevailing assumptions) and discourage others (which are illogical within the prevailing assumptions). Gergen (1985) argued that the assumptions of the prevailing belief system have more of an effect on the explanations developed to explain the events in the world than do any objective *facts*. Thus, understanding the evolving nature of human ideas may help put the current constructivist revolution into context.

Three distinct eras illustrate the evolving nature of the history of human believing (Mahoney, 1991). The first era grew out of the mystical, mythical, and supernatural world of early man (labeled by Mahoney as a prementation stage) around the sixth century B.C. (see Figure 1.1). This era took two directions, each based on similar assumptions. The first, religion, emphasized the value and power of faith in a higher power and took hold in the development of the first world religions — Buddhism and Zoroastrianism. These early religious systems paved the way for the development of Islam, Christianity, and other modern religions. The second direction, rational philosophy, drew attention to the power of thinking and reason.

The assumptions of this first era forged a prevalent belief system that influenced how reality, knowledge, and action were explained. The ontological premises of dualism (reality in distinct dimensions: the physical and the nonphysical; the mental and the spiritual), idealism (reality an idea-based abstraction), and realism (reality a singular and stable entity external to human thought) emerged. The epistemological principles of rationalism (knowledge based in reason) came to dominate the manner in which we developed knowledge of the world.

These emerging assumptions allowed a *new* way to look at the world. People could now draw distinctions between the physical world and the spiritual world, between body and mind, and between real and illusory. New explanations and, thus, new knowledge developed. The gods (the spiritual world) or man's will (the mind) caused life experiences. New solutions to problems "suddenly" became apparent. Effective change efforts were prayer, faith, thinking, effort, and/or reasoning. The pragmatic effect of this era was to promote the areas of philosophy (holders and discovers of knowledge) and religion (practitioners of that knowledge) as legitimate entities with important cultural roles.

The next significant changes in human belief systems did not occur for almost 19 centuries (Mahoney, 1991). Emerging from the Dark and Middle ages, it was the Enlightenment of the Renaissance that ushered in the second era of human thought, the "modern" period. Empiricism and the scientific revolution dominated this era (see Figure 1.1). The assumptions of this era argued for an ontological position in which knowledge (truth) was objective fact independent of the person or the observer. These stable and objective laws were universal principles, discoverable objective observation, reason, for-

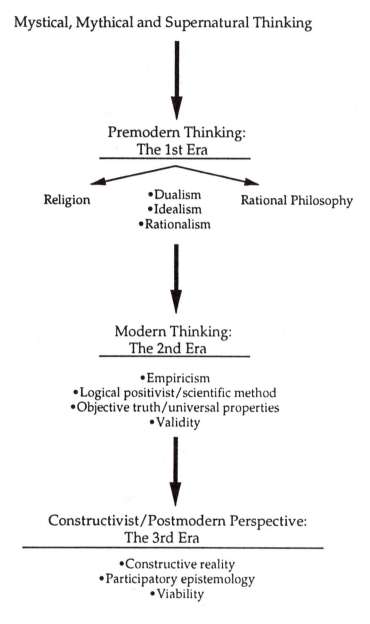

FIGURE 1.1. The Eras of Human Believing

mal logic, and rational thought. Science was a logical and empirical method for developing hypotheses, empirically gathering objective data, assigning meaning to those data, and developing theories.

One consequence of the scientific era was to solidify scientific and professional knowledge as *the* legitimate source of understanding the world. Through the logical process of science we could discover that which was true and explain the reality of the natural and psychological world. Scientific knowledge was assumed to be a mirror image of objective reality. The practice of science became the legitimate means for searching out the theoretical and empirical propositions that would describe the fundamental nature of the world. The knowledge developed through science became synonymous with *truth* (Houts, 1989).

The promise of the scientific era was appealing. Adherence to the path of discovery through the scientific method would reveal the wonders of nature, the fundamental principles of the world, and the universal rules by which our physical and psychological worlds work. Scientific knowledge would allow us to make accurate predictions about cause-and-effect relationships. Thus, we could, once appropriate technologies were developed, gain a mastery of the world (Gergen & Kaye, 1992). As this tradition took hold, it filled a void created by the decline in traditional religious values of the earlier era.

The impact of the *scientific* approach of believing cannot be underestimated. The logical positivist assumptions of this era have become synonymous with the methodology of science and systematic inquiry and have dominated our "scientific thinking" for centuries. The assumptions of the scientific revolution continue to dominate Western cultural, scientific, and professional thought and practice.

It was the dawn of the 20th century that brought the meager beginnings of a third era. Increasingly theorists had to break the mold of traditional science to understand the complex problems of their fields. Theoretical advances in the areas of relativity, quantum mechanics, and the self-regulating universe introduced the notion of the relative, as opposed to the absolute, nature of observation (Capra, 1983; Hawkings, 1988). Heisenberg suggested that it was not a single order that made up science but rather a randomness. In biology, von Bertanlanffy (1968) suggested that living systems were self-regulatory and thus called into question the dualistic notion of the separation of mind and body with the advancement of general systems theory. In mathematics the notions of indeterminacy challenged the assumption of stability and order (Gleick, 1987).

These developments fueled a growing disenchantment with the singular definition of legitimate knowledge, science, and professional practice inherent in the prevailing logical positivist assumptions. The growing critique found support in earlier philosophical principles of Vico and Kant, among others. Vico (credited as the founder of constructivism) suggested that humans create order by projecting familiar categories onto unfamiliar particles. Kant (in the form of Kantian idealism) similarly suggested that the mind imposes its own inherent structures on the particulars of thought and action (Kant, 1783/1911). Vaihinger (1911/1924), the originator of the philosophy of *as is*— later adopted by Adler (1926/1972) and Kelly (1955)—argued that the object of ideas is not to portray reality but to provide us with an instrument for finding our way in the world.

Challenges to and critiques of the fundamental assumptions of absolute truth, objectivity, and validity (the hallmarks of the modern era) characterized this third era. What is unique is that the postmodern critique has focused attention on the epistemological and ontological assumptions of thinking. As modernistic assumptions came under scrutiny, new views of the origins of knowledge emerged. From an evolutionary perspective, Popper (1972b) suggested that theoretical knowledge thrives not because of its *truth* value but because of a process of natural selection. As in Darwinian theory, ideas that have comparative "fitness" survive and become part of scientific truth. From a historical analysis, Kuhn (1970) argued that knowledge and realities of science were as much historical and relative as they were absolute and true. He suggested that major theoretical changes do not follow the modernistic principles of formal logic. Instead, scientific change is more a function of changing and evolving social consciousness and values applied in different degrees at different times. Thus, stability in science may be due to the adherence of scientists to a common set of assumptions and practices over a time rather than to its truth and validity.

The postmodern perspective calls for a participatory epistemology that replaces the "modern" principle of validity with a constructivist concept of viability. The perspective of the observer and the object of observation are inseparable; the nature of meaning is relative; phenomena are context-based; and the process of knowledge and understanding is social, inductive, hermeneutical, and qualitative (Gergen, 1985). The search for truths shifts from stable and generalizable rules and principles to the constructed and contextualized reason for action (Mahoney, 1991). Emphasis is on the contextual and relative nature of reality and suggests that rather than discover reality we invent or co-construct it (Watzlawick, 1984). The postmodern perspective is increasingly finding its way into many of the academic disciplines, including: anthropology (Geertz, 1973), social psychology (Gergen, 1994; Sampson, 1989), hermeneutics (Gadamer, 1975), and literary criticism (Barthes, 1979; Derrida, 1976).

THE SCIENCE AND PRACTICE OF COUNSELING: THE LIMITATIONS OF LOGICAL POSITIVISM

There is no question that the era of logical positivism led to important discoveries in many fields. As in other sciences, the logical positivist promise of a universal understanding and stable truth in psychological science has remained elusive. The discovery of fundamental principles of the world has become increasingly difficult from within the narrow assumptions that are science in the modern era. As the complexity of behavior increases, the exceptions to our general rules grow. Instead of identifying the general rules that apply across people and situations, it is not uncommon for studies of similar behavioral phenomena to produce contradictory results that may be statistically significant but are practically unimportant.

For example, theory and research on the nature of successful counseling have consistently found that one of the most influential aspects of counseling is the quality of the relationship between client and counselor (Bergin & Garfield, 1994; Lambert, 1989; Orlinski & Howard, 1986). However, in a recent review of the counseling relationship research, Sexton and Whiston (1994) determined that our present state of knowledge in that area is characterized by mixed, contradictory, and inconclusive research results. In other cases we have found that most of the variance in clinical research is attributable to *error* or individual difference. As an example, consider a study of counselor response modes and client interaction, in which Hill and colleagues (1988) found that 1% of the variance in client rating of therapist helpfulness was related to counselor responses, whereas 36% to 43% was directly related to individual client differences! Interestingly, that 1% of accounted for variance was statistically significant and thus, from a logical positivist perspective, theoretically important.

The predominant theoretical models of counseling have had an equally disappointing track record. Like researchers, the counseling theorists assumed that when ideas were based on careful and rational induction, one could move from observation to *valid* theoretical description and explanation. Theory, like scientific observation, would be neutral and reflect an explanation of the world as it is. Unfortunately, this does not seem to be the case. For example, current empirical evidence suggests that for counseling outcome, all theoretical approaches are equally effective (Garfield & Bergin, 1994; Whiston & Sexton, 1993). In our search for understanding we constructed an apparently endless list of psychological constructs (e.g., self-esteem, co-dependency, self-actualization, irrational beliefs, self-efficacy). Even more discouraging is that the conceptual models used to explain psychological events differ significantly from culture to culture and rarely are universal (Lee, 1959, Lutz, 1982; Smith, 1981).

The increasing criticisms by minority cultures that mainstream theories do not represent their worlds further illustrates the disappointing state of our theoretical knowledge. The feminist perspective argued that individual and family counseling models do not account for the role of power in abusive and violent relationships and that theories do not address the cultural pressures on females (Bogard, 1986; Enns & Hackett, 1993). In a similar manner, the significant interest in multiculturalism calls for an expanded paradigm in which culture is a fourth force in the field of counseling (Pederson, 1994). Thus, regardless of the considerable time and effort devoted to the generation of universal theoretical constructs, we seem to have many more theories, constructs, and techniques but no better idea regarding the ways in which behavior works than we did before.

The struggles in applying the modernistic approach have had other major consequences. For example, there is now a serious split between counseling theory, research, and practice (Anderson & Heppner, 1986; Hoshmand & Polkinghorne, 1992; Howard, 1986). The field of counseling is increasingly divided into two camps, practitioners and researchers (Brown, 1989). At present it seems that counseling research has little or no influence on clinical practice (Barlow, 1981). The majority of practitioners do not read the research literature (Garfield & Bergin, 1994; Howard, 1986) or do not see the relevance of research to their practice (Falvey, 1989). In other cases practitioners ignore research findings because they lack any consistent and relevant guidelines for therapeutic change in practice setting (Howard, 1986).

These limitations of logical positivism have led us to some curious solutions. Whether with clients, students, or the results of a scientific study, the explanations attributed to these failures are most often focused on the *problem* of individual differences. When counseling interventions do not work, we attribute the failure to unique client characteristics, client resistance, or chance occurrences. When our theories are inadequate we develop new approaches (based on the same assumptions), with a new language, and new techniques that included whoever or whatever had been left out. When our educational interventions produce less than we hope, we can look to student resistance, profess the need for the student's personal development, or note a student's inability to integrate what we had to offer. It is rare that we consider the assumptions of the paradigm as the source of these difficulties.

From a *postmodern* perspective, these dilemmas are the result of the narrow *modernistic* assumptions of science that have progressively narrowed our understanding of the world (Gergen, 1991). Within those assumptions, most of our empirical and theoretical efforts have focused on the reorganization of information within and the assimilation of information into existing assumptions. This process is much like what Bateson (1972) called first-order changes. First-order changes represent an entrenchment in prior knowing structures and result in what Popper and Eccles (1977) has called a context of justification. Thus, we argue that it is the very assumptions on which we as professionals operate that limit and hinder our process of understanding and further the contradictory and unexplained events in our knowledge base.

THE CONSTRUCTIVIST PERSPECTIVE: A PARADIGM SHIFT FOR COUNSELING

It is becoming increasingly apparent that a radical departure from the traditional assumptions of the prevailing modern view is at hand. The challenge for counseling and psychology is to shift epistemic paradigms and make the necessary alterations in the assumptions that guide our thinking. A paradigm shift illustrates what Bateson (1972) called a second-order change: a change in the structure of the organization of knowledge through accommodation. The postmodern approach of constructivism is a metatheory that has the potential to become the foundation of a new paradigm of understanding counseling practice, systematic inquiry, and professional training (Mahoney, 1991).

Constructivism is from the Latin word *construere*, which means to interpret or analyze (Mahoney, 1991, p. 96) in a manner that places emphasis on person's active creation and building of meaning and significance (Mahoney & Lyddon, 1988). Constructivists view knowledge as an invented and constructed meaning system rather than a free-standing, stable, external entity (Neimeyer & Lyddon, 1993). Therefore, it is not the degree to which knowledge corresponds to objective reality (a modernistic view) but instead utility and viability of knowledge that is the measure of its value (Anderson, 1990; Howard, 1991).

Constructivist thought is not a single approach but rather a continuum of beliefs that range from radical to more socially based orientations. Radical constructivists argue that knowledge and reality are individually generated and limited not by the external world but by the nature of the organism itself. The social constructionist paradigm focuses on the process by which people come to describe, explain, and account for the world in which they live (see Hayes & Oppenheim, Chapter 2). It is within the process of interpersonal communication that knowledge develops and the evolving sets of meanings that explain the world evolve (Hoffman, 1990). The primary location of the *truths* we have empirically sought is thus based in the realm of social interaction rather than in the intrapsychic world of the individual or the *true* nature of reality (Gergen, 1985; Harré, 1987).

A paradigm shift along constructivist lines requires a *dramatic* refocusing of the theoretical models we construct to explain culture, gender, human development, and behavior change. Radical changes in practice, research, and training would follow. The details of a constructivist paradigm shift are presented in the chapters that follow. The following five areas of change embody the challenge of a constructivist paradigm shift and form the basis of this volume.

Change in Counseling Practice

Constructivist counseling practice emphasizes the philosophical context as opposed to the clinical techniques of therapy. Emphasis is on the meaning that develops in the ongoing narratives developed by clients and counselors. Personal meanings and the interpersonal contexts are of primary concern. In each case, it is the counseling relationship that is the forum for change (Mahoney, 1991; Sexton & Whiston, 1994). Constructivist counseling practice shares the postmodern belief in the rejection of an ultimate truth. Thus, the process of assessment and the categorization of dysfunction are based on criteria of viability rather than an absolute external criterion (Neimeyer, 1993). The viability of behaviors is considered within the broader spectrum of a client's personal narratives rather than those specific thought processes, emotional units of expression, or acts of functional behavior (White & Epston, 1990). The goal of counseling interventions is more adaptable and viable personal constructions rather than the elimination and revision of cognitive distortions or corrective emotional experiences (Neimeyer & Harter, 1988).

The evolution of constructivist therapies is occurring across a wide spectrum of therapeutic areas including constructivist family therapy (e.g., Bateson, Jackson, Haley, & Weakland, 1956; Boscolo, Cecchin, Hoffman, & Penn, 1987; Efran, Lukens, & Lukens, 1990; Hoffman, 1990; Tomm, 1987a, 1987b), personal construct theory (e.g., Kelly, 1955; Neimeyer & Neimeyer, 1987), narrative psychology (White & Epston, 1990), structural-developmental approaches (Mahoney, 1991; Ivey, 1986; Rigazio-DiGilio & Anderson, 1994), and as an evolution of cognitive approaches (e.g., Mahoney & Lyddon, 1988; Neimeyer, 1993). These constructivist advances in counseling practice are addressed in Part II. In Chapter 6, Gordon and Efran outline the process of psychological change and the important role of language in the therapeutic process. The remaining chapters in this part focus on the practice of counseling in the varied settings in which we practice (cultural counseling, vocational counseling, school guidance).

Change in the Methods of Psychological Research

A postmodern perspective emphasizes a multitude of—rather than a single—methodological approaches to inquiry. It is not that logical positivism is thrown out. Instead, each systematic approach is an alternate social perspective with different strengths and limitations. Current research practices would take their place alongside phenomenological inquiry (Giorgi, 1985) and narrative analysis (Polkinghorne, 1988; Sarbin, 1986). While encompassing a multiplicity of paradigms, the postmodern view of inquiry would retain the emphasis on systematic, methodologically sound inquiry. It would, however, be based on a participatory epistemology in which viability replaces objectivity as the goal. In Part III of this book the process of systematic inquiry from a constructivist perspective is addressed. Nelson and Poulin (Chapter 10) provide a broad-based view of constructivist research while Daniels and White (Chapter 11) address the notion of measuring therapeutic change.

Alternative Models of Professional Training

Educating and training counselors and psychologists become the process of creating experiences and developing, guiding, and sharing meaning systems. Rather than students learning and educators teaching a fixed body of knowledge, the process of learning is embedded within social discussion and reflection. Instead of students learning and copying the meanings of the master therapists, the focus is on developing dialogue in which the students are participants who must understand events and make meaning by expanding their understanding of therapeutic events (White & Daniels, 1994). What the educator contributes is not the *right* way but the professional meaning system and the logic and rationale behind a model. The role of the educator becomes that of introducing new perspectives and alternative meaning systems rather than teaching fixed and static knowledge in a one-way communication process. This does not herald a return to *anything goes* or *whatever is comfortable*. Instead, the focus of education changes from the dissemination of information to the development of and alternation of meaning systems through social conversation and dialogue. The issues of constructivist principles of education and training are addressed in Chapter 13 (Lovell & McAuliffe). In Chapter 14, Winslade, Monk, and Drewery put these principles into practice with a training program based exclusively on constructivist principles.

Development of Constructivist Models of Supervision

Supervision also takes on a different form. With an emphasis on social conversation and construction through dialogue, the supervisor becomes a conversation manager who focuses on the development of alternative perspectives. The goal of supervision is expanding the narrative structure with which the student understands clients. Reflection and meaning-making through dialogue are the primary methods of clinical supervision (Daniels & White,

1994). In Chapter 12, Neufeldt outlines four main principles of constructivist supervision.

Development of Integrated Models of Behavior and Behavior Change

As a metatheory, the constructivist approach offers the opportunity to pull together the increasingly diverse theoretical models that make up our profession. Under the constructivist epistemology many of our constructions (e.g., multiculturalism, gender, specific counseling approaches) become not different, but variations on a constructivist theme. Mahoney (1991) proposed that constructivist metatheory has emerged as a particularly promising candidate for the exploration and integration of our various and seemingly diverse psychological theories. The unification potential of constructivism is probably nowhere more evident than in understanding the process of counseling and behavior change. In the arena of research, constructivism might serve as an umbrella that unites qualitative and quantitative approaches into a broad-based model of inquiry (Hoshmand & Martin, 1995). The result of such an integration is a unified profession based on common ontological and epistemological foundations. The potential of integration as well as the challenges of adopting constructivist thinking is the basis of Chapter 15.

CONCLUSION

In this time of epistemological change, the professions engaged in psychological science stand at a crossroads that poses two very difficult choices. One is to remain tied to our current assumptions and continue to look for universal and fundamental truths. Along this road, we would continue to look toward the development of new tools and instruments to answer the compelling and challenging contradictions with which we are faced. The other road calls for us to seek ways of applying the postmodern assumptions embodied in constructivism (Gergen, 1985; Mahoney, 1989). The challenging alternative of constructivism is a science based on the premise of participatory and recursive critique of the very process of knowing. This is a road on which the ways of knowing are as much a topic of attention as are the facts that become established.

The constructivist road requires us to challenge our assumptions about the objectivity, reality, and the very nature of knowledge. This road also invites a fundamental reappraisal of both the theoretical and the therapeutic assumptions of behavior change (Mahoney & Lyddon, 1988). While challenging, this road offers a model of understanding and inquiry that might provide an epistemological leap for our profession. This leap is that of a second-order change or a paradigm change for the psychological sciences. This last road is not easy and may involve resistance and struggle since constructivism requires reformulating our beliefs about reality, objectivity, and thus, our most dearly held beliefs. It is this second road that is the subject of this volume.

REFERENCES

Adler, A. (1972). *The neurotic constitution*. Freeport, NY: Books for Libraries Press. (Original work published 1926)

Anderson, W. P., & Heppner, P. P. (1986). Counselor applications of research findings to practice: Learning to stay current. *Journal of Counseling and Development, 65,* 152–155.

Anderson, W. T. (1990). *Reality isn't what it used to be*. San Francisco: Harper and Row.

Barlow, D. H. (1981). On the relation of clinical research to clinical practice: Current issues, new directions. *Journal of Consulting and Clinical Psychology, 49,* 147–155.

Barthes, B. B. (1979). From work to text. In J. Harari (Ed.), *Textual strategies* (pp. 73–81). Ithaca, NY: Cornell University Press.

Bartley, W. W. (1984). *The retreat to commitment* (2nd ed.). LaSalle, IL: Open Court.

Bateson, G. (1972). *Steps to an ecology of mind*. New York: Ballantine.

Bateson, G., Jackson, D., Haley, J., & Weakland, J. (1956). Toward a theory of schizophrenia. *Behavioral Science, 1,* 251–264.

Bergin, A. E., & Garfield, S. L. (Eds.). (1994). *Handbook of psychotherapy and behavior change* (4th ed.). New York: Wiley.

Bogard, M. (1986). A feminist examination of family systems models of violence against women in the family. In J. C. Hansen & M. Ault-Riche (Eds.), *Women and family therapy* (pp. 34–50). Rockville, MD: Aspen Systems.

Boscolo, L., Cecchin, G., Hoffman, L., & Penn, P. (1987). *Milan systemic family therapy*. New York: Basic Books.

Brown, M. T. (1989). Healing the split: Mental health counseling research and practice. *Journal of Mental Health Counseling, 11,* 116–120.

Capra, F. (1983). *The turning point*. New York: Bantam.

Christenson, A., & Jacobson, N. S. (1993). Who (or what) can do psychotherapy: The status and challenge of nonprofessional therapies. *Psychological Science, 5* (1), 8–14.

Daniels, M. H., & White, L. J. (1994). Human systems as problem-determined linguistic systems: Relevance for training. *Journal of Mental Health Counseling, 16,* 105–119.

Derrida, J. (1976). *Of grammatology* (G. C. Spivak, Trans.). Baltimore, MD: Johns Hopkins University Press.

Efran, J. S., Lukens, M. D., & Lukens, R. J. (1990). *Language, structure, and change: Frameworks of meaning in psychotherapy*. New York: Norton.

Enns, C. Z., & Hackett, G. (1993). A comparison of feminist and non-feminist women's and men's reactions to nonsexist and feminist counseling: A replication and extension. *Journal of Counseling and Development, 71,* 499–509.

Falvey, E. (1989). Passion and professionalism: Critical rapprochment for mental health research. *Journal of Mental Health Counseling, 11,* 86–95.

Gadamer, H. G. (1975). Hermeneutics and social science. *Cultural Hermeneutics, 2,* 307–352.

Garfield, S. L., & Bergin, A. E. (1994). Introduction and historical overview. In A. E. Bergin & S. L. Garfield (Eds.), *Handbook of psychotherapy and behavior change* (pp. 3–18). New York: Wiley.

Geertz, C. (1973). *The interpretation of cultures.* New York: Basic Books.

Gelso, C. J., & Carter, J. A. (1985). The relationship in counseling and psychotherapy: Components, consequences, and theoretical antecedents. *Counseling Psychologist, 13*(2), 155–243.

Gergen, K. (1982). *Toward transformation in social knowledge.* New York: Springer-Verlag.

Gergen, K. (1985). The social constructionist movement in modern psychology. *American Psychologist, 40,* 266–273.

Gergen, K. (1994). *Toward transformation in social knowledge* (3rd ed.). Thousand Oaks, CA: Sage.

Gergen, K. J. (1991). *The saturated self.* New York: Basic Books.

Gergen, K. J., & Kaye, J. (1992). Beyond narrative in the negotiation of therapeutic meaning. In S. McNamee & K. J. Gergen (Eds.), *Therapy as social construction* (pp. 166–185). Newbury Park, CA: Sage.

Giorgi, A. (1985). *Phenomenology and psychological research.* Pittsburg, PA: Duquesne University Press.

Gleick, J. (1987). *Chaos.* New York: Penguin Books.

Harré, R. (1987). Enlarging the paradigm. *New Ideas in Psychology, 5,* 3–12.

Hawkings, S. W. (1988). *A brief history of time: From the big bang to black holes.* New York: Bantam.

Hill, C. E., Helms, J. E., Tichenor, V., Speigel, S. B., O'Grady, K. E., & Perry, E. S. (1988). Effects of therapist response modes in brief psychotherapy. *Journal of Counseling Psychology, 35,* 222–233.

Hoffman, L. (1990). Constructing realities: An art of lenses. *Family Process, 29*(1), 1–12.

Hoshmand, L. T., & Martin, J. (1995). Concluding comments on therapeutic psychology and the science of practice. In L. T. Hoshmand & J. Martin (Eds.), *Research as praxis* (pp. 235–241). New York: Teachers College Press.

Hoshmand, L. T., & Polkinghorne, D. E. (1992). Redefining the science-practice relationship and professional training. *American Psychologist, 47,* 55–66.

Houts, A. C. (1989). Contributions of the psychology of science to metascience: A call for explorers. In B. Gholson, W. R. Shadish, Jr., R. A. Neimeyer, & A. C. Houts (Eds.), *Psychology of science: Contributions of metascience* (pp. 47–88). New York: Cambridge University Press.

Howard, G. S. (1986). *Dare we develop a human science?* Notre Dame, IN.: Academic Publications.

Howard, G. S. (1991). Cultural tales: A narrative approach to thinking cross-cultural psychology, and psychotherapy. *American Psychologist, 46,* 187–197.

Howard, G. S., & Conway, C. G. (1986). Can there be an empirical science of human action? *American Psychologist, 41,* 1241–1251.

Ivey, A. E. (1986). *Developmental therapy: Theory into practice.* San Francisco: Jossey-Bass.

Kant, I. (1911). *Prolegomena zu jeder Kunftigen Metaphyskik.* Werke, Volume 4. Berlin: Konigliche Preussishe Akademie der Wissenschaften. (Original work published 1783)

Kelly, G. A. (1955). *The psychology of personal constructs* (Vol. 1). New York: Norton.

Kuhn, T. S. (1970). *The structure of scientific revolutions* (2nd ed.). Chicago: University of Chicago Press.

Kuhn, T. S. (1977). *The essential tension.* Chicago: University of Chicago Press.

Lambert, M. J. (1989). The individual therapist's contribution to psychotherapy process and outcome. *Clinical Psychology Review, 9,* 469–485.

Lee, D. (1959). *Freedom and culture.* Englewood Cliffs, NJ: Prentice Hall.

Lutz, C. (1982). The domain of emotion words in Ifaluk. *American Ethnologist, 9,* 113–128.

Mahoney, M. F., & Lyddon, W. J. (1988). Recent developments in cognitive approaches to counseling and psychotherapy. *Counseling Psychologist, 16,* 190–234.

Mahoney, M. J. (1989). Participatory epistemology and psychology of science. In B. Gholson, R. A. Neimeyer, A. Houts, & W. Shadish (Eds.), *Psychology of science and metascience* (pp. 138–164). Cambridge: Cambridge University Press.

Mahoney, M. J. (1991). *Human change processes: The scientific foundations of psychotherapy.* New York: Basic Books.

Neimeyer, G. J. (1993). The challenge of change: Reflections on constructivist psychotherapy. *Journal of Cognitive Psychotherapy: An International Quarterly, 7,* 183–194.

Neimeyer, G. J., & Lyddon, W. J. (1993). Constructivist psychotherapy: Principles into practice. *Journal of Cognitive Psychology: An International Quarterly, 7*(3), 23–42.

Neimeyer, R. A., & Harter, S. (1988). Facilitating individual change in personal construct therapy. In G. Dunnett (Ed.), *Working with people* (pp. 174–185). London: Routledge.

Neimeyer, R. A., & Neimeyer, G. J. (Eds.). (1987). *Personal construct therapy casebook.* New York: Springer.

Orlinsky, D. E., & Howard, K. I. (1986). Process and outcome in psychotherapy. In S. L. Garfield and A. E. Bergin (Eds.), *Handbook of psychotherapy and behavior change* (3rd ed., pp. 311–381). New York: Wiley.

Pederson, P. B. (1994). Multiculturalism as a fourth force in counseling. *Journal of Counseling and Development, 70,* 1–2.

Polkinghorne, D. E. (1988). *Narrative knowing and human sciences.* Albany: SUNY Press.

Popper, K. R. (Ed.). (1972a). *Objective knowledge: An evolutionary approach.* London: Oxford University Press.

Popper, K. R. (1972b). Of clouds and clocks. In K. R. Popper (Ed.), *Objective knowledge: An evolutionary approach.* London: Oxford University Press.

Popper, K. R., & Eccles, J. C. (1977). *The self and its brain: An argument for interactionism.* New York: Springer.

Rigazio-DiGilio, S. A., & Anderson, S. A. (1994). A cognitive-developmental model for marital and family therapy. *The Clinical Supervisor, 12,* 93–118.

Sampson, E. E. (1989). The deconstruction of the self. In J. Shotter and K. F. Gerfen (Eds.), *Texts of identity* (pp. 1–19). London: Sage.

Sarbin, T. (Ed.). (1986). *Narrative psychology.* New York: Praeger.

Sexton, T. L., & Whiston, S. C. (1994). The status of counseling relationship: An empirical review, theoretical implications, and research directions. *The Counseling Psychologist, 22*(1), 6–78.

Smith, J. (1981). Self as experience in Maori culture. In P. Heelas & A. Lock (Eds.), *Indigenous Psychologies* (pp. 45–160). London: Academic Press.

Taylor, C. (1971). Interpretation and the sciences of man. *The Review of Metaphysics, 25*(1), 3–51.

Tomm, K. (1987a). Interventive interviewing: Part I. Strategizing as a fourth guideline for the therapist. *Family Process, 26*(1), 3–14.

Tomm, K. (1987b). Interventive interviewing: Part II. Reflexive questioning as a means to enable self-healing. *Family Process, 26*(2), 167–184.

Vaihinger, H. (1924). *The philosophy of "as if."* New York: Routledge & Kegan Paul. (Original work published 1911)

von Bertanlanffy, L. (1968). *General systems theory.* New York: George Braziller.

von Foerster, H. (1984). On constructing a reality. In P. Watzlawick (Ed.), *The invented reality* (pp. 41–61). New York: Norton.

von Glasersfeld, E. (1984). An introduction to radical constructivism. In P. Watzlawick (Ed.), *The invented reality* (pp. 17–40). New York: Norton.

Watzlawick, P. (Ed.). (1984). *The invented reality: Contributions of constructivism.* New York: Basic Books.

Whiston, S. C., & Sexton, T. L. (1993). An overview of psychotherapy outcome research: Implications for practice. *Professional Psychology: Research and Practice, 24*(1), 43–51.

White, L., & Daniels, H. (1994). Human systems as problem-determined linguistic systems: Relevance for training. *Journal of Mental Health Counseling, 10*(1), 105–119.

White, M., & Epston, D. (1990). *Narrative means to therapeutic ends.* New York: Norton.

Wittgenstein, L. (1969). *Philosophical investigations* (3rd ed.) (G. Anscombe, Trans.). New York: Macmillan.

CHAPTER 2

Constructivism: Reality Is What You Make It

Richard L. Hayes and Ramona Oppenheim

Postmodernism is challenging the great narratives of Western civilization (Derrida, 1982; Foucault, 1972; Lyotard, 1983). As such, it represents a general loss of faith in the modernist enterprise as leading to the rational planning of an ideal social order and the consequent standardization of knowledge and production. It is the argument of the postmodernists that the near total focus of the modernist enterprise on individual freedom has obviated attention to the larger social context within which such changes take place. Thus, from an epistemological, metaphysical perspective, postmodernism suggests that the sources of our uncertainty should be systematically exposed and that there be a restructuring of the intellectual life in order to attend fully to the meaning of a lack of secure intellectual markers.

Although no single unifying framework has yet arisen to guide such restructuring, several confluent positions are associated with postmodernism. In particular, postmodernists reject the pictorial (iconic) metaphor of knowledge in favor of a constructivist (architectural) metaphor (Lyotard, 1983). Despite its rising popularity, however, constructivism is not new. Indeed, many of those responsible for founding modern psychology would today be considered constructivists. Furthermore, counseling and supervision models derived from such a perspective have existed for some time, for example, Kelly's (1955) personal construct psychology or the deliberate psychological education offered by Mosher and Sprinthall (1970).

As suggested in Chapter 1, what is new is that constructivism is supported by the larger intellectual, social, and political context embodied in postmodernism (see Botwinick, 1993; Conner, 1987; Guba & Lincoln, 1990; Jencks, 1986; Kvale, 1992; Lyotard, 1983; Parry, 1993; Rickey, 1967). The growing interest in alternative epistemologies, fostered by the postmodern turn in the social sciences, is currently being merged with counseling's long-standing claim to a developmental focus (Hayes, 1994). The result has been the emergence of newer forms of counseling and psychotherapy based on a constructivist developmental psychology. Constructivism offers a distinctly different approach to the traditional relationship between knowledge and reality. Importantly, this shift in perspective is now sufficiently widely appreciated as to constitute a genuine revolution in counseling.

The purpose of this chapter is to orient the reader to the set of assumptions that frame a constructivist approach and to set the stage for their application in subsequent chapters to counseling practice, research, supervision, and education. In particular, this chapter is intended (1) to offer a comprehensive definition of constructivism, especially related to counseling and supervision; (2) to elaborate the common principles that underlie different approaches to constructivism; (3) to identify the range of theoretical notions that can be captured within this definition; and (4) to draw some implications for taking a constructivist approach to counseling and supervision.

AN ALTERNATIVE EPISTEMOLOGY

A growing number of thinkers across the behavioral sciences have increasingly rejected the modernist principles of science (see Chapter 1). They abandoned the notion of an objective universe and, like the ancient skeptics before them, argued that it is logically impossible to establish the truth of any particular piece of knowledge. Because each claim to know the truth is itself subject to comparison with yet another claim, we never get to see the constraints of the world. As some have noted, the fish is the last to discover water. Instead, what we experience, and thus come to know, is necessarily built up of our own building blocks and can be explained in no other way than in terms of our own ways and means for building. In this sense, reality is what you make it. Accepting the impossibility that science can yield satisfactory answers to ontological questions, the constructivist turns to considerations of epistemology.

As early as the 18th century, Vico (1710) noted that "as God's truth is what God comes to know as He creates and assembles it, so human truth is what man comes to know as he builds it, shaping it by his actions" (p. 5). This idea—that the only way to know a thing is to have made it—was reasserted by Kant (1783/1911) near the end of the same century when he noted that nature is "the collective conception of all objects of experience" (p. 295). In the centuries that followed, Dewey (1910), Hegel (1830/1975), Heidegger (1927/1962), James (1890), Vaihinger (1911/1924), and Wittgenstein (1969) all proposed a similar epistemic notion of reality as constructed. They argued for an experiential world that makes no claim whatsoever about truth in the sense of correspondence with an ontological reality. Rather, what is

TABLE 2.1. Contrasting Nature of Selected Issues from Positivist and Constructivist Approaches

Nature of	Approach	
	Positivism	Constructivism
Being	Knowable	Unknowable
Fact	Discovery	Convention
Knowing	Why	That
Knowledge	Representative, discovered, objective, certain	Constructed, invented, perspective, ambiguous
Language	Representational, mediates social reality	Formative, constitutes social reality
Learning	Reactive, consequential	Proactive, anticipatory
Memory	Stored and retrieved, recollective	Socially reconstructed, interpretive
Motives	Reasons for actions	Prospects for actions
Reality	Singular, knowable, objective	Multiple, transitory, contextual
Research	Evaluate practice	Improves practice
Science	Discovery of universal laws, value-free, natural	Creation of particular knowledge, value-laden, human
Scientific method	Empirical, control of variables, intervention	Hermeneutical, exploitation of possibilities, multi-method
Self	Individual, separate, isolated	Decentered, embedded, situated
Theory	Theory is built on facts	Facts are derived from theory
Thinking	Computational	Argumentative
Truth	Formal, verifiable	Functional, viable

known cannot be the result of a passive receiving, but originates as the product of the activity of the knower. This constructivist perspective asserts that we do not discover reality as something out there or hidden within ourselves; rather, we invent it (Watzlawick, 1984). Although constructivists are not of one mind, especially related to their assumptions about change and causation, a set of common principles can be articulated that provide a meaningful contrast with the positivist approach. Table 2.1 outlines the core differences between the positivist and constructivist perspectives.

COMMON PRINCIPLES FOR A CONSTRUCTIVIST APPROACH

While the approaches that fall under the umbrella of constructivism are diverse, they do share six common principles. These principles reflect the assumptions of postmodernism as applied to the development, maintenance, and change of human behavior.

Development Is Contextual

Counselors have generally accepted one or the other of two competing views of human development (Hayes, 1986): "environmental" and "maturational" (Kohlberg & Mayer, 1972). Theorists in the first of these traditions accept an exogenous (Green, 1989) paradigm by which they attempt to explain development in terms of learning, which is believed to be controlled by environmental factors (cf. Bandura, 1986; Pavlov, 1927; Skinner, 1971; Thorndike, 1913; Watson, 1919). In the second of these traditions, theorists accept an endogenous paradigm, wherein development is conceptualized as a qualitative property of the organism itself (cf. Adler, 1926/1972; Erikson, 1950; Freud, 1936/1946; Jung, 1928; Rogers, 1961). Critically, both perspectives adhere to the positivist notions outlined above.

At the turn of the century, Baldwin (1902/1897), Cooley (1902), Dewey (1910), and James (1890) argued for an alternative to the positivist's dichotomization of individual and environment. Noting that humans are creatures living in a time and place with other creatures, they argued that development is neither wholly a consequence of events that have happened to us nor wholly the result of inner urgings. Instead, they argued that development takes place in a social context and proposed a view of human knowing as both encouraged and bounded by the social context in which such understanding arises. The process of knowing emerges in the light of interaction between ourselves and our personal surroundings. Thus, person and world are not separate, not even in interaction, but rather are inextricably linked in transactions with one another (Basseches, 1984; Gibbs, 1979; Mead, 1934; Riegel, 1979; Viney, 1990; Vygotsky, 1934/1986).

Individuals Are Producers of Their Own Development

Although the basic tenets for a truly constructivist developmental psychology can be found in the work of many of those identified above — especially that of James Mark Baldwin (1902) — it is in the genetic epistemology of Jean Piaget (1936/1954, 1926/1955) that one finds its most explicit expression. Piaget explored the idea that as biological organisms, humans inherit two basic functions: organization and adaptation. Organization refers to the tendency for all living things to attempt to order their processes; in effect, organisms organize. Once the object has been experienced, it is brought into awareness as a part of the way we think. Thus, learning is the outcome of organizing our experience with objects.

The second function is the tendency of living things to make modifications in response to changing environmental conditions in anticipation of desired outcomes. The test of truth, therefore, is not correspondence with reality, but rather viability. As von Glasersfeld (1991) put the issue, "What matters is not to match the world, but to fit into it in spite of whatever obstacles or traps it might present" (p. 16). Thus, humans adapt in order to enhance their potential to reap positive outcomes from an anticipated environment and, as such, operate as self-organizing systems. In addition to Piaget's (1936/1954) genetic epistemology, notable attempts to describe the nature of this self system can be found in Kelly's (1955) personal construct psychology and Mead's (1934) symbolic interactionism.

Cognition Is an Active Relating of Events

Constructivists maintain that there are certain structuring tendencies inherent to human nature by which people attempt to make sense of their experiences within themselves and of the world in which they live (Bartlett, 1932; Hayek, 1952; Kelly, 1955). Reality is constructed through experience and thereby represents a relationship between the self and the world. Therefore, human development represents the course of our attempts to make sense of those changes going on around us—to understand what it means "to be me in a world like mine at a time like this."

Underlying this notion of basic mental structures is the concept of cognition. Cognitions represent internally organized systems of relations, which comprise a set of rules for processing information or connecting events in personal experience. Cognitive thinking is the active relating of events. By contrast, researchers operating from a positivist perspective have focused on the products of clients' cognitions rather than on the cognitive process itself. Although cognitive-behavioral counselors (see, for example, Beck, 1976; Ellis, 1962; Lazarus, 1976; Meichenbaum, 1977) have been interested in "faulty thinking," "decision-making processes," and "reasoning powers," they have tended to focus their attention on the influence of cognition on behavior as guides to prescribing treatments that focus on changing what the client knows.

The difference between the cognitive-behavioral and the constructivist approaches amounts to studying what the client knows rather than how the client is knowing it. As Mahoney and Lyddon (1988) explained:

> Central to the constructivist formulations is the idea that, rather than being a sort of template through which ongoing experience is filtered, the representational model [of the individual] actively creates and constrains new experience and thus determines what the individual will perceive as "reality." (p. 200)

Meaning-Making Is Self-evolution

The idea of transactions going on between people and their environments leads the constructivist to a particular notion of cognitive development. Each person's self-regulating system emerges as a consequence of new states of equilibrium that were created by the previous self-regulatory system. Therefore, disequilibration serves as a stimulus to development, while equilibration is its goal. Development can be seen from this view as the natural outcome of attempts to make stable sense of a changing world. As a result of this recurring cycle of equilibration-disequilibration-equilibration, development takes a path that may best be described as a spiral. The outer turns are analogous to the person's attempts at the integration of novel experiences to existing structures. In each evolutionary turn, the spiral moves to a new level of organization analogous to the movement to a higher stage of development (Langer, 1969, pp. 95–96).

Although constructivists are not of one mind about the notion of stages, specifically, any use of the term is reserved to refer to "qualitative differences in children's modes of thinking or of solving problems at different ages" (Kohlberg, 1969, p. 352). Where developmental stages are hypothesized, each of these stages is understood as providing a "structured whole" (Piaget, 1960, p. 14) that represents an individual world view or frame of reference for meaning-making. Each succeeding stage represents the capacity to make sense of a greater variety of experience in a more adequate way. Thus, each stage is a more differentiated, comprehensive, and integrated structure than the one before it. From a constructivist approach, development is understood as successively more complex attempts to make meaning of the facts of one's social experience.

Reality Is Multiform

The implication of this constructivist model of cognitive development is that individuals within a particular stage of development view reality in ways that are similar with regard to structure but may be vastly different with regard to content. In this way, each level of cognitive development might be viewed as a culture of cognitive structure. Nonetheless, because the sets of events from which one composes a life are experienced uniquely, each person's life can be viewed as its own grand narrative (Howard, 1990; Mair, 1988; Polkinghorne, 1993; White & Epston, 1990).

If we understand individual history as the construction of a personal social narrative, then all actions are essentially incomplete, susceptible to limitless interpretations by evermore imaginative interpreters. Therefore, the test of truth is pragmatic — it is the viability or practical utility of knowledge that makes it "true." From a constructivist perspective, the individual serves as his or her own historian in confronting the past either as menacing and unknown or as an organizing framework of thought and feeling that must be assimilated into present structures. Thus, the truth can never really be known because, as Botwinick (1993) explained, "it is always being presented in the present within the context of the present. Thus the truth lies within the set of truths that can be brought to bear upon a single event" (p. 131). Seen in this way, problems represent unsuccessful attempts to resolve difficulties and point to potential limitations in one's current way of knowing.

Language Constitutes Reality

As has been argued, a postmodern world is characterized by changing perspectives, with no underlying frame of reference. To find one's place in such a world, therefore, requires the development of a reliable, consensual system for negotiation. Language, the postmodernists teach us, provides the system necessary for grounding our understanding of the self in relation to the other. "But if, instead of thinking of language as being used in this way—to 'make contact' with those around us," Shotter (1992) cautioned, "we still insist upon thinking of our sentences as pictures, in which we can see the structure of the 'things' they represent, then we can be misled ourselves in fundamental ways" (p. 64).

Note, for example, how the positivist's claim to an objective reality supports a language wherein one has "viewpoints" rather than "opinions," or "takes a perspective" rather than "has a bias," or clients are "seen" rather than "related to," or where saying "I see" means "I understand." The postmodernist argues that rather than take the position that "seeing is believing," one might say that "believing is seeing." It is in this way that language shapes our conversations. Language does not permit the accurate representation of a world "out there," but rather is a symbol system for expressing sets of assumptions about our understanding of that world. Language does not mimic reality; rather, language constitutes reality, with each language constructing specific aspects of reality, each in its own way. Rorty (1983) argues that the various vocabularies we use or the particular perspectives we take are instruments for coping with things rather than ways of representing their intrinsic nature. Thus, one vocabulary is better than another not because it corresponds more closely to "reality" but rather because a given vocabulary works better in a particular situation for a given purpose.

When we enter the process of description, however, we invariably rely on conventions, which both expand and constrain what can be communicated. In effect, the words we choose reveal the ontological presumptions of a culture. Because clients actively construct their social world, the client's history is not so much a record of one's life experience as it is a living representation of how one is experiencing life. Understanding the world is thus a product not of the world as it is, but of a historical text. The constructivist's recognition of the social construction of discourse on the world (Gergen, 1991) points to the problem inherent in negotiated understandings across the boundaries of race, gender, ethnicity, culture, or personal experience. Constructivism encourages the development of a language of difference that would permit one to understand the Other as the self, recognizing the inseparability of our knowledge of one another.

A CONFLUENCE OF TRADITIONS: COUNSELING AND HUMAN DEVELOPMENT

Our analysis of the emergence of constructivism, at least in the present century, shows two definable if not separate paths of theory construction — one derived through research in human development and the other through clinical practice. Although participants in each arena were, at various times, aware of work being done by the others, it is not until recently that any deliberate and substantive attempts have been made to connect theorizing across these two enterprises.

While Piaget and his adherents focused their attention on theory construction in human development, clinicians were independently elaborating constructivist models of therapy. Although the works of Alfred Adler (1926/ 1972), Harry Stack Sullivan (1953) and the object relations theorists (e.g., St. Clair, 1986) point in the general direction of a constructivist therapy model, perhaps only George Kelly's (1955) psychology of personal constructs satisfies our current understanding of a truly constructivist approach to counseling and psychotherapy (Neimeyer, 1985).

As presented in *The Psychology of Personal Constructs,* Kelly's (1955) work represented the first systematic attempt to articulate a constructivist theory of clinical practice. Viewing knowledge as invented and evolving, Kelly hypothesized that the construing efforts of individuals were socially embedded. Further, he believed that a client's stories and metaphors functioned to establish continuity of meaning in the client's lived experience. The goal of his therapy, therefore, was to assist the client in developing a perspective shift or conceptual reframing that could permit new courses of action. As with Piaget (1936/ 1954), the breadth of Kelly's (1955) work and its profound implications for understanding human functioning have given rise to a host of dedicated adherents.

Although not all of today's constructivists will lay claim to having been influenced directly by either Piaget (1936/1954) or Kelly (1955), it is clear that many who are having an impact on this field today share a common intellectual history with these two pioneers. These theorists cover a broad range of interests and applications. They range from extensions of personal construct theory, to structural-developmental cognitive therapies, to constructivist family therapy, to narrative reconstruction, to social constructionist therapy, and beyond to sets of therapeutic interventions that remain to be developed sufficiently to permit classification. Nonetheless, they all share the basic constructivist perspective that humans actively create their own particular reality.

TOWARD AN INTEGRATED DIFFERENTIATION: CONSTRUCTING CONSTRUCTIVISM

As tempting as it may be to codify the elements differentiating these specific practices, a postmodern approach to counseling suggests that such integration may be premature, if not inappropriate. Taken metaphorically, our understanding of the events that comprise a constructivist movement is a function of where we are "standing" at the time. Consider, for example, the challenge to early astronomers of mapping the stars in the evening sky. Assuming that each star occupies a fixed point on a stable plane, creating an "accurate" map is seemingly the task of marking the relative position of each to the other on a flat piece of paper and checking the resulting map for several days to ensure its accuracy.

Today, of course, we understand several things that complicate such a project. First, neither the platform from which such observations are made (Earth) nor the evening sky against which the stars are arranged is flat. As ancient mariners well appreciated, what one sees in the sky at night is, in part, a function of where one is located on the surface of the planet at the time. Moreover, the view changes as the position of the planet changes relative to the sun around which the Earth travels.

To complicate matters further, we know today that the stars are not of equal size, nor equidistant. Further, if we recognize that what we see is actually the light emitted from the star and not the star itself, then, given the very long time (thousands of years) it takes light to reach our eyes from objects at such great distances (billions of miles), a moving star is never located today where it appears to be when we see it. What we really see at night is closer to a historical recreation of an arrangement of stars. If we recognize that light actually curves as it passes through the universe, then stars never actually were where they appear to have been (sort of like looking at a stick that appears to bend as it is immersed in water). If we understand further that stars die, then the light coming from any star tells us only that the star once existed and not necessarily that it does now.

So when we look at a fixed constellation of stars in the night sky, what we "see" is our representation of a set of relationships that we impose on light sources that we intercept at a given moment in time while traveling through space. Understood in this way, a constellation is only our understanding of a set of relationships that exist because of where we—not they—are located. When we consider that some of our favorite authors on the subject (our stars) have long since died, that all authors on the subject are no longer as they "were" at the time of their writing, and that different readers will be in "different place-times" (see Hawking, 1988) as they consider each work, then the best we can hope for is a reliable, rather than a verifiable, map of the constructivist terrain to guide our study.

Having offered this caution, how are we to attempt to show a causal connection between the set of principles that have emerged and the various adherents to a constructivist position? Suffice it to say that a constructivist movement, if there has ever been such a thing, is now only vaguely aware of itself, especially within counseling and psychology. Nonetheless, it is possible to identify persons and/or events that can provide points by which to map an initial portrait of the landscape. Rather than a linear, march-of-history account so compatible with the positivism that constructivism challenges, a different metaphor seems appropriate: a topographical map of the territory that shows the position taken by each theorist relative to the others, creating a map of relational rather than objective perspectives. A view across that landscape to-day indicates a unity of criticism and a diversity of alternative formulations of constructivism.

All adherents to a constructivist approach maintain the central epistemo-logical position of knowing as meaning construction. Nonetheless, they appear to have a friendly disagreement about the nature, if not the construction, of reality.

First and foremost, we may differentiate the constructivists from their positivist counterparts by their position vis-à-vis the ontological nature of reality. Having done so, we may now position the constructivists relative to one another in how far they travel from the ontological position that separates them from the positivists.

Mahoney (1991) has made a distinction between critical and radical constructivists. Critical constructivists argue that we live in an unknowable, but nevertheless inescapable, real world. These constructivists embrace a position of hypothetical realism, suggesting that we cannot choose to be the self-sufficient sole creators of our own experience. Rather, we must co-create, through an interactive interdependence with our social and physical environments, our own personal realities. We are literally bounded by an ultimately unknowable world that imposes constraints on the viability of our constructions. Guidano (1987), Hayek (1952), Kelly (1955), Mahoney (1991), Piaget (1936/1954), and Weiner (1985) are all cited as critical constructivists, although Piaget is claimed by the radical constructivists as well.

Alternatively, radical constructivists embrace the classical notion of ontological idealism. That is, they take the position that there is no reality that extends beyond the individual's own experience, believing instead in the absolute unknowability of a world beyond our own system for knowing. This position elevates to new heights the idea that the individual is entirely self-organizing. Therefore, the human mind is an autonomous knowing system that is closed with respect to input from any outside world. We are essentially the architects of our own reality and ideally we choose to participate with others to create realities within which we can thrive. In addition to von Glasersfeld (1984), representatives of this position include Maturana and Varela (1987), von Foerster (1984), and Watzlawick (1984).

An illustration may help to clarify what may be nothing more than a family squabble about the nature of reality.

Three baseball umpires are asked to describe how they decide whether a given pitch is a "strike" or a "ball." Says the first umpire, "I call 'em as they are."

"But how do you know," objects the second umpire. "I call 'em as I see 'em."

"But how can you be so certain," chimes in the third umpire. "They ain't nothing 'til I call 'em."

On review, our first umpire accepts that reality and truth are objective and can be one and the same. Moreover, he believes that he can tell the difference. Our second umpire, however, accepts that reality is constructed but remains silent on the issue of an independent reality. He recognizes the limitations of the situation but believes that some "truths" may be better than others. Our third umpire accepts that both truth and reality are subjective. He accepts not only that reality is constructed but that it arises as a consequence of personal experience rather than as an a priori condition. Implicit in his comments is that truth and reality can be the same only through social dialogue and negotiation — if the fans, the players, and the team owners will accept that he has the right to make such a call, has the proper training to exercise that right, has the will to discharge his duties faithfully, has applied the agreed-upon criteria, and so forth as part of the general "culture" of baseball, then they can also understand how he came to make the call that he did and accept it as part of the larger reality of the game.

The first of our umpires is a positivist while the other two represent the extremes of what might properly be seen as a constructivist continuum. This

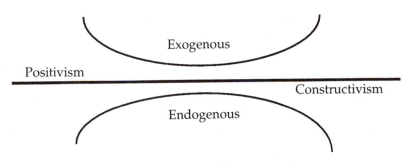

FIGURE 2.1. Charting the Constructivist Landscape

continuum may more properly be seen as a set of dichotomies that comprise the aforementioned ontological and epistemological positions and that chart the landscape of constructivism. Stretching out along the ontological dimension are the positivists and the constructivists, who are further differentiated by their position vis-à-vis a "negotiated reality." Orthogonal (if not perpendicular) to this vector lies the dichotomy of exogenous/environmental and endogenous/individual epistemologies noted above in differentiating developmental theories. Figure 2.1 charts these elements of the constructivist landscape in illustrating these relationships.

When the elements are charted in this way, one might usefully arrange various theorists within the plane of ontological and epistemological assumptions such that Beck (1976) and Lazarus (1976), for instance, would appear among the exogenous positivists, while both Freud (1946) and Rogers (1961) would appear among the endogenous positivists (see Figure 2.1). Although Piaget (1926/1955) is claimed by both radical and critical constructivists, he would appear in this scheme among the endogenous constructivists, while Gergen (1991), for example, might be found among the exogenous constructivists. Lying on a line between Gergen and Piaget, one might place Guidano (1987, 1991), Mahoney (1985, 1991), and Howard (1986, 1990). Between Rogers (1961) and Piaget (1936/1954), one might find a range of transpersonal psychologies represented by Maslow (1968) on the positivist side and Wilber (1985) on the constructivist side of the ontological-epistemological divide. Finally, between Beck and Gergen, one might reasonably place Ellis on the positivist side (despite his claims to the contrary) and Bandura just over the line on the constructivist side.

Finally, to add some depth and texture to our landscape, Lyddon (1995) has applied Pepper's (1942) root metaphor framework to contrasting constructivist theories along the dimension of causal assumptions associated with each of four different world views. Although space does not permit a full examination of his treatment of these issues here, it is instructive to consider that each theory might also be differentiated by its assumptions about causation and change: (1) Material constructivism takes a formistic world view and assumes that intrinsic and stable human properties account for cognitive functioning (e.g., von Glasersfeld, 1984; von Foerster, 1984). (2) Efficient constructivism takes a mechanistic world view and seeks understanding in the search for efficient cause-effect relationships (e.g., Bandura, 1986; Zimmerman, 1981). (3) Formal constructivism assumes a contextualist world view and assumes that reality emerges from a temporal flow of events that emerge from the stream of sociocultural-historical contexts in which humans are situated (e.g., James, 1890; Gergen, 1991). (4) Final constructivism assumes an organismic world view and assumes causation can be found in the inexorable movement of the organism toward some final, perfectible state of being through the dialectic of person-environment interactions (e.g., Kegan, 1982; Piaget, 1936/1954; Guidano, 1987, 1991).

Although this set of positions does not lie smoothly over the plane of our theories, each of these features, when applied theory by theory, does help to differentiate each usefully from any other. A complete explanation of how any particular theory comes to grips with the central developmental questions of human understanding, however, remains a central challenge. Because each form of constructivism is complex, it does not occupy a "single" position in our constellation of theories. As a consequence of their complexity, the various forms of constructivism are spread out along a set of dimensions. Forms that are close along one dimension/issue may be quite far apart on another. Recognizing that, as metaphors, these distinctions merely afford particular lenses through which to view each theory, we are reminded that the "truth" of any theory lies in its utility for understanding human functioning. Rather than being divisive, therefore, continued attempts to differentiate constructivist forms should only serve to enrich further what has already become a bountiful landscape.

IMPLICATIONS OF TAKING A CONSTRUCTIVIST APPROACH

The differences attending each of these theories notwithstanding, the assumptions that unite a constructivist epistemology of practice have profound implications for our conduct as counselors, educators, and supervisors.

Implications for Practice

If personality development is essentially the universal, ongoing process of meaning-making, then counseling should focus on development and the person's experience of this process. This notion of the self as a self-organizing system has profound implications for understanding human development and, in turn, for reconceptualizing counseling as something other than adjusting the client's reality to correspond more accurately to the real world (Carlsen, 1988; Feixas, 1990; Friedman, 1993; Goodman, 1984; Hayes, 1994; Ivey, 1986; Kegan, 1982; Kvale, 1992; Mahoney, 1985; Neimeyer, 1985; Saari, 1991).

The central implication of taking the constructivist's view of reality as a self-constructive activity is that development is essentially the task of mastering the facts of one's existence. As a consequence, constructivist counselors try to understand how clients make sense of personal experience, that is, how clients make meaning. It is to the client's struggle to understand the self and others, therefore, in the context of a shared social experience, that constructivist counselors turn their attention.

Because the client's reality represents a relationship between the client and the world as the client understands that world, true understanding combines knowledge with felt experience. In a way, the client's present concerns can be described as the rooting of the subject of inquiry in its immediate historical context. The chief means toward this end, however, is the reenactment of the past in the client's own mind. In reconstructing the past, the client serves as his or her own historian, which suggests the superimposition of a present context over the past. Thus client narratives may be seen more as fabrication than as re-creation (Howard, 1990; Noam, 1988). By contrast, Freud's (1946) explanation of the hysteria of his patients as an unconscious desire to merge with the aggressor can be seen instead as the social construction of an oppressive interpersonal event. It is not so much that clients have problems, therefore, as that they experience problems; how one understands and makes meaning of experience betrays the underlying logic of how one makes sense of one's own existence.

The implication of this perspective is that counseling should create a social context for reconstruction. The constructivist counselor attempts to provide a "holding environment" (Kegan, 1982, p. 256) for facilitating the client's development by acknowledging the client's reality and by supporting the client's efforts to restore some balance to the world as the client knows it. Questioning intended to uncover the client's meaning construction can facilitate such understanding. In so doing, constructivist counselors will want to focus more on present understandings in the service of future actions than on past actions in the service of present understandings. From a constructivist perspective, therefore, counseling takes the form of a dialogue between the client's structures and the structures of the environment, where the counselor may be understood as one of many elements in that environment (Gergen, 1991; Kelly, 1955). What clients learn in the course of counseling, even if they are unable to articulate it fully, is how theory-dependent their actions are. As Botwinick (1993) pointed out: "The nature of our actions are [*sic*] dependent upon the intellectual categories we employ to demarcate our world and the significant elements within it. That our theories are underdetermined by experience indicates the strategic role assigned to will in the making and remaking of our selves" (p. 124). In taking the perspective of the counselor as audience to the client, the client experiences himself or herself in new and potentially more developmental ways.

Implications for Research

Constructivists argue that truth and knowledge are constructions within the mind of the individual and that meaning-making and valuing are based on those constructions. Recognizing that structure is not static, research should be focused on the transformation of structure over time. The direction of structural change, however, is determined to a large extent by the total context, including space (immediate environment) and time (memories and anticipated) variables. Consequently, constructivists contend that the positivist's efforts to decontextualize behavior by trying to control for confounding variables is ineffective (at best) and invalid (at worst) when trying to understand individual behavior (Shotter, 1992; Steier, 1991).

If knowledge is a co-construction resulting from the interactive relationship between the observer and the observed, then researchers and their participants are inseparable aspects of any research design. The researcher is "the primary data-gathering instrument" (Lincoln & Guba, 1985, p. 39). Because mental phenomena have a relation to a content that is intentional in nature, all behavior is anticipatory rather than reactive. This intentionality establishes a person's way of being conscious of something. If reality exists at all, therefore, it has meaning only after it is perceived. As Geertz (1973) stated:

> Believing, with Max Weber, that man is an animal suspended in webs of significance he himself has spun, I take culture to be those webs, and the analysis of it to be therefore not an experimental science in search of law but an interpretive one in search of meaning. (p. 38)

The constructivist researcher, therefore, is engaged in a search for the deep structure that underlies the construction of meaning as expressed in specific mental phenomena.

Recognizing that what we know is that which has served us well, the test of all knowledge is its utility for the individual. Knowledge is useful if it stands up to experience and enables us to make predictions and bring about necessary change. Having given up the positivist's self-deception of predicting and controlling behavior, the constructivist no longer seeks external validity as a legitimate concern with regard to research design. As an alternative, the researcher considers the perspective of the user of the generalization — seeking epistemological harmony with the reader's experience — as a natural basis for generalizations (Lincoln & Guba, 1985). Therefore, research is useful if it stimulates readers to transform their own construction of reality in order to integrate the meaning of experiences as constructed by others.

Such real-world research arises from the lived experience of the participants, who share in the definition of questions for study, help to formulate alternatives, and are fully engaged in the analysis and interpretation of any findings. In reconceptualizing research from this perspective, internal validity becomes credibility; external validity (generalizability) becomes transferability (focus on maximizing description of context rather than minimizing it through control of variables); reliability becomes dependability; and, rather than control for instrumentation in method, the constructivist does a dependability audit to account for changes in strategy or methodological concerns over time (Lincoln & Guba, 1985). Rather than a search for grand unifying narratives in a system of similarities, a constructivist approach celebrates the unity to be found in a diversity of individual narratives.

Implications for Education and Supervision

Critical to a constructivist view of how we think is that experience is the necessary condition for development, although experience itself is not enough. Because we tend both to organize and to adapt, we must necessarily interact with the environment. Thus, each person's experience must be of a kind that presents genuine cognitive conflict for him or her. This conflict should present a discrepancy to some optimal extent between the individual's existing mental structures and present experience.

The realization that neither problems nor solutions are ontologically correct is the consequence of recognizing that our particular realities are self-constructions. Because constructivism accepts the possibility of multiple realities, counselors no less than clients should engage in a process of continual self-reflection. Because the problems encountered by professional practitioners are frequently complex, Schön (1987) has argued that professional education should be centered on enhancing the practitioner's ability for "reflection-in-action." Similarly, supervision will necessarily involve a reciprocal understanding of the other and will focus on the form of the relationship between the supervisor and the supervisee. A central feature of supervision, therefore, will involve negotiating the relationship over time in service of education as the development of both participants to the relationship.

If we understand that development is a liberating function, in that it expands the basis on which our present reality is constructed, then we should seek those social relationships that will support such expansion/liberation most fully. A constructivist perspective leads us to conclude that democracy is the social structure that best provides the proper context for such development. Whether in counseling, conducting research, or engaging in teaching or supervision, the constructivist's assertion of the impossibility of objective reality supports continual expansion of forums for democratic decision making to enable new possibilities to become crystallized and be acted upon. As argued by Dewey (1916/1944), "democracy is primarily a mode of associated living, of conjoint communicated experience" (p. 87). What Dewey is saying is that democracy begins in conversation because in conversation one must take the other into account. Acting in the context of a public decision-making process helps group members consider the opinions of others and place responsibility on members for the consequences of their actions (Haan, 1977).

Rather than being a powerless person with boundless desires, the postmodern individual is an empowered person with bounded desires. Bounded by the realization that his or her present understanding is necessarily limited, but having realized the nature of his or her own construction, the individual is empowered to change that world. By becoming developmental educators within a deliberate democratic community, constructivist counselors will accept the challenge to empower clients to work together to realize communities of their own making (Hayes, 1993).

The implication of meeting the challenge of a postmodern world from a constructivist perspective is that counselors should become developmental educators who are involved in the development of deliberate democratic institutions. The expansion of the self as a meaning-making system should be the proper aim of education and of a truly developmental counseling practice. Critical self-reflection coupled with ongoing dialogue among group members is a central element in democratic efforts to find unity in diversity and a logical extension of constructivism to educational practice.

Finally, participation in democratic social structures may be viewed as an ethical imperative for self-development. Rather than engage in a professional practice that serves to isolate the client from undo influence by the counselor, as current ethical practice demands, a postmodern ethics would recognize that counselor and client are inextricably entwined in at least a dual relationship. By the recognition of their very existence, each is engaged in a definition of the other that serves to define the self as well. Thus the task for the constructivist counselor is not avoiding dual relationships and minimizing the possibilities for exploitation, but rather recognizing the multiple relationships that define the counselor's and client's experience of each other and maximizing the exploitation (i.e., "to put [it] to productive use" [Webster's Ninth New Collegiate Dictionary]). The question is not how to avoid dual relationships but rather to ask what kind of relationship we want to have.

A CONCLUDING THOUGHT

Constructivism does not create or explain any outside reality — no objective world facing the subjective. The apparent separation of the world into pairs of opposites is constructed by the subject, and that paradox opens the way into autonomy as the recognition of one's ownership of his or her particular reality. Understanding that problems represent unsuccessful attempts to resolve difficulties helps point to potential limitations in one's current way of knowing. In exploring the means by which we create our experiential world, however, we can increase our awareness of both the limitations and opportunities that our present understanding provides. Recognizing that we cannot escape our own constructed reality, counseling from a constructivist perspective is nothing less than an attempt to create the conditions for such exploration. In a world that is coming increasingly to recognize its social as well as its biological interdependence — one that celebrates rather than merely tolerates diversity — counselors can do no less than to risk themselves in relationships with others. In so doing, we may come closer to living the truth we attempt to understand.

REFERENCES

Adler, A. (1972). *The neurotic constitution.* Freeport, NY: Books for Libraries Press. (Original work published 1926)

Baldwin, J. M. (1902). *Social and ethical interpretations in mental development.* New York: Macmillan. (Original work published 1897)

Bandura, A. (1986). *Social foundations of thought and action.* Englewood Cliffs, NJ: Prentice-Hall.

Bartlett, F. C. (1932). *Remembering.* Cambridge: Cambridge University Press.

Basseches, M. (1984). *Dialectical thinking and adult development.* Norwood, NJ: Ablex.

Beck, A. (1976). *Cognitive therapy and the emotional disorders.* New York: International Universities Press.

Botwinick, A. (1993). *Postmodernism and democratic theory.* Philadelphia: Temple University Press.

Carlsen, M. B. (1988). *Meaning-making: Therapeutic processes in adult development.* New York: Norton.

Conner, M. B. (1987). *Postmodern culture: An introduction of the contemporary.* Oxford: Blackwell.

Cooley, C. H. (1902). *Human nature and the social order.* New York: Scribner's.

Derrida, J. (1982). *Margins of philosophy.* Chicago: University of Chicago Press.

Dewey, J. (1910). *How we think.* Boston: Heath.

Dewey, J. (1944). *Democracy and education.* New York: Free Press. (Original work published 1916)

Ellis, A. (1962). *Reason and emotion in psychotherapy.* New York: Lyle Stuart.

Erikson, E. H. (1950). *Childhood and society.* New York: Norton.

Feixas, G. (1990). Personal construct theory and the systemic therapies: Parallel or convergent trends? *Journal of Marital and Family Therapy, 16,* 1–20.

Foucault, M. (1972). *The archeology of knowledge.* New York: Harper Colophon.

Freud, S. (1946). *The ego and the mechanisms of defense.* New York: International Universities Press. (Original work published 1936)

Friedman, S. (Ed.). (1993). *The new language of change: Constructive collaboration in psychotherapy.* New York: Guilford Press.

Geertz, C. (1973). Thick description: Toward an interpretive theory of culture. In R. M. Emerson (Ed.), *Contemporary field research: A collection of readings* (pp. 37–59). Prospect Heights, IL: Waveland Press.

Gergen, K. (1991). *The saturated self: Dilemma of identity in contemporary life.* New York: Basic Books.

Gibbs, J. (1979). The meaning of ecologically-oriented inquiry in contemporary psychology. *American Psychologist, 34,* 127–140.

Goodman, N. (1984). *Of mind and other matters.* Cambridge, MA: Harvard University Press.

Green, M. (1989). *Theories of human development: A comparative approach..* Englewood Cliffs, NJ: Prentice-Hall.

Guba, E. G., & Lincoln, Y. S. (1990). Can there be a human science? Constructivism as an alternative. *Person-Centered Review, 5,* 130–154.

Guidano, V. F. (1987). *Complexity of the self: A developmental approach to psychopathology and therapy.* New York: Guilford Press.

Guidano, V. F. (1991). *The self in process.* New York: Guilford Press.

Haan, N. (1977). Two moralities in action contexts: Relationships to thought, ego regulations, and development. *Journal of Personality and Social Psychology, 36,* 286–305.

Hawking, S. (1988). *A brief history of time: From the big bang to black holes.* New York: Bantam Books.

Hayek, F. A. (1952). *The sensory order.* Chicago: University of Chicago Press.

Hayes, R. L. (1986). Human growth and development. In M. Lewis, R. L. Hayes, & J. Lewis (Eds.), *An introduction to the counseling profession* (pp. 36–95). Itasca, IL: Peacock.

Hayes, R. L. (1993). A facilitative role for counselors in restructuring schools. *Journal of Humanistic Education and Development, 31,* 156–162.

Hayes, R. L. (1994). Counseling in the postmodern world: Origins and implications of a constructivist developmental approach. *Counseling and Human Development, 26*(6), 1–12.

Hegel, G. W. F. (1975). *Logic* (W. Wallace, Trans.). Oxford: Clarendon Press. (Original work published 1830)

Heidegger, M. (1962). *Being and time* (J. Macquarrie & E. Robinson, Trans.). New York: Harper & Row. (Original work published 1927)

Howard, G. S. (1986). *Dare we develop a human science?* Notre Dame, IN: Academic Publications.

Howard, G. S. (1990). Narrative psychotherapies. In J. K. Zeig & W. M. Munion (Eds.), *What is psychotherapy?* (pp. 199–201). San Francisco: Jossey-Bass.

Ivey, A. E. (1986). *Developmental therapy: Theory into practice.* San Francisco: Jossey-Bass.

James, W. (1890). *The principles of psychology.* New York: Holt, Rinehart & Winston.

Jencks, C. (1986). *What is postmodernism?* New York: St. Martin's Press.

Jung, C. G. (1928). *Contributions to analytic psychology.* New York: Harcourt.

Kant, I. (1911). *Prolegomena zu jeder kunftigen Metaphysik. Werke,* Vol. 4. Berlin: Konigliche Preussische Akademie der Wissenschaften. (Original work published 1783)

Kegan, R. (1982). *The evolving self.* Cambridge, MA: Harvard University Press.

Kelly, G. A. (1955). *The psychology of personal constructs.* New York: Norton.

Kohlberg, L. (1969). Stage and sequence: The cognitive-developmental approach to socialization. In D. Goslin (Ed.), *Handbook of socialization theory and research* (pp. 347–480). Chicago: Rand McNally.

Kohlberg, L., & Mayer, R. (1972). Development as the aim of education. *Harvard Educational Review, 43,* 449–496.

Kvale, S. (Ed.). (1992). *Psychology and postmodernism.* Newbury Park, CA: Sage.

Langer, J. (1969). *Theories of development.* New York: Holt, Rinehart & Winston.

Lazarus, A. (1976). *Multimodal behavior therapy.* New York: Springer.

Lincoln, Y. S., & Guba, E. G. (1985). *Naturalistic inquiry.* Beverly Hills: Sage.

Lyddon, W. J. (1995). Forms and facets of constructivist psychology. In R. Neimeyer & M. Mahoney (Eds.), *Constructivism in psychotherapy* (pp. 69–92). Washington, DC: American Psychological Association.

Lyotard, J. (1983). *The postmodern condition: A report on knowledge.* New York: Basic Books.

Mahoney, M. J. (1985). Psychotherapy and human change processes. In M. J. Mahoney & A. Freeman (Eds.), *Cognition and psychotherapy* (pp. 3–48). New York: Plenum Press.

Mahoney, M. J. (1991). *Human change processes: Notes on the facilitation of personal development.* New York: Basic Books.

Mahoney, M. J., & Lyddon, W. J. (1988). Recent developments in cognitive approaches to counseling and psychotherapy. *The Counseling Psychologist, 16,* 190–234.

Mair, M. (1988). Psychology as storytelling. *International Journal of Personal Construct Psychology, 1,* 125–138.

Maslow, A. H. (1968). *Toward a psychology of being* (2nd ed.). New York: Van Nostrand.

Maturana, H. R., & Varela, F. J. (1987). *The tree of knowledge.* Boston: Shambhala.

Mead, G. H. (1934). *Mind, self, and society.* Chicago: University of Chicago Press.

Meichenbaum, D. (1977). *Cognitive behavior therapy.* New York: Plenum.

Mosher, R. L., & Sprinthall, N. S. (1970). Psychological education in secondary schools. *American Psychologist, 25,* 911–924.

Neimeyer, R. A. (1985). *The development of personal construct psychology.* Lincoln: University of Nebraska Press.

Noam, G. (1988, Spring). A constructivist approach to developmental psychopathology. In D. Nannis & P. Cown (Eds.), *Developmental psychopathology and its treatment* [special issue] (pp. 110–121). *New Directions for Child Development* (No. 39). San Francisco: Jossey-Bass.

Parry, T. (1993). Without a net: Preparations for postmodern living. In S. Friedman (Ed.), *The new language of change: Constructive collaboration in psychotherapy* (pp. 428–459). New York: Guilford Press.

Pavlov, I. (1927). *Conditioned reflexes.* New York: Dover Books.

Pepper, S. C. (1942). *World hypotheses.* Berkeley: University of California Press.

Piaget, J. (1954). *The origins of intelligence in children.* New York: International Universities Press. (Original work published 1936)

Piaget, J. (1955). *The language and thought of the child.* Cleveland: World Publishing. (Original work published 1926)

Piaget, J. (1960). The general problem of the psychological development of the child. In J. M. Tanner & B. Inhelder (Eds.), *Discussion on child development: A consideration of the biological, psychological, and cultural approaches to the understanding of human development and behvior* (Vol. 4). New York: International Universities Press.

Polkinghorne, D. (1993, January). Narrative configuration in qualitative analysis. Paper presented at the annual meeting of the Qualitative Research Interest Group, Athens, GA.

Rickey, G. (1967). *Constructivism: Origins and evolution.* New York: Braziller.

Riegel, K. F. (1979). *Foundations of dialectical psychology.* San Diego: Academic Press.

Rogers, C. (1961). *On becoming a person.* Boston: Houghton Mifflin.

Rorty, R. (1983). Method and morality. In N. Haan, R. N. Bellah, & P. Robinson (Eds.), *Social science as moral inquiry* (pp. 155–176). New York: Columbia University Press.

Saari, C. (1991). *The creation of meaning in clinical social work.* New York: Guilford Press.

St. Clair, M. (1986). *Object relations and self psychology: An introduction.* Monterey, CA: Brooks/Cole.

Schön, D. (1987). *Educating the reflective practitioner.* San Francisco: Jossey-Bass.

Shotter, J. (1992). "Getting in touch": The meta-methodology of a postmodern science of mental life. In S. Kvale (Ed.), *Psychology and postmodernism* (pp. 58–73). Newbury Park, CA: Sage.

Skinner, B. F. (1971). *Beyond freedom and dignity.* New York: Knopf.

Steier, F. (Ed.). (1991). *Research and reflexivity.* Newbury Park, CA: Sage.

Sullivan, H. S. (1953). *The interpersonal theory of psychiatry.* New York: Norton.

Thorndike, E. L. (1913). *Educational psychology.* New York: Columbia University Press.

Vaihinger, H. (1924). *The philosophy of "as if."* New York: Routledge & Kegan Paul. (Original work published 1911)

Vico, G. (1710). *De antiquissima Italorum sapientia.* Stamperia de classici Latini, Naples, 1858, Chapter 1, Section 1.

Viney, L. (1990). Psychotherapy as shared reconstruction. *International Journal of Personal Construct Psychology, 3,* 437–456.

von Foerster, H. (1984). On constructing a reality. In P. Watzlawick, (Ed.), *The invented reality: How do we know what we believe we know: Contributions to constructivism* (pp. 41–61). New York: Norton.

von Glasersfeld, E. (1984). An introduction to radical constructivism. In P. Watzlawick (Ed.), *The invented reality: How do we know what we believe we know: Contributions to constructivism* (pp. 17–40). New York: Norton.

von Glasersfeld, E. (1991). Knowing without metaphysics: Aspects of the Radical Constructivist position. In F. Steier, (Ed.), *Research and reflexivity* (pp. 12–29). Newbury Park, CA: Sage.

Vygotsky, L. S. (1986). *Thought and language* (Kozulin, Trans.). Cambridge, MA: MIT Press. (Original work published 1934)

Watson, J. B. (1919). *Psychology from the standpoint of a behaviorist.* Philadelphia: Lippincott.

Watzlawick, P. (1984). *The invented reality: Contributions to constructivism.* New York: Norton.

Weiner, M. L. (1985). *Cognitive-experiential therapy: An integrative ego psychotherapy.* New York: Brunner/Mazel.

White, M., & Epston, D. (1990). *Narrative means to therapeutic ends.* New York: Norton.

Wilber, K. (Ed.). (1985). *The holographic paradigm, and other paradoxes: Exploring the leading edge of science.* Boston: Shambala.

Wittgenstein, L. (1969). *Philosophical investigations* (3rd ed.). (G.E.M. Anscombe, Trans.). New York: Macmillan.

Zimmerman, B. J. (1981). Social learning theory and cognitive constructivism. In I. E. Siegel, D. M. Brodzinsky, & R. M. Golinkoff (Eds), *New directions in Piagetian theory and practice* (pp. 39–49). Hillsdale, NJ: Erlbaum.

CHAPTER 3

The Social Construction of Culture and Its Implications for the Therapeutic Mind-Self

William M. Wentworth and Carlene M. Wentworth

This chapter follows the distinction described by Guterman (1994, 1996) between constructivism and social constructionism: The former applies to individual processes in a social environment, the latter to social processes and products that emerge *between* individuals in the course of interaction. We take the sociological approach of social constructionism and claim that it forms the conditions within which contructivism occurs. Social constructionism is not, however, another form of top-down social determinism. It has immediate implications for the theory and practice of counseling precisely because it specifies the mutual and reciprocal causal link that ties the social realm to the interior workings of individuals (cf. Gergen, 1985; Lyddon, 1995). This chapter intends to provide some steps toward a *social* theory of the therapeutic process. Further, by the means of such a social theory — as compared with a psychological theory — we intend to help connect the therapeutic process to the everyday lives of people who are only temporarily clients.

THE CONCEPT OF CULTURE

A certain portrayal of culture is developing from the discourse among several schools of thought, and this idea is expressed in an eclectic vocabulary (e.g., "epistemic communities," Holzner, 1968; "habitus," Bordieu, 1972; "structure," Giddens, 1984). Some of these perspectives are constructionist, others not. However it is expressed, this emerging concept of culture has become central to the social constructionist perspective. This concept is one in which culture bounds physical space and concurrently acts as the algorithm of conversion between the social and personal spheres. At the social level, culture is seen as immanent in the patterns of interaction that arise among people. It exists there in a manner analogous to the way self-reproductive information is immanent in DNA, or grammar intrinsic to language usage. Culture also becomes a part of the person as a result of immersion in daily life. How? Internalized culture provides a means to organize the myriad pieces of experience. But this similarity of social origin does not make us social psychological twins. The particulars of individuals' lives are of course diverse, leading to the inevitable differences among mind-selves. The thread of culture runs through this array of individuality; it allows for a more or less easily *negotiated* (Berger & Luckmann, 1966; Gergen, 1982) sense of living in a shared world.

The "Context" as a Unit of Culture

Culture results from the actions of individuals *on* external, persisting patterns of social relationships (i.e., social structures). Culture production is accordingly dependent on the stability of those underlying social structures. At the same time individuals act on social structures, they act *in* them, creating and re-creating the patterns (see Giddens, 1984, on such recursive organization of conduct). Thus, culture production is at once individual and eminently social. What is important to grasp from this discussion is that all intelligible conduct is situated. We do not act on and in, say, "U.S. society"; that remains an abstraction from the here and now. Rather, we act on and in the immediacy of mutually monitoring, face-to-face interaction, in a definite setting. Likewise, the culture (re)produced *in situ* is not, say, "Western culture," in its totality. By attending to the specifics of interaction, a small world is framed in the midst of the larger environment. This partially segregated social place is the immediate frame of reference for the mutual interpretation of participants' activity. Thus culture is always and unavoidably created and implemented in units called *contexts*. The context is a situation- and time-bounded rule-resource set that acts as an arena for human activity (Wentworth, 1980, p. 92; and cf. Giddens, 1984).

Culture mediates our conceptions of reality and, hence, culture influences the thoughts, feelings, and actions that arise in our moment-by-moment experience. The concept of context (as a unit of culture) is of critical importance to the practice of counseling. Context implies that we do not have to change all of culture to change the meanings and conditions of our lives, but we must change some of it. Further, a context is "portable," meaning it can be reconstructed outside the boundaries of the therapy situation. The concept can thus provide a theoretical underpinning for a social theory of the therapeutic process.

DEFINITIONS OF CULTURE

Before we proceed with the chapter, the concept of culture must be further clarified. "Culture" carries so much connotative baggage that the term invites quibbling. We will not attempt, in so short a space, to peel away its political meanings. We will set those aside and focus on social science usage. In the social sciences, the idea of culture is used in two domains: (1) the older, descriptive, or taxonomic definitions that always use the term culture, and (2) the newer, theoretically functional understandings that have emerged from affinities among structuralism, dialectical sociologies, and social constructionist writings, and that use several terms (the eclectic vocabulary mentioned above) to refer to the idea of culture (cf. Rossi, 1983).

Older Definitions

Culture has been defined in many ways since 1865 when it was first used in a way that would be familiar to social scientists today (Kluckhohn, 1964, p. 166). Not until well into this century did it become a standard conceptual category across the several social sciences. Generally, these older definitions depict culture as a taxonomic classification — a conceptual bin, really, into which are thrown a disparate assortment of the defining and idiosyncratic aspects of a society. In this approach, culture is typically divided into the "nonmaterial" (e.g., a song, a theology) and the "material" (e.g., a pot, a behavior), with the entirety defined much as follows: Culture is the beliefs, values, behavior, and material objects shared by a particular people (e.g., Henslin, 1995).

As a taxonomic category, culture has no fruitful theoretical function; it is merely a convenient descriptor that allows one society to be differentiated from another. Further, it can be said that this usage really talks about the constructs of a culture, not the culture itself. This older form of the definition is still used frequently where no conceptual framework is required to explain social processes.

Newer Definitions

In this chapter, we will rely on a newer, theoretically functional understanding of culture. Here culture is seen as the grammar that organizes the bits and pieces of life and thereby makes them into meaningful wholes. Thus, words, behaviors, beliefs, values, material objects, and so forth are not culture. These are patterned and acquire significance only insofar as they are generated and mutually related by the grammar that is culture. As described here, culture is an open rule system that functions to make an intimate connection among individuals and between individuals and social structure. Let us briefly look at the meanings of "open" and of "intimate" as used in this definition.

Life contains and expresses cultural rules, but no cultural rule tells you the next thing to do, think, or feel. Culture only puts the person in interpretable space. The interpretive process and behaviors based on it are "open" to the dispositions and decisions of the individual. The fact of open rules means that the relationship between society and the individual is not deterministic. Put differently, individuals are not governed by culture; they unavoidably act (and think and feel) in relation to culture. Thus, culture forms the medium for dialectical processes that drive a flow of meaning from within institutions to within individuals, and back again. This interchange can occur precisely because culture is internalized as the framework of the individual mind-self. Cultural ties among a people are thus "intimate" because they constitute and then attach to the very essence of a person's social being.

Starting with a model of the social construction of reality, this chapter will use the concepts of context (as a unit of culture), identity (as a situation specific presentation of the mind-self), power, and negotiation to sketch the *social* processes of therapy.

A CONSTRUCTIONIST MODEL

The constructionist model to be presented is adapted from the classic work of Peter Berger and Thomas Luckmann (1966). Their model (see Figure 3.1) interrelates human biology, social structure, culture, and the mind-self in a remarkably straightforward dialectical conjunction. As human groups lend order to their social lives, and act on and witness the ensuing pattern, they unavoidably abstract, construct, and exemplify culture.

At the center of the model is socially constructed reality. The relation of culture to "reality" is direct and causal. Reality is a culturally engendered perspective that we live as if it were *actual* (i.e., independent of our mutual, historical, collective effort). When we apply the cultural grammar to everyday life, the physical, temporal, cognitive, emotional, social, linguistic, and intentional aspects of the social world are unified or made whole. We do not live culture, we live reality. Reality is the meaningful "whole" apperceived by persons who interact and share a cultural grammar.

This constructionist model may be read in the following way: The biological person naturally *externalizes* our species' creative capacity through behaviors oriented toward others and, with them, creates *order* in the environment. This order is *social structure*. Now, biological persons and their structural creation exist simultaneously. Structure acts back on its creators to impart a persisting measure of recognizability to the mutual relations among persons.

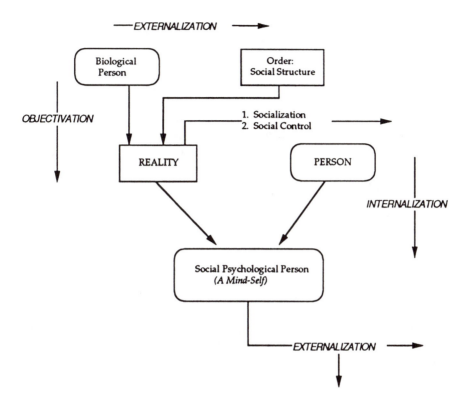

FIGURE 3.1. The Social Construction of Reality. Adapted from Berger and Luckmann, 1966.

Individuals act on and react to the regularity conferred by structured relations. From this exchange with the social environment, they gradually abstract culture. Using their emerging version of culture as a guide, and in the process of *objectification* (making meaning in concert with others), they negotiate a shared *reality*.

Socially constructed, historically arbitrary reality is no mere chimera. "Reality" carries in it the willful force of all its co-creators, the plausibility of its socially accepted legitimacy, the sheer weight of its existence, and the momentum of its history (however short or long). With all the power of reality, our creation acts back on the *person* through the primary process of *socialization*, and secondarily, through the ongoing, situated processes of *social control*.

Embedded in structure and influenced by reality, and being biologically adapted to do so, the person "brings" this meaningful order inside. This occurs as the process of *internalization:* importing the basic structure of the mind (culture) and the contents of the self (knowledge) from society. The *social psychological person* thus emerges from a state of naive biological capacity into encultured personhood.

Reality now forms the background of members' biographical experiences. *Externalization* continues to occur. In encultured persons the process of externalization is no longer merely a generalized species capacity to participate in the creation of social order: Encultured persons externalize actions, thoughts, and feelings shaped by and for their particular society. Once the base process of externalization is affected by internalized culture, the remaining processes (depicted in the constructionist model) serve to *re*construct the social basis of those experiences. The processes depicted in the above model are everywhere present all the time among wide-awake, conscious, interacting persons — making culture and reality continuously available.

POWER AND STRUCTURE

Social structures dispose encultured individuals toward certain expected ways of doing, thinking, and feeling. Put simply, there is a strong tendency for members of a society to be unsurprising. Structural predisposition is *ongoingly accomplished* by distributing the social resources for interaction unequally among established roles and statuses. Examples of these resources include authority, prestige, knowledge, wealth, rank, socially evaluated personal attributes, and demeanor. It should be noted from the examples that we do not react to the material world directly. Social resources are immaterial qualities attached by culture to the material world.

This predisposing inequality of resource distribution constitutes the power dimension of social life. Established power relations promote the reproduction of structural patterns of doing, thinking, and feeling. In the face of established power relations, encultured individuals are less likely to recognize their own creative powers and more likely to be blinded to any feasible avenues for change. That is, persons tend to take the existing pattern of relations for granted, and as an unchangeable given. The litany of the reified consciousness is: "That's the way life is. What can I possibly do?"

Despite social power but because of the open nature of cultural rules, individuals in interaction can redistribute social resources in limited ways. Redistribution can modify local structures and cultural contexts when it is accomplished repeatedly, over time by individuals in interaction. Given the existing balance of power, such change is always difficult. And change is risky. The individual risks alienation (or excommunication) and the disorientation of anomie. The ultimate risk to the structure is dissolution (e.g., divorce).

STRUCTURE AND CULTURE

Multicultural society and multiculturalism reflect structurally based perceptions about the degree of unity within a society. By saying that these phenomena are structurally based, we impute a structural cause beneath the realm of their reality to the people of a society. This structural cause is the existing, predisposing inequality of resource distribution. Such inequality creates separate — even divergent — lives for segments of the same society.

Social Structural Differentiation

"Structure" comprises segmented yet integrated parts within a functioning whole. The fact of structural segmentation creates natural eddies of cultural knowledge (persisting differences of perspective within the organization of a structure's parts). This is so because individuals act on their part of structure, and in relation to what, from their place, they grasp as the whole of structure, to abstract culture. The degree to which this knowledge is isolated and specialized relative to the component parts of structure reflects the strength of subcultural or — at a greater extreme — "multicultural" tendencies within that society.

The component parts of what we now, rather hopefully, call "multicultural" society exist within an interactional field characterized by severe inequalities of power. The persistence of those inequalities has led to "multicultural*ism*": the political recognition of stratified societal structure and, therefore, heterogeneities of culture.

Structural and cultural heterogeneity is most noticeable in the way that a society is divided into operative types. These types can be based on heritage (race and ethnicity), gender, and class. Religion, occupation, and age are also markers of differentiation, but they vary widely in their significance across societies. With the exception of heritage, the rest of these types are not usually counted as culturally distinct. Yet the greater the structural inequalities between types (e.g., income and educational disparities between classes), the greater are the actual cultural differences. Any form of extreme inequality within a society is a basis for genuine "multiculturality" (several separate cultures within one politically inclusive boundary), whether named such and politically recognized or not. However, less extreme effects of structural differentiation extend to the level of the individual, even in relatively homogeneous societies.

"Negotiation" as a Central Feature of All Interaction

Structural heterogeneity creates between persons, but especially between persons of different social-cultural type, what is known as the problem of attaining intersubjectivity. In discussing the Berger and Luckmann (1966) model above, we stated that the processes of reality construction are ongoing, occurring everywhere and all the time. Here, we are saying that the construction process, while continuous, is not seamless. That is, the differentiation of structure implies a distribution of cultural contexts; the result is the construction of individually unique mind-selves, each with its own more or less distinct set of social origins. Hence, in addition to biological diversity within a population, each person has at least a slightly different cultural perspective. These differences impose the necessity of *negotiation* on all reality construction. Every interaction represents such a negotiation: a working out of the details of meaning that join the involved persons. In the long run, members strive to reduce negotiation to the routine of recipe and expectation. That is, joined members seek to apply the same contextual (cultural) rules and achieve repeatedly similar interactional outcomes. Such limiting of creative behavior by the constraints of social structure is never total (i.e., deterministic). Two common yet striking examples of routinization are "learning" a job and "getting to know" a stranger.

Negotiation produces an evolving reciprocal and shared (not identical and common) definition of the situation. Because of negotiation, situations and longer-lasting relationships are said to be "emergent," even as they are conservatively stabilized by their past (e.g., by previously evolved reciprocal expectations, norms, and contextual culture, etc.). Persisting, intimate negotiation effects changes in the involved mind-selves, and can create greater similarity of cultural perspective. Theoretically, however, negotiation can never achieve perfect symmetry between mind-selves. The symmetry that does arise from interaction always occurs by degree. When the negotiation processes are blocked, anger or confusion and distress often result.

THE SOCIOCULTURAL EMERGENCE OF THE MIND-SELF

This section discusses the social psychology of mind-self formation as a sociocultural emergent (Harré & Gillett, 1994; Mead, 1962). A social psychology of the mind-self is not its psychology. That is, we will write about the way the mind-self functions within the frames of contextual culture; we will not discuss the way the mind-self functions within itself. However, any such functioning is dependent on the socioculturally elicited organization of the mind-self. This section examines the functional components of the adult mind-self.

First, and for the sake of comparison, the simpler childhood structure is briefly considered. Second, the organization and aptitudes of the adult mind-self are illustrated at somewhat greater length. Dialogue with this organization undergirds the counseling process and must therapeutically influence it. Thus, this section acts as a necessary introduction for the concluding section on culture construction in the context of therapeutic interaction.

The Social Psychological Structure of Children

Very young children are generally more approachable and more vulnerable than adults (Fraiberg, 1959), for two reasons. First, children have no reflexive capacity that allows them to put the distance of judgment between themselves and events (see Figure 3.2; the absence of reflexivity is signified by the hyphen between mind and self). They can only employ pre- and proscriptions learned from significant others in very literal ("rigid") fashion (Maier, 1969, chap. 3). If these canons are broken, children's emotions (fear, guilt, shame) tend to attach them more strongly to the offending events (cf. Wentworth & Ryan, 1992), for example, sexual and physical abuse. Second, children are incapable of buffering the environment by fronting an identity. What they are is what you see, to modify the cliché a bit. The absence of social psychological structures (as contrasted with the diagram of the adult in Figure 3.2) does not deny that certain psychological mechanisms will be available to protect children, but these function only after severe threat (e.g., post trauma memory loss, emotional numbness, acting out, etc.) and not proactively as do identity structures.

The Social Psychological Structures of Adults

Adult social psychological structures attend to the nuances of interpersonal boundary exploration typical of interactional negotiation. Identities filter the exchange between a person's mind-self and the situation. The manipulation of an identity by the mind buffers the self from direct contact with the situation. This is a reflexive relation signified by the "hyphen" between mind and self in Figure 3.2.

Current Identity. A *current identity* is a highly specialized, situation-specific presentation of self that may not be reflective of "who we really are." It is the manner in which a person assumes a particular role in a structure. But there is another effect of identity presentation that pertains to the construction of cultural contexts.

Because cultural rules are open and contexts are emergent, current identities are negotiated, not determined. The process of interactional negotiation

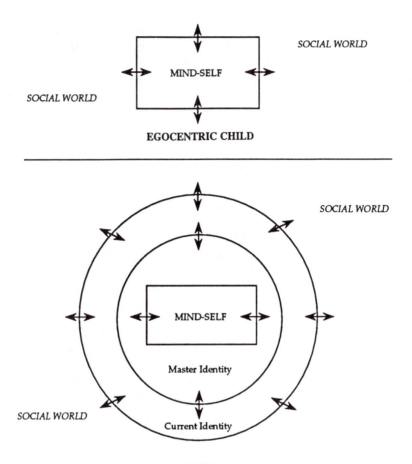

FIGURE 3.2. Structure of the Social Mind in Relation to Age.
Double-headed arrows indicate exchange between environments.

constructs the precise identity fronted, and a single person can behave, think, and feel differently in similar cultural contexts, when different others are present. Different cultural contexts can "bring out" very different aspects of the same person as the current identity is negotiated in the here and now of that social place. This social-psychological operation of "fronting" an identity has implications for therapy. The formation of current identities is the source of the interpersonal flexibility that is at the basis of therapy-influenced change. But the question then arises: What *individual qualities* and what *structured expectations* govern the degree to which a person varies the presentation of the self across cultural contexts?

Individual Qualities. Within the social-psychological framework, the question concerning individual qualities makes the assumption of a potential for far more variation in self-presentation than is typical. The question really asks, therefore, how we so regularly stay within the bounds of a single, recognizable personality. The answer goes back to two personal attributes that can be applied as social resources — the person's implicit image of authority about the self and the habit of reflexive judgment.

Authority of self. The relatively simple social behaviors of the very young child are directly susceptible to temperament and nearly impervious to social control. Still, as we live, an inevitable me-ness envelops our sense of what we do, think, and feel. Our sense of me-ness normally resides in the taken-for-granted background of experience. We do not fully grasp that it has been the structured regularity of our social lives that imposes so much of our objective sense of self on us. That is, we are not conscious of internalization having occurred, while we may well recognize that at various times we have deviated from expectations and resisted social control. This disjuncture, small though it can be, encourages some sense of ownership of who we are becoming; *there is no necessity for a parallel perception of control over the process.* In short, for better or for worse our selfness is reified. Additionally, societal mores and laws can reinforce this reified self: We can be taught that we have the *right* to unimpeded selfhood. Hence issues the constraining authority of the self that is both an origin and a standard for our own social being. Even with the loss of egocentrism, we necessarily and habitually take our developed sense of me-ness as an unquestionable reference point. And with wonderful human paradox, this self-referencing occurs even when the habitual me-ness is understood by the person to be individually and socially questionable (e.g., when the unreliability of the person is a given). For example, a person can have low self-esteem and not question this particular quality of self. The authority of self sustains a low opinion of self!

Reflexive judgment. As egocentrism is lost and the ability to "take the attitude of the other" is gained, an "unreliable" person can continue, by authority of self, the childish overdependency on others for cues about negotiating a current identity. A self-authority in which our me-ness is perceived as unreliable reduces the individual's positive influence on the negotiation of a current identity, giving others more power. But to use the full power of self-authority we must put some distance between ourselves and immediate social influences. In that moment of distancing, we judge the impact of the situation on the self. We may alter our social tactics subsequent to this appraisal, thereby purposefully altering our current identity. This is a function of reflexivity.

Reflexive judgement is not a constant feature of adult consciousness. Occasionally we all "get carried away" by the flow of social circumstances and things "get out of hand." Whereas adults in general are capable of reflexive judgment about self-in-situation, the frequency of its use is a matter of individual habit pattern.

Structured Expectations and the Master Identity. Despite the identity-molding capacity of reflexivity, some elements of an individual's identity are less negotiable than others. The second part of the question asked several paragraphs ago inquired after the structured expectations that govern the presentation of self. And so we are brought to consider *master identity*. The characteristics of a master identity are that it is relevant in multiple contexts (or before multiple others), its traits are ascribed as features of the bearer, and its expected presentation is supported by social control.

Master identities are clusters of symbols that belong more to society than to the individual (on whom they are affixed by authority of society). Race and gender are examples of some strongly held, global master identities. Physician, counselor, and professor are more local master identities. Others behave toward a master identity in impersonal, stereotyped ways. However, the internalization of these symbols can incorporate them into the self. When they are internalized, we lay a personal claim to these template symbols, by authority of the self. That is, we accept the rituals of stereotyped conduct as appropriate and perhaps desirable. (The paradigmatic statement of this social/personal relationship might be: "You know me as male, and I *am* a man.") We are consistently encouraged by self and other to fulfill the expectations of our master identities. Even as we negotiate a current identity, we are "kept in our place" by the boundaries of our master identity.

The Functions of "Identity" in Culture Construction

We have seen that in its presentation, the mind-self is emergent, partitioned into a series of "current identities," and layered into master and current identities. This social-psychological structure has several implications for culture construction, particularly in the light of the concept of context.

Culture is not a physical thing to behold; it is a rules-resource-based process. Culture is constructed by persons in interaction who act on what they perceive to be life's objective regularities. These perceptions, however, are variable. We noted earlier that structural segmentation imparts a heterogeneity of cultural perspectives onto the population of members. That is, each person acts, thinks, and feels in terms of internalized social origins and present structural location. It was also noted that heterogeneity necessitates interactional negotiation. Heterogeneity is thus the ultimate precursor for the master and current identities that represent the mind-self in the negotiation of ongoing reality.

These identities, in turn, add another variable element in culture construction. As current identities emerge in different situations, and as differing master identities interact, the contextual rules of culture are modified.

In fact, the meanings of contextually generated identities — along with their behaviors, thoughts, and feelings — are sometimes so specific that they are not easily recountable in other settings. We even have a set phrase for this phenomenon of specificity. After trying in vain to convey the humor, for example, of another social setting, we give up in frustration and say, "Well, you just had to be there!" Everyone knows exactly what this means, so it acts as a face-saving etiquette for backing away from unsuccessfully telling a particular story.

Yet, the context (as a unit of culture) accounts for structural and cultural continuity as well as situational uniqueness (Wentworth, 1980, pp. 105– 108). Aspects of the macroworld (including master identities) are drawn on by individuals (often not in conscious fashion) in constituting the contextually framed reality of the microworld. Institutional roles, discrete items of information, and the like, are objectively available resources. Contextual realities are composed in the presence of social control efforts by individuals who have internalized existing cultural rules. Stated differently, cultural contexts propagate social institutions and they are idiosyncratic in terms of the motives and capacities represented in the identities of context participants.

CONCLUSION: THE THERAPEUTIC CULTURAL CONTEXT AS STRUCTURED INTERACTION BETWEEN MIND-SELVES

Cultural constructionism offers an opening toward a social theory of the therapeutic process, and its relationship to the everyday life of those who are temporarily "clients." Because cultural constructionism theoretically relates social interaction with the social psychological processes of identity manipulation and self-formation, its principles hold equally for individual, family, and group counseling. This concluding section will draw on the preceding sections and lay out a sketch of therapy as an intentional use of sociocultural and social psychological processes (cf. Hamer, 1995; Ivey, 1994).

The constructionist position emphasizes the sociocultural origins of the mind-self. Constructionism, additionally, makes explicit the power and resource imbalance existing between society and the social psychological person. It thus lays bare the root of the predicament of personal change. Let us state this problem as if from the client's viewpoint:

> What I think, do, and feel are not mine alone; they are part of the social world and that world will resist any of my efforts to change my place in it. Furthermore, I myself am a part of that world and that world is a part of me. Even in the face of emotional pain and dysfunction, I may resist losing my anchorage — my only known place — by means of any personal change. And being constrained by that anchorage, I may not be able even to conceive of healthy, alternative acts, thoughts, and feelings.

Such constraints, while powerful, are not deterministic. Self-consciousness allows for the possibility of autonomous change. If the world cannot be made to change by direct confrontation, the person can reorient himself or herself to it and negotiate change — but at the cost of effort and risk.

Any change we intentionally undergo is made more achievable when others, especially "significant" others, support the process of alteration. This is an avenue toward increased social power for the individual, what has recently been called "empowerment" (but that term does not express the insight that empowerment is as much a social derivation as powerlessness). The therapist can provide the support of a significant other for the client. But structural segmentation presents an inherent obstacle to this achievement in therapy.

The structurally established roles of "therapist" and "client" bring two strangers together in a secondary relation. Based on role relations alone, interaction always begins with substantial, mutual subjective distance. Such differences initially manifest themselves as a wary lack of rapport. But in addition, persons of separate cultural lineages have unlike fundamental perspectives. Only surface conversation can ensue with such differences intact. However, mutual cultural differences lead to sometimes impalpable interactional misjudgments that prevent closing the intersubjective gap. Gaining rapport or trust is merely the first step. It does not set aside any internalized cultural differences. It is the responsibility of the therapist to overcome such dissimilarities. It is possible to draw the rough outline of a general method for increasing the chances of intersubjectivity in the therapeutic setting. This is a method by which the therapist approaches the client's world for understanding. This sketch can be done most quickly using the metaphor of therapist-as-anthropologist. This metaphor has been specifically derived both to cross-cultural divides and to maintain the judgment of the professional. Our assumption about this metaphor is that it describes an appropriate stance all the time, not just when there are obvious markers of cultural difference between client and therapist (cf. Atkinson, Morten, & Sue, 1989).

During fieldwork, the good anthropologist must start with a minimum of presuppositions, and refrain from jumping to conclusions. Tentative hypotheses certainly give direction to the ongoing inquiry, but in a field study they must be treated as sensitizing markers needing further evidence (cf. Clark, 1995; Spradley, 1979; Wentworth 1980). Why take this degree of care? The object of such research is to disclose an exotic world as it is lived, known, felt, and constructed by its native members. Approaching that world with one's own presuppositions produces a *rough translation* of everyday life — a mere caricature of the unique original, and indeed one limited by values from the examining society. The careful anthropologist is able to write about this exotic reality with the exquisite sensitivity of lived experience contemplated from another (anthropological) perspective. However, the anthropologist must pass through the exotic world, and, to remain an anthropologist, must come out of that reality with valid insights that further the aims of anthropology.

The therapist-as-anthropologist explores the patient and his or her "exotic" world as it is (i.e., without presuppositions). We believe that this methodological approach is theoretically warranted by the function of the therapist. To wit, the therapist helps clients live their own lives in their own worlds. This means the therapist works with the client as a unique person and not as some image cloned from the therapist's own values or from cultural stereotypes. Successful therapy moves past the client's situated, current identity and makes direct, deeper contact with the mind-self in terms of its own cultural realities. The actual therapeutic process begins when the therapist learns how to observe the reality of the client's world and to fathom its vernacular mores.

To do so means constructing a unique cultural context for the assembly of a trustworthy current identity in close relation to the client. This unique, highly situated identity is the therapist's socially presented face, one that sometimes eclipses the master identity of "therapist." That is, the new identity is lived authentically and embodied with emotion; it is no mere con, no artificial tool.

Neither the personhood of the therapist nor the therapeutic role is compromised as the new identity emerges from negotiating one's self toward sharing a cultural context with the client. The new identity is regulated by the therapist, and it lacks sovereignty. It functions as the nexus between the master identity of "therapist" and the client's current identity. This identity construction is, however, mutual. The client too is revising her current identity in reciprocal relation to that of the therapist. Via the construction of these new context-specific identities, the therapist can attain an empathetic understanding of the client, glimpse the contexts of the client's world, and discern key elements of the client's mind-self. Then the therapy can begin to bear the fruit of a more healthful client.

However, no one reading this chapter need be reminded that a healthy "client" is different from a healthy person. Ideally, therapy will end with a healthy person, not just a healthy client. Successful attempts at therapy-engendered personal change will have been aided by the following progression:

1. The exploratory attitude (therapist-as-anthropologist) of the therapist
2. The construction of a unique client-centered, therapy-oriented cultural context
3. The sensitive negotiation of new current identities that provide the therapist with a window on the client's self
4. The intentional emergence of new contextual rules in the here-and-now of therapy, but applicable in the client's world
5. The internalization of those healthful cultural guidelines by the client
6. Through practice and feedback, the provision of the specific behavioral, cognitive, and emotional means to transfer the cultural context of therapy to the client's full world and everyday life (a process of recontextualization)
7. A period of continued intimate support from the therapist *qua* "significant other"

The last element is especially necessary during the period of initial adjustments between the new contextual rules gained in therapy and the established (change-resistant) micro-structures of the client's everyday life. In short, clients must gain the authority of self to construct a different set of cultural units, with their concomitant identities, for their everyday lives, and thereby reconstruct themselves. But this fresh authority of self only grows from the fertile soil of therapeutic skill in culture construction.

REFERENCES

Atkinson, D. R., Morten, G., & Sue, D. W. (1989). *Counseling American minorities: A cross cultural perspective.* Dubuque, IA: Wm. C. Brown.

Berger, P., & Luckmann, T. (1966). *The social construction of reality.* Garden City, NY: Doubleday.

Bordieu, P. (1972). *Outline of a theory of practice.* Cambridge: Cambridge University Press.

Clark, A. J. (1995). An examination of the technique of interpretation in counseling. *Journal of Counseling & Development, 73,* 483–490.

Fraiberg, S. H. (1959). *The magic years.* New York: Scribner's.

Gergen, K. J. (1982). *Toward transformation in social knowledge.* New York: Springer-Verlag.

Gergen, K. J. (1985). The social constructionist movement in modern psychology. *American Psychologist, 40*, 266–275.

Giddens, A. (1984). *The constitution of society.* Berkeley: University of California Press.

Guterman, J. T. (1994). A social constructionist position for mental health counseling. *Journal of Mental Health Counseling, 16*, 226–244.

Guterman, J. T. (1996). Reconstructing social constructionism: A response to Albert Ellis. *Journal of Mental Health Counseling, 18*, 29–40.

Hamer, R. J. (1995). Counselor intentions: A critical review of the literature. *Journal of Counseling & Development, 73*, 259–270.

Harré, R., & Gillett, G. (1994). *The discursive mind.* Thousand Oaks, CA: Sage.

Henslin, J. (1995). *Sociology: A down to earth approach.* Englewood Cliffs, NJ: Prentice-Hall.

Holzner, B. (1968). *Reality construction in society.* Cambridge, MA: Schenkman.

Ivey, A. E. (1994). *Intentional interviewing and counseling.* Pacific Grove, CA: Brooks/Cole.

Kluckhohn, C. (1964). Culture. In J. Gould and W. Kolb (Eds.), *A dictionary of the social sciences.* Glencoe, IL: Free Press.

Lyddon, W. J. (1995). Cognitive therapy and theories of knowing: A social constructionist view. *Journal of Counseling & Development, 73*, 579–585.

Maier, H. W. (1969). *Three theories of child development.* New York: Harper & Row.

Mead, G. H. (1962). *Mind, self and society.* Chicago: University of Chicago Press.

Rossi, I. (1983). *From the sociology of symbols to the sociology of signs: Toward a dialectical sociology.* New York: Columbia University Press.

Spradley, J. P. (1979). *The ethnographic interview.* New York: Holt, Rinehart & Winston.

Wentworth, W. M. (1980). *Context and understanding.* New York: Elsevier.

Wentworth, W. M., & Ryan, J. (1992). Balancing body, mind and culture: The place of emotion in social life. In D. Franks and V. Gecas (Eds.), *Social perspectives on emotion*, Vol. 1 (pp. 25–26). Greenwich, CT: JAI Press.

CHAPTER 4

Gender, Social Constructionism, and Psychotherapy: Deconstructing Feminist Social Constructions

Linda Terry Guyer and Lonnie L. Rowell

The field of psychotherapy began struggling visibly with the inclusion and exclusion of sex and gender in theory and practice in the early 1970s (Chesler, 1972; Firestone, 1970; Gornick & Moran, 1971), and this struggle is intricately tied to the feminist critique of psychology. As a movement that linked political and social activism and personal growth in the service of women, feminism embarked on a course bound to bring it into conflict with the dominant forms of psychotherapy found in the first half of the 20th century (Rowell, 1992).

In the past 30 years, feminism and social constructionist theory within the discipline of psychotherapy have achieved a kind of marriage and have profoundly influenced taken-for-granted social truths about sex and gender. This marriage is based, in part, on challenges posed by both feminism and social constructionism to an objectivist psychology, that is, a psychology that applies the rules and methods of empiricism to formulate true theoretical positions about human behavior. The feminist movement, in its pursuit of alternative systems of knowledge, has evolved into an intelligibility of women's meanings concerning an increasingly wide range of socioeconomic, personal, political, psychological, spiritual, and cultural experiences. In this context, the feminist movement has encouraged women (and men) to "shake off" the patriarchal mode of thought, and the starting point for feminist psychotherapy was the interplay between ideology and treatment and the tension between the political and the personal.

Although these efforts have long been recognized as, to say the least, a daunting project, the disciplines of psychology (Flax, 1987; Gergen, 1991; Hare-Mustin & Maracek, 1990; Jordan, Kaplan, Miller, Stiver, & Surrey, 1991), counseling (Enns & Hackett, 1993), and family therapy (Bograd,

1991; Epston & White, 1992; Goodrich, Rampage, Ellman, & Halstead, 1988; Luepnitz, 1988; Myers-Avis & Braverman, 1994) now have all offered directions for the integration of feminist and social constructionist perspectives into theory and practice. Taken together, these directions represent an effort to socially construct a new set of meanings about gender and gender relations. In general, the common premise across disciplines is that gender distinctions are more powerfully guided by sociocultural conventions than by biological imperatives. In addition, this view holds that these constructed gender arrangements have favored men and been inequitable to women. Psychotherapy theories and practices are seen to have perpetuated these inequities and are called on to reshape themselves to better reflect the realities of both halves of humanity, to correct distortions in diagnosis and treatment caused by gender stereotypes, and to equalize the opportunities to access power between men and women.

In general, gender is one of the flashpoints in what some see as an increasingly sharp-edged debate within psychotherapy between postmodern, narrative-oriented theorists and practitioners and adherents to a more objectivistic scientific perspective (Howard, 1991; Kendler, 1994; Smith, 1994). This chapter has two central concerns: first, the relationship between feminism and social constructionism, with a set of "historically situated interchanges" (Gergen, 1985) involving conflicting efforts to create — or to defend existing, intersubjectively shared — social constructions of meaning and knowledge about gender; and second, how these interchanges have influenced, and might continue to influence, trends in psychotherapy. The purpose of this chapter is to assess these new constructions for their contributions and limitations within psychotherapy and to propose alternative directions for psychotherapy theory and practice where shortcomings are noted.

FEMINISM AND SOCIAL CONSTRUCTIONISM IN PSYCHOTHERAPY

Psychotherapy has risen to the status of a mainstream institution in the postmodern era in the United States and most Western countries. Feminism and social constructionism have found an increasingly comfortable fit with psychotherapy as the values of the postmodern world bring them into alignment. The less fettered a particular subdiscipline has been by the early history of the field of psychotherapy, the more central feminist-social constructionism ideas and practices have become. For example, the most integrative linking of social constructionism, feminism, and family therapy came with the introduction of White's narrative therapy (Epston & White, 1992). White's articulation of the dominant cultural discourse of psychotherapy as a political and problem-generating conversation forwarded a framework and methodology for deconstructing or "breaking down" personally constraining cultural narratives and "reauthoring" one's life (Epston & White, 1992). A "narrative" (White, 1992) refers to individuals', families', or societal descriptions of experience and the meanings people ascribe to experience. Personal gender narratives in therapy are evaluated by the clients for their effects on their problems, on their views of themselves in relationship, and on their views of others' views of themselves in relationship.

The feminist social constructionist position takes as given that the patriarchy discourse is dominant and that patriarchy is having a pernicious effect on people's lives. Narrative therapy has become the endorsed therapy for linking social constructionism, feminism, and psychotherapy (Myers-Avis & Braverman, 1994; Roth & Chasin, 1994; Weingarten, 1991).

Perhaps feminist constructions in psychotherapy's greatest contribution to the gender dilemma conversation has been to create a safe environment in which to express feelings and beliefs that were previously unseen and unheard. If women previously experienced disqualification through subordination, psychotherapy has been a primary vehicle for helping women develop sufficient confidence to address their experience and change it. Giving validity to the realities of rape, violence, and sexual abuse without blaming women and excusing men has been accomplished through the acceptance and institutionalization of rape counseling, domestic violence programs, and protection for victims. Women's development of a sense of entitlement to request increased participation of men in family life and to have their opinions honored also are encouraged in psychotherapy today. The valuing of personal choice about singlehood, divorce, and sexual identity and partnership has become a part of the dominant discourse of psychotherapy. While therapy outcome research is not sufficiently developed, there is documentation of increased satisfaction in couples' relationships through more flexible gender role assignments and partnership arrangements (Goodrich et al., 1988; Roth & Chasin, 1994; Walters, Carter, Papp, & Silverstein, 1988); of women's increased sense of personal power and competence in the public world, and ability to protect themselves in the private world (Goodrich, 1991; Imber-Black, 1989; Laird, 1989); and of men's increased flexibility and sense of fulfillment with changing gender demands (Jenkins, 1995). Women's voice is very much heard through the effects of feminist social constructionism in psychotherapy.

However, the feminism–social constructionism relationship seems itself to have become a new privileged social discourse, and now shows its own exclusiveness. In family therapy, thoughtful critiques of the feminist social constructionist position are often dismissed as deriding of feminism, as self-serving and misguided, and as merely backlash (Philipson, 1993). Yet, some challenges to the glorification of this relationship are beginning to appear. Critiques of feminism (Coyne, 1992; Kaminer, 1993; Pittman, 1992) and postmodern influences (Held, 1995; Rosenau, 1992; Smith, 1994) are advising that the effects of this trend require critical examination.

We identify two particular areas of tension in the feminism–social constructionism linkage that create dilemmas for theory and practice in psychotherapy. The first tension derives from the origins of feminism as a social and political movement with an agenda to improve the position of women and with a determination to wage an ideological struggle against sexism and patriarchy (Gornick & Moran, 1971; Millett, 1970; Mitchell, 1974; Morgan, 1970). While specific goals and strategies have varied widely within the movement, feminism is a prescriptive and intervention-oriented movement. In contrast, social constructionism emerged as a description of how "to know" the social world and the relational effects of its workings (Gergen, 1985). As an epistemological position, social constructionism does not prescribe a direction or a methodology for change. Those attracted to this postmodern "understanding" like the openness and sense of expanded possibilities. Detractors paint it as "dizzy and disoriented" (Smith, 1994, p. 408). The marriage of feminism and social constructionism has resulted in a body of thought that criticizes patriarchal discourse for its ideological and self-serving, singular-truth world-view, yet has replaced it with another ideological and self-serving, singular-truth world-view. In addition to having generated a conceptual paradox, the pragmatic effect in psychotherapy is to have redefined psychotherapy as a political institution in which all male behavior is criticized and all female behavior is preferenced.

The second tension derives from a stated belief that the feminist–social constructionist position considers the social good while focusing on and defining what is good for the female half of humanity. Feminism has taken as given that both men and women would benefit from the outcomes of its political agenda and that a social restructuring based on "equality" would be good for society. Social constructionism, as a description, does not take a position on social good. In its broadest social perspective, social constructionism cautions us about how to evaluate what is considered true and who holds truth within and across social groups. In its narrowest social perspective, it has been understood to mean that all difference is equally valid. The effect of this second tension shows itself in psychotherapy, which is traditionally focused on personal well-being, or at most on relationship well-being, in a reaffirmation of a "me-orientation" to assessing the effects of change. The feminist–social constructionist inquiry in psychotherapy does not adequately address the question of social responsibility and the deferring of personal preference for cultural functioning purposes.

These two significant tensions are reflected in four key interrelated constructions that undergird a feminist social constructionist orientation. To continue a critical examination of the effects of this orientation in psychotherapy and to consider alternative understandings to enhance psychotherapeutic practice, the next section applies the tools of social constructionist analysis to the four feminist social constructions.

DECONSTRUCTING FEMINIST SOCIAL CONSTRUCTIONS

Within social constructionist theory, the constructions of a cultural discourse or personal narrative are explored and altered through deconstructive procedures. Deconstructive procedures allow for the experience of "difference, that is, the opening up of spaces for what is not said and heard through conversation" (Lax, 1992). Meaning ascribed to social situations can either constrain or expand possibilities.

> Deconstruction [in therapy] has to do with procedures that subvert taken-for-granted realities and practices, those so-called "truths" that are split off from the conditions and the control of their production, those disembodied ways of speaking that hide their biases and prejudices, and those familiar practices of self and of relationship that are subjugating of person's lives. (White, 1992, p. 121)

Although this chapter is not a fully dimensioned deconstruction, we aim to "break down" now favored, yet unchallenged descriptions and meanings of gender relations. This deconstruction is particularly concerned with making distinctions between ideology and sufficient social reality and between individual and societal well-being. Alternatives and expansions to current feminist social constructions are offered to increase the possibilities for improved gender relationships through a socially responsible psychotherapy.

Gender Relations Are a Problem

Whether one embraces or rejects this view, there are probably few people in the United States who would not be aware that there is an ongoing cultural debate about the treatment of women by men. As the history of feminism portrays, the social ordering of gender privileges men and disadvantages women. The problematic nature of this ordering, specifically for women, has been voluminously described in the literature of feminism. Whether gender relations are a problem for men is known only through women's literature and a small cohort of feminist men's literature.

This construction is a response to what feminists experienced as the historically privileged view that biology orders male-female relationships, that this ordering naturally selects for male's greater competence for positions of dominance, and that this ordering is not a problem. "Historically privileged" has referred, in academic and activist feminist circles, to the past 2,000 years, or since hierarchical, competitive societies overpowered partnership societies (Eisler, 1987). In the early stage of the contemporary feminist movement, more direct forms of expression were used to make this point. For example, Millett (1970) proclaimed that

> what goes largely unexamined, often even unacknowledged (yet is institutional-ized nonetheless) in our social order, is the birthright priority whereby males rule females. . . . However muted its appearance may be, sexual domination obtains nevertheless as perhaps the most pervasive ideology of our culture and provides its most fundamental concept of power. (p. 25)

Millett criticized patriarchy as the form of "sexual politics" through which men establish their power and maintain control. As she described it, the sys-tem of male domination and female subjugation is achieved through socializa-tion, perpetuated by ideology, and maintained by institutions.

Evidence of generalized acceptance of the construction "gender relations are a problem" shows itself in the attention given in political, public informa-tion, and social service institutions to the themes of domestic violence, abor-tion rights, sexual harassment, divorce and single-parent families, sexual abuse, and male-female communication. The "problem" has been increasingly defined through public institutions as men's bad behavior. The pragmatic effect of this reality is that men and women experience each other as adversar-ies and are having serious difficulty getting along in the workplace and in personal relationships.

These relationship difficulties have become the work of psychotherapy. Psychotherapy is social discourse organized around "having personal prob-lems," and the question that guides the therapeutic conversation is, "Is this a problem for me?" or, at most, "Is there a problem for us?" Psychotherapy's focus on the individual and interactional levels of relationship does not ask what effect promoting this type of social reality has on the larger picture of cultural interdependence and functioning.

We also suggest that psychotherapy has centered on the belief that most behavior is determined through social processes, and that biology, as related to gender, is less influential. The question in psychotherapy has been, "Is this biological and, therefore, not changeable (except by medication), or is this social and, therefore, changeable through therapy?" Feminist social construc-tionists have believed that "what has been constructed can be reconstructed, albeit with considerable effort. Gender and sexual orientation thus should be understood as changeable ideologies rather than as biological facts" (Herek, 1987, p. 82).

Although family therapy has shifted the focus from the decontextualized individual to interactional patterns among family members, therapy is still oriented to personal or relationship satisfaction. Feminist social constructionists have highlighted that definitions of satisfaction and health are guided by cultural prescriptions. However, the goal of feminist social constructionists in therapy is to "step outside" the cultural constraints for personal well-being. Missing in psychotherapy in general, and even more intensely in feminist social constructionism, is the attention to social responsibility and ideas and practices that invite a family or individual to consider its/his/her contribution to cultural or societal survival and thriving. In the psychotherapeutic relationship, feminist inspired or not, the interplay between anthropological, sociological, interactional, and individual social contexts is most often considered only through the psychotherapeutic lens.

We are not proposing a reconstruction of gender relationships along masculinist rather than feminist lines. We adhere to the construction "gender relations are a problem." We also realize that attention had to be called to the devaluing and marginalizing of women's experience. We do suggest a more realistic construction: that gender relationships have been continually evolving rather than constant and have not necessarily been a problem throughout history. Feminist social constructionists have imposed a current reality about the meaning of gender organization on the past. In this context, cross-gender relations are primarily defined against the backdrop of an all-encompassing evil system: patriarchy. As we see it, there is insufficient evidence to regard current gender dilemmas as stemming from other than recent and co-evolving developmental societal changes. These developmental trends may be an outgrowth of shifts in multilevel contexts that include greater control over biology; an increasingly industrialized, formally educated, and technologically driven culture; and an expanding celebration of individual rights and self-determination (Gergen, 1991; Segal, 1987). This view lifts the blameful implications and puts gender problems in an evolutionary frame.

Answers to the natural-versus-cultural debate over sex and gender have tended to rely on a muddled assumption that the truth about this can be both known and shaped to serve particular interests. The socially responsible question is, given that essential biological structures have remained the same over time (although the constraints related to these structures have changed considerably) and that social values and behaviors do change over time, what is the most useful reality about sex and gender relationship possibilities that addresses questions of cultural continuance and well-being? We believe that feminist social constructionist ideas and practices in psychotherapy have tended to close off conversation on this question.

The Discourse of Patriarchy Organizes Cultural Relationships

Patriarchy used to be understood to mean a social system in which leadership descended through kinship via senior males (Gailey, 1987). Patriarchy as a construction of feminist ideology currently asserts that authority is accorded to men through all institutions of influence including government, law, religion, health care, and the family and that it pervades social belief systems. The narratives about how the world should be that emerge from this discourse reflect men's perspectives and, therefore, define power and knowledge in a way that supports those perspectives and renders others marginal or invisible.

The mediated meaning of patriarchy has changed from benign to overwhelmingly negative. The ideology of the feminist critique of patriarchy is about an evil, oppressive system, willfully and conspiratorially designed by white men to serve their own interests. This understanding of social organization spawned corollary constructions that counter historical constructs of gender relations as balanced and complementary. For example, feminism has portrayed motherhood as a burden rather than a reward and responsibility. Women have been controlled by men through sex and reproduction and men hold the resources that give women the power to mother adequately (Chodorow, 1978; Dinnerstein, 1976; Glen, 1987). Importantly, also, men are viewed as perpetrators and oppressors, and women as victims. Bad men have been taken as evidence that men as a class need to be reeducated and fixed.

In psychotherapy, the feminist social construction of ill-willed patriarchy has become institutionalized. The feminization of psychotherapy by the increasing presence of women as practitioners, the continuing prevalence of women as consumers, and the defining of psychotherapy as a profession of caretaking (Philipson, 1993) is accompanied by a variety of beliefs and applications that pathologize men's behavior and normalize women's behavior.

While the patriarchy-as-oppressor construction is not universally accepted among psychotherapists, differing views are silenced or marginalized now. The goal for men is to accept more responsibility for their oppressive behavior and to be more emotionally vulnerable. The goal for women is to accept less responsibility for men's behavior and to take care of themselves instead of others. In other words, the social "truth" is that women are giving more than they are getting in relationships. The narrative of psychotherapy defines women as victims and then uses the process of therapy to help them get out of victimhood. The distinction between a woman's personal narrative of victimhood and a social reality of victimhood is no longer examined. For men, the trend in psychotherapy has been to shame them into therapy in order to have them own their bad behavior and then invite them to redefine masculinity to include feminine qualities. Many psychotherapeutic programs and strategies embracing the feminist social construction of ill-willed patriarchy have not been successful. Domestic violence programs provide a highly visible example.

Domestic violence programs offer discouraging data on modifying the behavior of male batterers (Jacobson, 1993). The models for helping male batterers focus on anger management and ownership of responsibility for controlling mean behavior. The failure of women to leave these men is ascribed to male intimidation and lack of economic and personal resources, which keep the women from acting. These realities are based on the notion that men have all the power, and women have none. Meaning is now ascribed to the situation through women's eyes. This reality insufficiently attends to more complex and closer-to-truth realities of relational power. Many couples continue to be drawn to each other in love and attraction, with each often responding out of a desperation for closeness. The point is not to be forgiving about bad behavior but to put back into the gender dilemma a more interactional perspective that includes both men's and women's experiences.

Our recommendations for reconstructing the construction of ill-willed patriarchy include, first, the perspective that patriarchy is no longer the dominant discourse. The feminist reality, if not dominant, is as influential as masculinist reality in the discourse of psychotherapy. Second, we recommend a view of male-female relationships that rejects the oppressor-victim dichotomy and adheres more to the view of power as relationally developed. Embracing this reality relies on understanding that women's described deference to men's emotional vulnerability is not part of victimhood but part of a power balance between men's physical strength and women's emotional strength. Men's violence against women should be examined in relation to men's violence against other men and themselves in response to the experience of betrayal or emotional abandonment by a woman, not in relation to women's physical violence against men, in order to construct a fuller relational narrative.

Equity Means Sameness in Access to Influence, Participation, Behavior, and Meaning-Making

"Equity" is a core ideological assumption in the United States. That feminism organizes itself around this premise is a reminder of how ideologies and discourses interweave and how even a discourse identified as a revolutionary movement cannot step outside the dominant cultural discourse. Different meanings of equity in feminism have been privileged by different types of feminism. Radical feminists and antipsychotherapy feminists saw equity as a restructuring of all social institutions and a reshaping of the structures that arrange work-home relationships. Liberal or cultural therapists, often represented in psychotherapy by psychodynamic psychologists and humanistic counselors, saw equity as an adaptation of current institutional structures to equally value the essential differences between men and women, and include women and women's resources, and to invite men to escape the confines of traditional male gendering. Postmodern and social constructionist feminists see sameness and difference as socially mediated. Equity, also, is a construction and can, therefore, be reconstructed to open up and reshape men's and women's possibilities and social institutions. This construction includes a vision of partnership, equal valuing of all contributions to social, economic, and political functions and cross-gender access to whatever one chooses.

The sameness-difference conversation in psychotherapy shows itself in conflicted conversations about roles of economic providership and childrearing and in patterns supporting physical and emotional protection. Clients bring in narratives that affirm that either gender can choose to fill either role or can develop or harness the personal resources to "do it all." The goal of therapy for men and women, individually or coupled, is to become more flexible in their role behavior.

More subtle, though, are some implications and effects of the equity-as-sameness meaning on values commonly expressed in therapy. Feminist social constructionists support, first, that fathers should be more involved in families, childrearing, and household responsibilities. The rationale is not that such involvement would be good for the children but that it would be good for mother. Second, in these social constructions, men are incompetent in emotional expressiveness. Psychotherapy with men is often about helping to acknowledge and express feelings of vulnerability. The implication is: Women do this better and can better judge that men need to develop these skills. Third, women must be affirmed for their competence as single parents and for their ability to raise men. It seems, again, that equity is for women's interest and does not consider men's, male children's, or female children's interests in current and future cultural history.

We suggest a reconstruction of the construction of equity as sameness to equity as a time and culture-bound social reality. We suggest abandoning the debate about whether men and women are more biologically or socially determined for a recognition that social discourse will position itself in this debate according to the cultural purposes of the times. Although the cultural purposes of the postmodern era have guided us to a blurring of gender boundaries, perhaps this blurring has gone too far. Psychotherapy should take a less authoritative position on how the sameness/difference complementary works or should work. We recommend a position of tentativeness, or not-knowing, about the biological versus socialization/social discourse debate. Clients can be invited to take their own positions on the sameness/difference question and consider the social effects of their positions, when appropriate.

The Institution of Psychotherapy Reproduces Socially Constructed Gender Relations

The process of psychotherapy is a gendered interaction no matter how many participants or what genders are in the room or what clinical theoretical framework the therapist prefers. Both therapists' and clients' unique individual and family experiences and their interactional and cultural situations are influenced by both dominant discourse and personal narratives about how men and women relate to each other. The construction of psychotherapy guides expectations about how caretaking is to be provided and received, how emotional experience is to be expressed, and how personal authority is to be managed.

Feminist analysis has attended to gender bias in the psychotherapeutic relationship. This analysis has addressed male therapist bias toward women (Gergen, 1988; Goodrich et al., 1988; Hare-Mustin & Maracek, 1990; Walters et al., 1988), women therapist bias toward men (Bograd, 1991), the effects of feminist bias in counseling relationships (Enns & Hackett, 1993; Nelson, 1993), and women's issues as therapists (Libow, 1986; Warburton, Newberry, & Alexander, 1989). Further examination of this literature shows that the focus is almost exclusively on women's well-being. The concern is either that men will restrict women's growth by preconceived truths about women's qualities or that women will disadvantage themselves as therapists by accommodating to male behavior that should be challenged. The literature most often does not attend to how female or male therapists might restrict or misunderstand men's behavior through the therapeutic process. On the contrary, this literature focuses on the power of maleness in the psychotherapy relationship and the need to use the position of the therapist to break traditional gender patterns. Again, the feminist social construction of psychotherapy as a gendered relationship has imposed women's meaning on how that relationship should work and what the goals of men and women should be.

The gendered relationship of psychotherapy has also either focused on the dyadic relationship of one client and one therapist or on the therapist as reflecting a gender idea, but not a gendered person. In other words, what is not elaborated is the complex and inevitable effects of multiple alliances and coalitions in couple and family therapy. For example, if a female therapist takes a position in male-female couple therapy that the male partner needs to express his feelings more openly and directly, how can an alliance between the female partner and the therapist be prevented? This commonly preferenced view often results in men leaving therapy and being labeled resistant or avoidant.

In the feminist construction of the gendered psychotherapy relationship, women are not to be criticized for being "overinvolved" with their children, and men are not to be invited into parenting in a way that demeans the female parent (Goodrich et al., 1988; Luepnitz, 1988; Walters et al., 1988). This view does not allow for criticism of women's behavior or for an alliance with men. We suggest that many treatment impasses are a result of gender bias that feminizes the psychotherapy relationship.

We recommend a reconstruction of the construction of psychotherapy as a gendered relationship to include men's experience of the therapy relationship. The discourse of psychotherapy, although credited to men for its inception, fundamentally offers a female problem-solving narrative. Talking about emotional experience and relationships has been considered women's province. While men have increasingly participated in it (voluntarily and involuntarily), the premises of psychotherapeutic problem solving often run counter to preferred male narratives of problem solving, which are doing- rather than talking-oriented. Action-oriented change processes, such as the Twelve Step programs, are increasingly considered insufficient to handle substance abuse problems without psychotherapy. The imposition of psychotherapy as the solution for men as well as women is increasingly defining other approaches to change as adjunctive and rendering undiscussable the fact that men may respond better to doing than to talking programs. We recommend that therapists expand the therapeutic conversation to allow for problem-solving approaches that acknowledge gender variations in fit.

CONCLUSION

Although Geertz (1973) reminded us some time ago that an ideology as a cultural narrative has a coherence, that coherence does not necessarily contain a sufficiency of reality. As feminism, social constructionism, and psychotherapy have evolved and become interwoven, they have created a coherent narrative for the postmodern world. This narrative includes feminism as a political theory serving the interests of women; social constructionism as a descriptive metatheory about knowledge; and psychotherapy as a cultural institution to help people "make it" in society. This chapter has taken the position that although each of these discourses has contributed significantly to opening cultural and personal possibilities in the midst of major social transformations, the constructions of the interwoven discourse need to be challenged for their closeness to "reality" and social responsibility.

Fundamental to this challenge is the recognition that feminist social constructionism forms an ideology, and an ideology narrows descriptions of reality. Ideology names the structure of situations in such a way that the attitude contained toward them is one of commitment (Geertz, 1973). Feminist social constructionism as an ideology and social constructionism as a way of knowing present a contradiction in purposes. Social constructionism opens up possibilities for giving meaning to experience. Feminist social constructionism closes possibilities for giving meaning to experience.

This definition does not imply that an ideology, specifically feminist social constructionist ideology, does not contain truth. However, there is significant evidence of replacing masculinist discourse, which excludes the experience of women, with feminist discourse that excludes, or at the least marginalizes, the experience of men. A critique of psychotherapy for its failures to reflect the experiences and realities of both men and women must be articulated.

Another challenge relates to a more practical problem. An authoritative position of a pernicious patriarchy as the truth about the world cannot be reconciled with a view that takes the plurality of descriptions of social reality as its core belief. While there is disagreement within psychotherapy on how political or value-neutral the therapy process can be, all therapists accept the imposition of the therapist's positions on clients' lives as an ethical issue. Feminist social constructionism does not wrestle adequately with the ethical implications of its ideological stance.

Finally, feminist social constructions seemed to offer the promise of a relational understanding of social experience and a direction for viewing power as having a positive face and with potential for equitable distribution and interpersonal accountability. Family therapy, in particular, was founded on an understanding of relationship behavior as reciprocally influencing and of power as defined by the relationship. However, family therapy, along with psychology and counseling, now asserts that power can be objectively defined as the privilege of men and that women cannot be held as accountable as men for their position in the culture balance. The social historian (Foucault, 1980) regards power as inherent in social discourse. All culture-defining discourses embed meanings of power in what is known and not known and in who shares those knowledges and who does not. This social constructionist view differs from feminist social constructionism, which sees power as defined unilaterally by special interests and as a social relationship that can be eradicated. The problem for psychotherapy is that it falls short of contributing to greater interpersonal accountability and to a cultural rebalancing of the excessive focus on the individual. In this regard, we find ourselves aligned with Parry (1993).

> Psychotherapy also shares a great deal of responsibility, I must say, for the singularity of focus on the inner person and his or her personal satisfaction, almost as life's *summum bonum* . . . the relational therapies have not yet adequately capitalized on their own potentialities for addressing the full implications of coming to terms with the indispensable importance of the other for one's own well-being. As the challenge of the other cries out to be met, lest the postmodern be apocalypse rather than opportunity, the relational therapies (and family therapy particularly), are perhaps the best equipped, both theoretically and clinically, to meet that challenge. (p. 441)

The promise of feminist social constructionism in psychotherapy continues to be its contribution to "shaking up" notions of truth about human behavior and relationships that marginalized women's experience. It is time now to reconsider reality to incorporate both men's and women's experience, and develop a fuller vision of how men's and women's constructions of relationships can support maximizing personal well-being as well as social responsibility for a culturally thriving future.

REFERENCES

Bograd, M. (1991). *Feminist approaches for men in family therapy.* New York: Basic Books.

Chesler, P. (1972). *Women and madness.* New York: Doubleday.

Chodorow, N. (1978). *The reproduction of mothering: Psychoanalysis and the sociology of gender.* Berkeley: University of California Press.

Coyne, J. (1992). Letters to the editor. *Family Therapy Newsletter, 16,* 7.

Dinnerstein, D. (1976). *The mermaid and the minotaur.* New York: Harper & Row.

Eisler, R. (1987). *The chalice and the blade.* New York: Harper & Row.

Enns, C. Z., & Hackett, G. (1993). A comparison of feminist and non-feminist women's and men's reactions to nonsexist and feminist counseling: A replication and extension. *Journal of Counseling and Development, 71,* 499–509.

Epston, D., & White, M. (1992). *Experience, contradiction, narrative and imagination (1989–1991).* Adelaide, South Australia: Dulwiche Centre Publications.

Firestone, S. (1970). *The dialectic of sex: The case for feminist revolution.* New York: Morrow.

Flax, J. (1987). Postmodernism and gender relations in feminist theory, *Signs, 12,* 621–643.

Foucault, M. (1980). *Power/knowledge: Selected interviews and other writings.* New York: Pantheon.

Gailey, C. W. (1987). Gender and ideology. In M. M. Ferree & B. B. Hess (Eds.), *Analyzing gender* (pp. 32–67). Newbury Park, CA: Sage.

Geertz, C. (1973). *The interpretation of cultures.* New York: Basic Books.

Gergen, K. (1985). The social constructionist movement in modern psychology. *American Psychologist, 40,* 266–275.

Gergen, K. (1991). *The saturated self: Dilemmas of identity in contemporary life.* New York: Basic Books.

Gergen, M. M. (1988). *Feminist thought and the structure of knowledge.* New York: New York University Press.

Glen, E. N. (1987). Gender and family. In M. M. Ferree & B. B. Hess (Eds.), *Analyzing gender* (pp. 348–380). Newbury Park, CA: Sage.

Goodrich, T. J. (Ed.). (1991). Women and power. Special Issue. *Journal of Feminist Family Therapy, 3.*

Goodrich, T. J., Rampage, C., Ellman, B., & Halstead, K. (1988). *Feminist family therapy: A casebook.* New York: Norton.

Gornick, V., & Moran, B. K. (Eds.). (1971). *Women in sexist society: Studies in power and powerlessness.* New York: New American Library.

Hare-Mustin, R., & Maracek, J. (1990). *Making a difference: Psychology and the construction of gender.* New Haven, CT: Yale University Press.

Held, B. S. (1995). *Back to reality.* New York: Norton.

Herek, G. (1987). On heterosexual masculinity: Some psychical consequences of the social construction of gender and sexuality. In M. Kimmel (Ed.), *Changing men: New directions on men and masculinity* (pp. 68–82). Newbury Park, CA: Sage.

Howard, G. S. (1991). Culture tales: A narrative approach to thinking, cross-cultural psychology, and psychotherapy. *American Psychologist, 46,* 187–197.

Imber-Black, E. (1989). Rituals of stabilization and change in women's lives. In M. McGoldrick, C. Anderson, & F. Walsh (Eds.), *Women in families: A framework for family therapy* (pp. 451–470). New York: Norton.

Jacobson, N. J. (1993). *Men who batter: A report of research.* Paper presented at American Association for Marriage and Family Therapy Conference, Anaheim, CA.

Jenkins, A. (1995). *Invitations to responsibility: The therapeutic engagement of men who are violent and abusive.* Adelaide, South Australia: Dulwiche Centre Publications.

Jordan, J. V., Kaplan, A., Miller, J. B., Stiver, I., & Surrey, J. (1991). *Women's growth in connection: Writings from the Stone Center.* New York: Guilford Press.

Kaminer, W. (1993, October). Feminism's identity crisis. *Atlantic Monthly,* pp. 51–68.

Kendler, H. H. (1994). Can psychology reveal the ultimate values of humankind? [Comment]. *American Psychologist, 49,* 970–971.

Laird, J. (1989). Women's stories: Restorying women's self-constructions. In M. McGoldrick, C. Anderson, & F. Walsh (Eds.), *Women in families: A framework for family therapy* (pp. 427–450). New York: Norton.

Lax, W. (1992). Postmodern thinking in clinical practice. In S. McNamee & K. J. Gergen (Eds.), *Therapy as social construction* (pp. 69–85). Newbury Park, CA: Sage.

Libow, J. (1986). Training family therapists as feminists. In M. Ault-Riche (Ed.), *Women and family therapy* (pp. 16–24). Rockville, MD: Aspen.

Luepnitz, D. (1988). *The family interpreted: Feminist theory in clinical practice.* New York: Basic Books.

Millett, K. (1970). *Sexual politics.* New York: Doubleday & Co.

Mitchell, J. (1974). *Psychoanalysis and feminism.* New York: Random House.

Morgan, R. (Ed.). (1970). *Sisterhood is powerful.* New York: Random House.

Myers-Avis, J., & Braverman, L. (1994). Integrating feminist and narrative ideas into training and supervision. Paper presented at American Association for Marriage and Family Therapy Annual Conference, Chicago, IL.

Nelson, M. L. (1993). A current perspective on gender differences: Implications for research in counseling. *Journal of Counseling Psychology, 40,* 200–209.

Parry, A. (1993). Without a net: Preparations for post modern living. In S. Friedman (Ed.), *New language for change* (pp. 428–459). New York: Guilford Press.

Philipson, I. J. (1993). *On the shoulder of women.* New York: Guilford Press.

Pittman, F. (1992). It's not my fault. *Family Therapy Newsletter, 16,* 56–63.

Rosenau, P. M. (1992). *Post-modernism and the social sciences: Insights, inroads, and intrusions.* Princeton, NJ: Princeton University Press.

Roth, S., & Chasin, R. (1994). Entering one another's worlds of meaning and imagination. In M. F. Hoyt (Ed.), *Constructive therapies* (pp. 190–216). New York: Guilford Press.

Rowell, L. (1992). *Evolving approaches to feminist therapy: A qualitative study.* Unpublished doctoral dissertation, University of Southern California, Los Angeles.

Segal, L. (1987). *Is the Future Female? Troubled thoughts on contemporary feminism.* London: Virago.

Smith, M. B. (1994). Selfhood at risk: Postmodern perils and the perils of postmodernism. *American Psychologist, 49,* 405–411.

Walters, M., Carter, B., Papp, P., & Silverstein, O. (1988). *The invisible web: Gender patterns in family relationships.* New York: Guilford Press.

Warburton, J., Newberry, A., & Alexander, J. (1989). Women as therapists, trainees, and supervisors. In M. McGoldrick, C. Anderson, & F. Walsh (Eds.), *Women in families* (pp. 152–165). New York: Norton.

Weingarten, K. (1991). The discourses of intimacy: Adding a social constructionist and feminist view. *Family Process, 30,* 285–305.

White, M. (1992). Deconstruction and therapy. In D. Epston & M. White (Eds.), *Experience, contradiction, narrative and imagination (1989–1991)* (pp. 109–151). Adelaide, South Australia: Dulwiche Centre Publications.

CHAPTER 5

From Microscopes to Holographs: Client Development Within a Constructivist Paradigm

Sandra A. Rigazio-DiGilio

What are the foundations on which the mental health profession is constructed? How do the aims of our profession mirror societal beliefs about healthy growth and adaptation? To what degree are the curative factors inherent in counseling theory, practice, and research consistent with societal notions regarding positive development? These questions require us to reflect on how our assumptions regarding development affect our professional culture. Without this understanding, our profession tends to conform to changing societal imperatives — primarily set forth by the dominant culture — as these shift over generations.

Traditional theories explicating human and systemic development exerted tremendous influence in the mental health field (cf. Baltes, Reese, & Lipsitt, 1980; Ginter, 1989; Ivey, Gonçalves, & Ivey, 1989; Ivey & Rigazio-DiGilio, 1991; Liddle, 1983; Weikel & Palmo, 1989). Over the last century, we have relied on these developmental models to guide theory, practice, and research. These models have come to serve as a basic platform undergirding the modern science of our profession.

As our profession moves toward a postmodern understanding of development and therapy, we have come to recognize that traditional North American and European frames of reference underlie most developmental models and therapeutic approaches (cf. Casas, Ponterotto, & Gutierrez, 1986; Ibrahim, 1985; Ivey, Ivey, & Simek-Morgan, in press; Pedersen, 1994; Rigazio-DiGilio & Ivey, 1995; Sue, Ivey, & Pedersen, 1996). This leads us to examine the nature and impact of the wider contextual forces (e.g., societal, political, cultural, generational, historical, economic) that influenced past scientific endeavors and the contemporary contexts that influence current theory, practice, and research. Such constructivist analyses attend to the wider context, the subject itself, and the transaction that occurs between the context, the subject, and the participant-observer.

This chapter presents a socially constructed view of client (i.e., individual and family) development. The constraints evident in traditional forms of scientific inquiry are noted and the core assumptions undergirding our mainstream developmental models are deconstructed. Additionally, an alternative set of assumptions based on constructivist principles is offered and one model of client development—built on these assumptions—is presented. Finally, a direct link between individual and family developmental theory and therapy is provided.

THE CONSTRAINTS INHERENT IN TRADITIONAL SCIENTIFIC INQUIRY

During the reign of positivistic ontology, there were three primary aims of science: reductionism, causal explanation, and prediction (Ainslie, 1993). To gain credibility within this predominant paradigm, social scientists attempted to imitate the way physical scientists investigated their terrain to find and label the "truth" about individual and family development (McWilliams, 1993). In so doing, they minimized human and interactional complexity and presented hierarchical, stage-specific conceptualizations of development that asserted high levels of predictability regarding normal and abnormal adaptation.

The microscope represented the tool of choice for scientific inquiry. The prevailing paradigm dictated that social scientists isolate their subject and concentrate within its boundaries to locate observable components, thereby reducing reality to those smaller ingredients thought to "reveal" world-governing principles. Since these scientists could not decipher development in a manner similar to the way biological science unraveled DNA, theoreticians substituted verifiable developmental theories with "best guess" theories (e.g., Duvall, 1977; Haley, 1963; Piaget, 1955; Solomon, 1973). Unfortunately, even when the locus of causal explanation shifted from the individual to the family, the primary emphasis still remained "the subject" (cf. Haley, 1963; Watzlawick, Beavin, & Jackson, 1967) versus "the subject in dialectic transaction" with various contexts over time (cf. Anderson, Goolishian, Pulliam, & Winderman, 1986).

These scientific endeavors at best identified critical transition points that occur for many individuals and families in North American and European societies and, at worst, stereotyped human and systemic development into normative and non-normative categories based on mainstream societal expectations. Following suit, mental health professionals tended to assess clients using these stereotypical growth processes as evaluative typologies. They did not broaden their scope of inquiry to include multicultural diversity, the voices of silent minorities, or the dialectic transactions that occur between clients and wider contexts. Instead, they helped maintain the status quo by assisting clients to become developmentally in sync with mainstream society rather than intervening at various levels of dialectic exchange (i.e., individual, family, institutions, wider contexts). Therefore, during the positivistic era, there was a failure—at all levels of inquiry and practice—to recognize the intimate relationship between the predominant context, the scientific enterprise it supported, the developmental theories it spawned, and the types of mental health practice it sanctioned.

DECONSTRUCTING CORE ASSUMPTIONS UNDERLYING TRADITIONAL THEORIES OF INDIVIDUAL AND FAMILY DEVELOPMENT

When one examines traditional individual (e.g., Kohlberg, 1969) and family (e.g., Duvall, 1977) developmental theories, the hegemonic effect of a positivistic ontology is evident. By deconstructing the primary assumptions undergirding such theories the limits of modernistic theorizing can be illustrated.

Assumption 1
Development Is Stage-Specific, Linear, and Hierarchical

The assumption that "development progresses in an orderly sequence, through definable stages . . . [and that] at each phase, previous development is not only added to but transformed into more complex, highly differentiated levels of functioning" (Agnew, 1985, p. 226) forms the basis of most traditional developmental theories.

Human Development. Human development is generally referred to as a sequential series of stages that individuals move through, toward higher levels of differentiation and complexity (cf. Bronfenbrenner, 1979; Werner, 1948). Erikson's psychosocial model (1963), Piaget's cognitive-developmental model (1955), Kohlberg's (1981) and Gilligan's (1982) moral development models, and Neugarten's adult development model (1976) represent examples of such linear conceptualizations that depict development from an individual psychological perspective and suggest that the degree of task resolution achieved at any one stage affects subsequent stages. Research shows, however, that early development and experience are not powerful or irreversible forces (cf. Emde & Harmon, 1984; Macfarlane, 1964).

The stages defined within traditional models of individual development are arbitrarily derived — influenced by the wider contextual environment in which specific theories emerged. The subjective nature of these stages is evident in political debates such as the abortion controversy (When does life begin?), the euthanasia dispute (When does life end?), issues of adolescent emancipation (When does a child become an adult?), and issues regarding the superiority of autonomous versus relational frames of reference (Is differentiation a higher developmental stage than intimacy for all individuals, in all families, and in all cultures?). Additionally, these models suggest that there are specific stages of development that we all strive for, and yet only a privileged few achieve. Responding to this latter modernistic assumption, Brim and Kagan (1980) state:

> Adult stages cast development as unidirectional, hierarchical, sequenced in time, cumulative, and irreversible — ideas not supported by commanding evidence. The facts, instead, indicate that persons of the same age, particularly beyond adolescence, and the same historical period are undergoing different changes; one person may show an increase in certain attributes while another shows a decline in the same aspects of behavior and personality. (p. 31)

Family Development. Family scientists also assumed that families moved through predictable stages of development, reaching higher levels of differentiation, organizational complexity, and hierarchical integration over time. Family life-cycle theories (cf. Barnhill & Longo, 1978; Haley, 1973; Hill & Rogers, 1964) relied on stage-specific formulations that defined changing constellations of families over time, usually following a couple through traditional patterns of marriage, childbearing, childrearing, and child launching.

In the 1970s, family scientists recognized that families did not proceed in an orderly fashion through any particular series of stages. For example, Aldous (1978) pointed out that theorized stages were neither descriptive nor prescriptive of family life cycles in general. It also became apparent that there was an arbitrary nature to stage-specific formulations that was influenced by wider contextual forces.

In an effort to deal with diverse family forms and still retain stage-specific formulations, some theorists attempted to modify life-cycle theories to reflect the various family structures represented in society (e.g., Carter & McGoldrick, 1989). For example: (1) In the 1980s, theorists finally incorporated a stage of single young adulthood for women; (2) an alternative life-cycle trajectory not based on childrearing was constructed to account for the 15% of contemporary marriages that now remain childless; and (3) a "re-nesting phase" was developed to incorporate the many young adults who now return home.

Another attempt to maintain the concept of stages and still attend to vari-

ations in family functioning was the development of family life-course models. Burr, Day, and Bahr (1993) describe these models as providing a variety
of trajectories that families can choose from, with each choice altering the life
course. While these models demonstrate variability in life course, they also
render life-cycle theories, packaged within a traditional framework, meaning-
less in that it becomes virtually impossible to capture the endless possibilities
open to any given family.

The concept of limitless variations leads to the notion that the structure
of family life comes to rest on a tenuous basis — the mutual feelings of two
individuals (Skolnick & Skolnick, 1994). Looking at systemic development
this way requires social scientists to move away from developing predictable
structures around increasing and ever-changing developmental options. Instead, they need to examine the dialectic meaning-making processes that occur within and among individuals, relationships, and the wider contexts in
which they live (cf. Feixas, 1990; Ivey, 1991; Neimeyer, 1985; Rigazio-
DiGilio, 1994a).

Stage theorists also suggest that families can perform more complex and
diverse tasks with the passage of time (Thomas, 1992). However, the specific
issues and tasks, the particular position within the wider context, and the style
of adaptation used vary among families. In fact, there is little validity in the
concept of organizational complexity. Some families may develop in this way,
while others will choose or be required to take a different life course. It appears, therefore, that traditional family development models do not capture
the complexity of several individuals developing within the same internal context, over the same temporal space, and within a particular wider context.

Assumption 2
Development Defines Normative and Nonnormative Adaptations

We are born into a socially constructed world. Traditional developmental theories often are used to establish boundaries for acceptable behavior, tasks, and
functions; to develop assessment and treatment protocols; and to define social policy. The categories we are socialized into and carry out serve to perpet-
uate predictability and stability. These categories then gain credibility and set
the standards for normal and abnormal behavior. Over time, the culture creates the continuum for normalcy and deviance and identifies the social consequences of differing positions on this continuum (Freud, 1994).

For example, Erikson's psychosocial theory suggests that mastering
autonomy is a precursor to developing intimacy, a construction devoid of
gender-sensitivity. Family development models define leaving home as an essential aspect of functional adjustment, a supposition that neglects generational and cultural variations as well as contemporary economic realities.

There are two primary concerns associated with this second assumption:

the issue of generalizability and the notion of emphasizing tasks and functions over meaning-making processes.

Generalizability. While the markers depicted in traditional theories may hold some validity, no theory can account for all variations inherent in the general population. For example, even though Levinson's (1978) study of adult male development focused solely on white middle-class men born before or during the depression, only 80% of the participants experienced the "mid-life transition" explicated in his theory. Further, Ryff (1986) speculates that men born after World War II — the first generation to be well educated and in dual-career marriages — may not even experience this period of personal reflection. In terms of family development, Mattessick and Hill (1987) stated that their developmental model was appropriate for one-half to two-thirds of America's families. While this was used as a point of validation, even a decade ago, one-third to one-half of American families did not relate to the traditional markers and developmental conflicts described in their theory.

While there is some consistency regarding how individuals and families develop over the life span, the normative value of most traditional theories is outweighed by their stereotypical application across contexts. Consider our country's sociopolitical reaction to unwed mothers. In 1989, 7 out of 10 black women between the ages of 15 and 35 had their first child before marriage (U.S. Bureau of the Census, 1991). This "modal" behavior runs counter to traditional developmental theories and is labeled "deviant" by many conservative political and religious groups. Or what of the Hispanic children labeled "deviant" for refusing to go to school (dysfunctional individual adaptation)? Their behavior is often seen as a reflection of their parents' failure to provide proper socialization and guidance (dysfunctional family adaptation). It is less often considered that neighborhoods, schools, or sociopolitical and economic frameworks strongly influence children's perceptions of their life chances, or that their deviant behavior may more accurately reflect a legitimate response to a devaluing and dehumanizing society (Agnew, 1985; Skolnick & Skolnick, 1994).

A primary result of our tendency to discount the fallacy of generalizability is summarized by Skolnick and Skolnick (1994):

> The family theories of the postwar era were descriptively correct insofar as they portrayed the ideal middle-class family patterns. . . . But they went astray in elevating the status quo to the level of a timeless necessity. In addition, these theories did not acknowledge the great diversity among families that has always existed in America. (p. 4)

In effect, this fallacy has done social scientists a disservice. By leading them to seek and hence to find structured patterns of development, it has blinded them to historical precedents for multiple legitimate family arrangements (Keller, 1971).

Tasks and Functions. Traditional models tend to frame development in terms of stage-specific tasks and functions and marginalize the process of individual and collective meaning-making (e.g., Duvall, 1988; Erikson, 1963). While the theories provide insight regarding temporal and behavioral changes that may occur over the life span, many insufficiently describe the cognitive and relational changes that accompany growth and development. The focus on tasks and functions appeared to satisfy a need to identify what was "expected" of individuals and families at particular stages in the life course. The power of this need emanates from definitions provided by early pioneers:

> A developmental task is a task which arises at or about a certain period in life, successful achievement of which leads to happiness and to success with later tasks, while failure leads to unhappiness, disapproval by the society, and difficulty with later tasks. (Havinghurst, 1953, p. 2)

This emphasis on tasks and functions failed to recognize that unique solutions to life's issues are reflective of natural and logical consequences that result from our idiosyncratic paths toward development and our distinctive meaning-making processes as these occur throughout the person-environment dialectic over time (Ivey & Rigazio-DiGilio, 1994). The importance of individual and collective meaning was only minimally acknowledged in traditional models, thereby perpetuating an external framework that discounted a person's or a family's own perceptions of experiences and goals. In effect, the emphasis on tasks and functions limited our capacity to recognize and embrace the multitude of options that could be chosen by any individual or family.

Assumption 3
Development Occurs Within Individuals and Within Families

Developmental theories fail to adequately address the dialectic, reciprocal, and transactive exchanges occurring between subject and environment that propel or hinder growth and adaptation (cf. Hayes, 1994; Lacan, 1978; Parry, 1993). When one relies on the microscope, contextual and inter-subjective issues coloring development are lost. While some traditional theories acknowledge immediate context (e.g., family, school, work), most ignore the wider contextual influences affected by and affecting development (Bird & Melville, 1994).

Constructivists reject this isolated and fragmented view of development and search to understand not only obvious contextual issues, but also hidden influences in the person-environment dialectic, such as shifting legal, educational, and vocational policies, and changing sociocultural expectations and attitudes (cf. Hunter, 1994; Luker, 1994; Riley, 1994; Rosen, 1994).

Assumption 4
Developmental Models Represent Approximations of Reality

The final assumption blinds us to the fact that developmental stages reflect, to a large degree, social and cultural inventions (Skolnick, 1994). These stages were created to fill some contextual purposes based more on sociopolitical than on biological or natural considerations. Therefore, our understanding of development is based not on truths, but rather on consensual social constructions (Freud, 1994).

For example, the construct of childhood originated in the 17th century with the emergence of the private, domestic family and formal schooling (Aries, 1962). The concept of adolescence was introduced at the end of the 19th century as the industrial revolution and public high schools made space for this life stage (Demos & Demos, 1969; Skolnick, 1994). Concepts about middle age (Sheehy, 1976), middle years of marriage (Duvall, 1988), grandparenthood (Cherlin & Furstenberg, 1994), and later marriage (Busse & Maddox, 1985) surfaced after World War II, approximately the same time as stage-specific developmental models began to appear.

Additionally, social scientists used narrow populations within limited generational cohorts to validate socially constructed perspectives and establish norms for acceptable behavior. By failing to account for the socially derived nature of their models or the narrowness of their samples, developmental theorists promoted ideas as representative of a larger reality. By confusing reality with theory, they implied that an objective and stable reality existed, and that the mark of maturity was the ability to correctly interpret that reality.

To illustrate, family sociologists now indicate that the 1940s and 1950s were actually deviant periods in terms of family life (i.e., traditional breadwinner, domestic wife, 2.4 kids) (Masnick & Bane, 1980). Ironically, this is when the major assumptions undergirding traditional models of family development were constructed and legitimized. Now, instead of seeing "nontraditional" family constellations (e.g., single-parent families, dual-earner families) as closely related to our historical roots (cf. Cherlin, 1981; Masnick & Bane, 1980), many mythologize the life-style depicted in the 1940s and 1950s into a collective ideal of what families should be (McWilliams, 1993). As such, diverse family forms appear counter to the established ideal.

This example illustrates how socially constructed images powerfully and reciprocally influence sociopolitical expectations and the direction of social science. For example, social scientists have not yet constructed alternative models of development that directly challenge the underlying assumptions of the 1940s and 1950s. In terms of individual development,

> all of the large scale theories were established in the first half of this century. . . . [While] life span developmental psychology has become more active in recent years, it has no major theory as a basis. . . . To some extent, there have instead been a number of organizing concepts within which much of the [traditional] material can be coordinated and understood. (Stratton, 1988, pp. 209 and 211)

In terms of family development, there have been major criticisms regarding how current models tend to omit a multitude of diverse family types or developmental trajectories. What tends to occur in response, however, is that we add or subtract stages to our traditional models to account for general trends, we modify these models to identify the supposed trajectories of diverse populations, or we integrate several models in an attempt to make them more comprehensive. However, we seldom challenge the undergirding assumptions of our stage-specific theories.

While it is true that the nineties have given rise to literature questioning the foundations of traditional models (cf. Guterman, 1994; Sue et al., 1996), alternative formulations that have hit mainstream literature or that have been sufficiently operationalized have yet to emerge. This phenomenon is associated with the introduction of a paradigmatic shift: Alternative conceptualizations introduced during paradigmatic transitions generate further confusion because they are not grounded in years of theoretical co-constructions that are linked to empirical investigations, clinical experience, and professional dialogue (Rigazio-DiGilio, 1994b, p. 206).

The monological perspectives perpetuated by traditional developmental models are now being repudiated by constructivists. These theorists use more holistic frameworks that integrate the transactions and meaning-making processes that occur among individuals, families, and the wider environment and that provide alternative explanations of how contextual and scientific factors influence the theory-building process (cf. Amatae & Sherrard, 1994; Auerswald, 1983; Falicov, 1988; Ivey, 1991; Luepnitz, 1988; Neimeyer & Hudson, 1985; Pedersen, 1994; Rigazio-DiGilio, 1994a). These lines of inquiry offer potential sources for more syntropic theories of human and systemic development. The dialectic assumptions undergirding these theories contain numerous perspectives, just like holographs. The feelings, behaviors, and beliefs of all those involved in a situation, as well as the various contexts influencing the situation, are used to interpret and view the multiple dimensions inherent in the many forms human and systemic development may take.

Before we move into a constructivist view of development, it is important to note that the trend toward this perspective has emerged as part of a dialectic exchange between the wider context, the scientific enterprise, and the mental health field. For example, Veroff, Douvan, and Kulka (1981) found that individuals now tend to find fulfillment by attending to inner experience and self-definition rather then by adhering to traditional roles. Further, our profession recognizes that no one model or set of assumptions can claim superiority, and that there is merit to integrating therapeutic models within and among disciplines (e.g., Rigazio-DiGilio & Ivey, 1991, 1993). These types of environments influence our shift to constructivism.

A CONSTRUCTIVIST APPROACH TO INDIVIDUAL AND FAMILY DEVELOPMENT

Unlike the linear, normative, and self-contained perspectives cast by traditional developmental models, constructivists focus on the dialectic and reciprocal aspects of human and systemic meaning-making (cf. Basseches, 1984; Berger & Luckmann, 1966; Bruner, 1986; Gergen, 1985; Hayes, 1994; Hoffman, 1990; Ivey, 1986; Kelly, 1955; Lacan, 1978; Mead, 1934; Sarbin, 1986; Vygotsky, 1962). Constructivist models reflect holistic perspectives that provide alternative understandings of how individuals and families make sense of and operate in their worlds. Such models see the person-environment dialectic as an integral factor in the growth and adaptation of individuals (cf. Berger & Luckmann, 1966; Carlsen, 1988; Gergen, 1985; Ivey, Gonçalves, & Ivey, 1989; Selman, 1980; Vygotsky, 1962), and families (cf. Anderson & Goolishian, 1988; Hoffman, 1990; Howard, 1991; Procter, 1985; Rigazio-DiGilio, 1994a, 1996; Rigazio-DiGilio & Ivey, 1991, 1993; Watzlawick, 1978, 1984).

Constructivist perspectives are analogous to holographic images that provide multidimensional lenses for reviewing the complexities of development. In this section, the assumptions undergirding constructivist models of individual and family development are defined and further elaborated using the work of Ivey and Rigazio-DiGilio regarding Developmental Theory (DT) (Ivey, 1986; Ivey & Rigazio-DiGilio, 1994) and Systemic Cognitive-Developmental Therapy (SCDT) (Rigazio-DiGilio, 1994a, 1996; Rigazio-DiGilio & Ivey, 1991, 1993; Rigazio-DiGilio, Ivey, Ivey, & Simek-Morgan, in press).

Assumption 1
Persons and Collective Systems Co-Construct Unique World-Views

Individuals and families rely on unique, co-constructed world-views to experience, understand, and act within their life space. Many terms are used to describe this concept as it applies to individuals, including "personal constructs" (Kelly, 1955), "personal theories" (Martin, 1994), and "cognitive-developmental orientations" (Ivey, 1986). In terms of families, constructs such as "family paradigms" (Reiss, 1981), "family construct systems" (Procter, 1978, 1981, 1985), "language-determined systems" (Anderson & Goolishian, 1988; Epstein & Loos, 1989), and "systemic cognitive-developmental orientations" (Rigazio-DiGilio, 1994a, 1996) are used to describe the collective world-views or fundamental and enduring assumptions families construct about their world. Common to all these terms is that the meanings a person or family derives from experiences are primarily filtered through a world-view. Because these world-views develop as part of the natural and logical consequence of our own unique journeys, the way in which each individual or family experiences, reacts to, and acts on the world is idiosyncratic.

According to Rigazio-DiGilio and Ivey (1991), individual and collective world-views can be conceptualized within two dimensions: cognitive-developmental *orientations* and cognitive-developmental structures. Regarding orientations, it is assumed that individuals and families develop within four main worlds that can be metaphorically anchored within neo-Piagetian constructs. These are the worlds of images and perceptions (*sensorimotor/experience*); visible things and concrete action and thought (*concrete/situational*); abstract and reflective reasoning (*formal/reflective*); and recursive awareness among self, system, and environment (*dialectic/systemic*). Each orientation influences language, feelings, perceptions, behaviors, and meaning-making in a unique way. It is the individual's and the family's dialogue within these worlds that leads to growth and adaptation and stabilization, or nonadaptation and "stuckness."

Structure relates to the preexisting schemes individuals or families co-construct about the world, the self, and others. The effectiveness of these schemes relates to the degree to which individuals or families can access each of the four orientations to deal with specific internal or external demands. Adaptive development is related to *flexible and varied* structures, wherein individuals and families can access a variety of orientations along their developmental journeys. Less adaptive development can occur when individuals or families overrely on one orientation in response to varying circumstances (*rigid structures*), or when their resources within all orientations cannot be effectively accessed (*diffuse or underdeveloped structures*). These cognitive-developmental structures are analogues to the permeable, rigid, and loose personal constructs defined by Kelley (1955).

Assumption 2
World-Views Develop in a Person-Environment Dialectic Transaction

Individuals and families do not develop as pawns of the environment. Nor do they develop independently of their external world. Rather, it is the transaction between individual, family, and environment that is the dynamic force of development (cf. Harland, 1987; Ivey, Gonçalves, & Ivey, 1989; Vygotsky, 1962).

Co-construction. Constructivist theory "represents a more complex worldview because it recognizes the need to shift back and forth between environmental and organismic reference points, assigning top priority to neither" (Prawat & Floden, 1994, p. 45). We co-construct individual worldviews by participating in the environment, and we co-construct collective world-views by participating in resonating experiences within relationships that evolve in the environment (Rigazio-DiGilio & Ivey, 1991, 1993).

The co-construction process that occurs between individuals, families, and wider systems reflects an ongoing negotiation process that affects every involved member and system. For example, Rigazio-DiGilio (1994a) postulates that the systemic cognitive-developmental orientation relied on by a family evolves via a co-constructive process that occurs among individual world-views, collective negotiations, and wider contextual forces. The common reality co-constructed by the family then influences, to varying degrees, the meanings, emotions, and actions a family and its members share in relation to their issues and over time.

This is true even though members intrapersonally operate from various orientations. A collective world-view does exist, which may represent an amalgamation of all individual orientations or a combination of some members or subsystems in the family (Rigazio-DiGilio & Ivey, 1991).

The degree of influence family members have on the co-construction of a collective world-view and, conversely, the degree of influence this worldview has on members are related to the concept of *embeddedness* — that is, the extent to which individuals, subsystems, families, and wider contextual environments are connected to one another at different points over the life span as well as the significance of the power differentials governed by this connectedness. If, for example, an individual's primary source of consensual validation is based within the family's collective orientation, then the member will be strongly influenced by this world-view and will assist in its continuation. If an individual's sense of self and others is primarily based in other contexts (e.g., work, culture), then this member will be less affected by, and affect less, the family world-view. Finally, if a family's sense of identity is more embedded in societal norms than in family ideology, then members will be guided by societal imperatives over their own values.

Equifinality. Unlike the predetermined perspective related to positivistic models, constructivism supports the notion of equifinality (Bavelas & Segal, 1982): In effect, people interacting in similar environments may render different interpretations, based on the power differentials that exist between person and environment and the developmental histories influencing each. Further, people interacting in different environments may develop similar points of view.

Given the concept of equifinality, it is difficult to view differences as deficits. In this sense, constructivists assume a positive stance toward individual and systemic adaptation. What used to be considered deviant behavior can be recast as natural and logical reactions to environmental, personal, and systemic inconsistencies, power differentials, or demands for change (cf. Ginter, 1989; Ivey, 1986; Rigazio-DiGilio, 1994a). This perspective enables people to view growth as an idiosyncratic journey and to recognize environmental and personal variables that contribute to further personal and systemic enhancement.

Assumption 3
Change Occurs in a Nonhierarchical, Recursive Manner

The path of change is an idiosyncratic journey through life. The specific world-views and the salient aspects of the person-environment transaction give rise to numerous life trajectories.

The Path of Change. Constructivists view the nature of development as nonlinear, recursive, and adaptive (cf. Basseches, 1984; Berger & Luckmann, 1966; Gergen, 1985; Hoffman, 1990; Lacan, 1978; Sarbin, 1986). Ivey and Rigazio-DiGilio (1991) hypothesize that adaptive individuals and families naturally revisit the four cognitive-developmental orientations as they need to in response to external and internal demands for change. In this way they select resources from the orientations that will best assist them to react to or act on these demands.

The Process of Change. The process of change is also a recursive proposition. People are influenced by and influence their environment. Piaget's (1955) concept of *equilibration* can be used to explain this process. Change is a product of interacting accommodative and assimilative forces that are held in symmetrical relationship. Individuals and families modify or transform preexisting world-views by relying on these forces to govern the amount, quality, and type of incoming data. The adaptive balance created represents a state of equilibration.

According to Rigazio-DiGilio and Ivey (1991), *accommodation* is the process by which cognitive-developmental structures are altered during environmental exchange. The ease with which individuals and families adapt to the thinking of others, their ability to see patterns that do not align with preconceived ideas, or their openness to learning from experiences signifies their degree of accommodation. *Overaccommodation* is associated with imbalance, wherein individuals and families possess diffuse schemes about the world and their relation to it. It is not unusual for them to "change" their minds or shared realities frequently, constantly constructing alternative world-views in response to minimal variations in their environments.

Assimilation is the imposition of an existing point of view on incoming data. Individuals and families attempt to alter the perceptions of others or shape experiences to fit their preexisting ideas. The tenacity of their beliefs can be indicative of the degree of assimilative reasoning being used to understand and operate in the world. Overassimilation is evident when individuals and families rely on outdated world-views that are no longer in sync with their developmental or situational needs.

Assumption 4
Developmental Impasses Reflect Incongruities Between World-Views and Contextual Demands

Individuals and families carry ways of understanding and relating to the world. Their preexisting world views influence the range of options they can access to react to or alter internal and external demands for change. If individuals and families can tap into resources that are congruent with or can alter existing demands, then adaptation and growth will occur. However, if their resources are not viable enough to deal with current developmental or situational pressures, then impasses and nonadaptation may result. "In these terms, the experience of . . . distress reflects the natural disequilibrium that occurs when there is a salient discrepancy between various life demands and adaptive capacities" (Lyddon, 1993, p. 219).

Ivey and Rigazio-DiGilio (1994) suggest that adaptation occurs through horizontal and vertical movement within and across the four cognitive-developmental orientations. *Horizontal development* promotes the mastery of cognitive, affective, and behavioral skills reflective of a particular orientation. Horizontal movement enables individuals and families to develop a firm base of understanding and operating within one orientation. *Vertical development* facilitates adaptation by enabling individuals and families to expand their range of options by tapping cognitive, affective, and behavioral skills associated with underutilized or unfamiliar orientations.

Adaptive individuals and families access the rich repertoire of thoughts, feelings, and behaviors inherent in various orientations as they respond to or act on their environment. During their development, they garner the flexibility to use multiple perspectives to understand and operate in their world. In terms of orientations, it is hypothesized that "individuals and families that access the unique vantage points available in all orientations will have a wide range of cognitive, emotional, and behavioral flexibility" (Rigazio-DiGilio & Ivey, 1993, p. 210). Conversely, individuals and families who have less access to multiple orientations will experience difficulties as they face unfamiliar circumstances. Developmental impasses arise when individuals or families rely on world-views that are not congruent with developmental or situational demands and when they cannot access other, more viable resources within alternative orientations to either adapt to or alter these demands.

The above assumptions provide a framework for the construction of developmental models that depart from the traditional, positivistic paradigm. Using this framework, and continuing with the work of Ivey and Rigazio-DiGilio (1994), the salient aspects of client development are now explored as these occur in the context of the therapeutic relationship.

CLIENT DEVELOPMENT AS A SOCIAL CONSTRUCTION

According to Ivey and Rigazio-DiGilio (1994), adaptive individuals and families repeatedly move through four cognitive-developmental orientations as they approach their world. They use the cognitive, behavioral, and affective *facilitative resources* within each orientation to react to or act on their environment. Two orientations relate to the world of experience and action (sensorimotor/experience; concrete/situational), and two relate to the world of thought and abstraction (formal/reflective; dialectic/systemic). Together, the four orientations represent the cognitive-developmental structure that clients move through, horizontally and vertically, to meet or alter their developmental and situational circumstances.

Distressed clients often face incongruities between their available cognitive-developmental orientations and their wider environments and are not able to move within and across other orientations to adapt to or alter their circumstances. Some clients may become embedded within a dominant orientation that is not in sync with how they need to interact with their wider context. Others may haphazardly and ineffectively access underdeveloped resources within several orientations. In either case, these clients tend to utilize *inhibitory resources* that do not promote effective interaction with and/or alteration of developmental and situational demands.

Cognitive-Developmental Orientations

As stated, four orientations are comprised within the individual and family cognitive-developmental structures proposed in the developmental models espoused by Ivey and Rigazio-DiGilio. Clinical and empirical evidence indicates that these cognitive-developmental orientations can be reliably identified within the natural language of individuals (Rigazio-DiGilio & Ivey, 1990) and families (Ivey & Ivey, 1990; Rigazio-DiGilio, 1994a; Rigazio-DiGilio & Ivey, 1991) as they dialogue in therapeutic contexts. Each orientation offers a unique vantage point from which to understand and operate. Further, each has facilitating resources, labeled *competencies,* and inhibitory resources, labeled *constraints.* These individual and collective orientations are described in detail in several works by Rigazio-DiGilio and Ivey (e.g., 1990, 1991, 1994).

To illustrate the idea of competencies and constraints, clients who can access the *sensorimotor orientation,* along with other orientations, can use their immediate sensory experiences — what they see, hear, and feel — to construct meaning and operate within their world. Competencies include the ability to engage in direct emotional experiences, to monitor emotional transactions without becoming bewildered, and to identify personal feelings. However, when *constrained* within this orientation, clients are easily overwhelmed by affective situations or minor variations in their world. This tends to restrict their cognitive and behavioral repertoire, making it difficult to meaningfully organize or act on sensory-based data.

As individuals and families interact with the environment, internal and intrafamilial dialogues are stimulated. The conversations, shaped by the individual's or family's cognitive-developmental structure and by the resources and constraints of the environment, form the essence of the world-view. Over time, the conversations become more internalized and exercise increasing influence over feelings, thoughts, and behaviors. According to Vygotsky (1934/1986), this internalization process explains how social versus biological determinants influence the development of a world-view.

Negotiating the Person-Environment Dialectic

Individuals and families are members of multiple dialectic relationships, reciprocally affecting one another. This dialectic-transactional view of human and systemic interaction offers an alternative conception of growth and adaptation to explain how individuals and families internalize and co-construct social reality, thus enhancing or revising their world-views through interaction with others (cf. Ivey, 1986; Rigazio-DiGilio, 1994a, 1996; Taylor, 1989).

Rigazio-DiGilio (1994a) uses four recursive phases to describe how mutual constructions are co-created between individuals, families, and wider contexts: system exploration, system consolidation, system enhancement, and system transformation. At the *system exploration* phase, the sensory worlds of individuals, relational systems, and wider contexts begin to merge, as each one shares perspectives, emotions, and behaviors. Power differentials affect the degree to which any individual, family, or context can influence another. As interactions continue, a unique blending of perspectives occurs that leads to *system consolidation*. Here, repetitive experiences evolve into a collective view of individuals, relationships, and wider contexts. This view organizes predictable and mutual ways of thinking, feeling, and acting.

At the *system enhancement* phase, each participant or system develops an increased awareness of the emerging mutual world-view and how this view influences each member and each system. They begin to reflect on and modify or enhance their collective perspective and the ways that participants function within this perspective. Further along in the process, participants and systems may develop an awareness of how mutual world-views are influenced by wider, perhaps hidden contextual factors. This type of awareness fosters alternative options not previously imagined and occurs within the *system transformation phase*. Participants and systems can examine the ramifications of mutual world-views without losing a sense of identity and can deconstruct and reconstruct these world-views as necessary. This framework also is directly applicable to the course of development that occurs within therapeutic alliances.

Given that individuals and families constantly move through and among these phases as they interact with their environments, it is inevitable that each person and family will develop a unique world-view. This model replaces a temporal-linear perspective with one that highlights the importance of the person-environment dialectic.

During adaptive transactions, major issues that arise recycle through this process. When this occurs, individuals, families, and other influential contexts develop the capacity to use varying options within each phase (e.g., sharing experiences and ideas; acting predictably; reflecting and analyzing; examining and revising). This capacity maximizes their ability to adapt to or alter internal and external demands for change.

Less adaptive transactions may result in developmental impasses within any one of the four cognitive-developmental processes, or in an oscillation between two phases. The resultant relationships become constrained by a lack of consensus regarding goals or the means for achieving goals. In these less adaptive relationships, participants become constrained within the limited resources of one or perhaps two developmental orientations. Professional assistance may be indicated to assist them to use resources within each developmental phase so they do not remain stagnant and constrained.

Before discussing how a constructivist developmental perspective can inform individual and family therapy, it is important to note that constructivist therapists recognize that the points of therapeutic intervention meant to alleviate developmental impasses are often found beyond the therapy context. That is, interventions can target individuals, families, wider contexts, and the dialectic transactions that occur among the three. This recognition is leading our field to introduce therapeutic approaches that synthesize individual, family, and network interventions within integrative and constructivist metaframeworks (cf. Amatae & Sherrard, 1994; Anderson & Goolishian, 1988; Falicov, 1988; Rigazio-DiGilio, 1994a).

DEVELOPMENTAL THEORY TO PRACTICE: CO-CONSTRUCTING INDIVIDUAL AND FAMILY THERAPEUTIC ENVIRONMENTS

A constructivist developmental perspective assumes that individuals and families are members of multiple dialectic relationships that reciprocally influence one another. Over time and in context, individuals and families co-construct world-views that reflect unique orientations toward themselves and their environment and that enable them to sustain lifelong development. When the world-view, the wider context, or the dialectic relationship(s) is rendered ineffective in generating appropriate solutions to life's demands, assistance may be needed. In individual and family therapy, an isomorphic process of reviving developmental growth and adaptation can occur.

According to cognitive-developmental theory, the central goal of therapy is to enable clients to access the resources found within each orientation so as to resume their developmental process. This is accomplished by first identifying which orientation the client primarily operates within and then providing a *matching environment*. Once clients develop stronger facility within their primary orientation, *mismatched environments* are co-constructed to promote access to underutilized or unfamiliar orientations, thus increasing the client's range of cognitive, behavioral, and affectual responses.

According to DT and SCDT, there are four environments that correspond with each of the cognitive-developmental orientations and that serve to enhance and expand the developmental capacities of the client — *directive, coaching, consultative,* and *collaborative*. These therapeutic environments are co-constructed through the use of developmentally oriented questioning strategies and therapeutic approaches that are tailored to the immediate and unique needs of clients. These strategies are defined in several works by Rigazio-DiGilio and Ivey (e.g., 1990, 1991, 1994).

The basic premise undergirding the idea of co-constructing environments relates to the concept of synchronicity. By providing environments that are tailored to client needs, the therapeutic process recreates the types of dialectic transactions that can propel development and adaptation.

The process of using therapeutic interventions that correspond with a client's predominant orientation is referred to as *style-matching*. After sufficient competency is developed within the primary orientation, style-mismatching questions and interventions are used to promote explorations of resources within underutilized orientations. As clients indicate that they are able to use these new resources, a style-matching posture is again assumed in order to establish an extended base.

The *style-shifting* process through all four orientations re-creates a positive developmental process. As the natural developmental processes are reestablished in the safety of the therapeutic alliance, clients are enabled to use these resources to continue with their developmental journeys.

CONCLUSION

The alternative developmental model presented rejects linear, hierarchical, and self-contained perspectives and instead embraces a recursive, dialectic framework that transcends stage-specific developmental tasks. Viewing client development within such a constructivist framework opens new perspectives for mental health theory, practice, and research. The wider contextual lens and the understanding of the person-environment dialectic promote a holistic understanding of human and systemic development, adjustment, meaning-making, and liberation. This multidimensional view of development is analogous to a holograph image. It can be viewed from many positions, each rendering new information to form a more comprehensive composite.

Research, theory, and practice associated with a constructivist paradigm must be developed to capture the potentialities inherent in alternative, nonpathological models of why clients seek therapy and the essential factors of effective practice — within and outside of the therapy office. These changes have the potential to transform our profession to better meet the challenges of the 21st century.

The socially constructed model of client development presented here is derived from an alternative perspective of growth and adaptation that claims no superiority over any other. Staying true to the constructivist movement, I hope to promote dialogue that will further enhance, extend, and revise these and other views of development.

REFERENCES

Agnew, J. (1985). Childhood disorders or the venture of children. In E. Button (Ed.), *Personal construct theory and mental health.* Cambridge, MA: Brookline Books.

Ainslie, G. (1993). A picoeconomic rationale for social constructionism. *Behavior and Philosophy, 2,* 63–75.

Aldous, J. (1978). *Family careers: Developmental change in families.* New York: Wiley.

Amatae, E., & Sherrard, P. A. (1994). The ecosystemic view: A choice of lenses. *Journal of Mental Health Counseling, 16,* 6–21.

Anderson, H., & Goolishian, H. (1988). Human systems as linguistic systems: Preliminary and evolving ideas about the implications for clinical theory. *Family Process, 27,* 371–393.

Anderson, H., Goolishian, H., Pulliam, G., & Winderman, L. (1986). The Galveston Family Institute: Some personal and historical perspectives. In D. E. Efron (Ed.), *Journeys: Expansion of the strategic-systemic therapies* (pp. 97–122). New York: Brunner/Mazel.

Aries, P. (1962). *Centuries of childhood.* New York: Random House.

Auerswald, E. (1983). The Gouveneur Health Service Program: An experiment in ecosystemic community care delivery. *Family Systems Medicine, 1,* 5–13.

Baltes, P., Reese, H., & Lipsitt, L. (1980). *Life-span developmental psychology.* Palo Alto, CA: Annual Reviews.

Barnhill, L. H., & Longo, D. (1978). Fixation and regression in the family life cycle. *Family Process, 17,* 469–478.

Basseches, M. (1984). *Dialectical thinking and adult development.* Norwood, NJ: Ablex.

Bavelas, J. B., & Segal, L. (1982). Family system theory: Background and implications. *Journal of Communication, 32,* 99–107.

Berger, P., & Luckmann, T. (1966). *The social construction of reality.* Garden City, NY: Doubleday.

Bird, G., & Melville, K. (1994). *Families and intimate relationships.* New York: McGraw-Hill.

Brim, O., & Kagan, J. (1980). *Constancy and change in human development.* Cambridge: Harvard University Press.

Bronfenbrenner, U. (1979). *The ecology of human development.* Cambridge: Harvard University Press.

Bruner, J. (1986). *Actual minds, possible worlds.* Cambridge: Harvard University Press.

Burr, W., Day, R., & Bahr, K. (Eds.). (1993). *Family science.* Pacific Grove, CA: Brooks Cole.

Busse, E. W., & Maddox, G. (1985). *The Duke longitudinal studies of normal aging, 1955–1980: Overview of history, design, and findings.* New York: Springer.

Carlsen, M. B. (1988). *Meaning making: Therapeutic process in adult development.* New York: Norton.

Carter, B., & McGoldrick, M. (1989). *The changing family life-cycle.* Boston: Allyn and Bacon.

Casas, J. M., Ponterotto, J. G., & Gutierrez, J. M. (1986). An ethical indictment of counseling research and training: The cross cultural perspective. *Journal of Counseling and Development, 64,* 347–349.

Cherlin, A. J. (1981). *Marriage, divorce, and remarriage.* Cambridge: Harvard University Press.

Cherlin, A. J., & Furstenberg, F. (1994). The modernization of grandparenthood. In A. Skolnick & J. Skolnick (Eds.), *Family in transition* (8th ed.) (pp. 104–116). New York: HarperCollins.

Demos, J., & Demos, V. (1969). Adolescents in historical perspective. *Journal of Marriage and the Family, 31,* 632–638.

Duvall, E. M. (1977). *Marriage and family development* (5th ed.). New York: Lippincott.

Duvall, E. M. (1988). Family development's first forty years. *Family Relations, 37,* 127–134.

Emde, R. N., & Harmon, R. J. (Eds.). (1984). *Continuities and discontinuities in development.* New York: Plenum Press.

Epstein, E. S., & Loos, V. E. (1989). Some irreverent thoughts on the limits of family therapy: Toward a language-based explanation of human systems. *Journal of Family Psychology, 2,* 405–421.

Erikson, E. H. (1963). *Childhood and society* (2nd ed.). New York: Norton.

Falicov, C. J. (1988). Learning to think culturally. In H. A. Liddle, D. S. Breunlin, & R. C. Schwartz (Eds.), *Handbook of family therapy training and supervision.* New York: Guilford Press.

Feixas, G. (1990). Approaching the individual, approaching the system: A constructivist model for integrating psychotherapy. *Journal of Family Psychology, 4,* 4–35.

Freud, S. (1994). The social construction of gender. *Journal of Adult Development, 1*(1), 37–46.

Gergen, K. J. (1985). The social constructivist movement in modern psychology. *American Psychologist, 40,* 266–275.

Gilligan, C. (1982). *In a different voice.* Cambridge: Harvard University Press.

Ginter, E. J. (1989). Slayers of monster-watermelons found in the mental health patch. *Journal of Mental Health Counseling, 11,* 77–85.

Guterman, J. T. (1994). A social constructionist position for mental health counseling. *Journal of Mental Health Counseling, 2,* 226–244.

Haley, J. (1963). *Strategies of psychotherapy.* New York: Grune & Stratton.

Haley, J. (1973). *Uncommon therapy: The psychiatric techniques of Milton H. Erikson.* New York: Norton.

Harland, R. (1987). *Superstructuralism.* London: Methuen.

Havinghurst, R. J. (1953). *Human development and education.* New York: Longmans, Green.

Hayes, R. (1994). Counseling in the postmodern world: Origins and implications of a constructivist developmental approach. *Counseling and Human Development, 26,* 1–12.

Hill, R., & Rogers, R. H. (1964). The developmental approach. In H. Christensen (Ed.), *Handbook of marriage and family therapy* (pp. 171–209). Chicago: Rand McNally.

Hoffman, L. (1990). Constructing realities: An art of lenses. *Family Process, 29,* 1–12.

Howard, G. S. (1991). Culture tales: A narrative approach to thinking, cross-cultural psychology, and psychotherapy. *American Psychologist, 46,* 187–197.

Hunter, J. D. (1994). The family and the culture war. In A. Skolnick & J. Skolnick (Eds.), *Family in transition* (8th ed.) (pp. 537–547). New York: HarperCollins.

Ibrahim, F. A. (1985). Effective cross-cultural counseling and psychotherapy: A framework. *The Counseling Psychologist, 12,* 625–638.

Ivey, A. E. (1986). *Developmental therapy: Theory into practice.* San Francisco: Jossey-Bass.

Ivey, A. E. (1991). *Developmental strategies for helpers: Individual, family, and network interventions.* Pacific Grove, CA: Brooks/Cole.

Ivey, A. E., Gonçalves, O. F., & Ivey, M. B. (1989). Developmental therapy: Theory and practice. In O. Gonçalves (Ed.), *Advances in the cognitive therapies: The constructive-developmental approach.* Porto, Portugal: Associacao dos Psicologos Portugeses.

Ivey, A. E., & Ivey, M. B., (1990). Assessing and facilitating children's cognitive-development: Developmental counseling and therapy in a case of child abuse. *Journal of Counseling and Development, 68,* 299–305.

Ivey, A. E., Ivey, M. B., & Simek-Morgan, L. (in press). *Counseling and psychotherapy: A multicultural perspective* (4th ed.). Needham Heights, MA: Allyn and Bacon.

Ivey, A. E., & Rigazio-DiGilio, S. A. (1991). Toward a developmental practice of mental health counseling: Strategies for training, practice, and political unity. *Journal of Mental Health Counseling, 13,* 21–36.

Ivey, A. E., & Rigazio-DiGilio, S. A. (1994). Developmental counseling and therapy: Can still another theory be useful to you? *The Journal for the Professional Counselor, 9,* 23–48.

Keller, S. (1971). Does the family have a future? *Journal of Comparative Studies, 23,* 174–196.

Kelly, G. (1955). *The psychology of personal construct.* New York: Norton.

Kohlberg, L. (1969). Stage and sequence: The cognitive-developmental approach to socialization. In D. Goslin (Ed.), *Handbook of socialization theory and research* (pp. 352–406). Chicago: Rand McNally.

Kohlberg, L. (1981). *The philosophy of moral development.* San Francisco: Harper & Row.

Lacan, J. (1978). *Four fundamental concepts of psychoanalysis* (2nd ed.). New York: Norton.

Levinson, D. (1978). *The seasons of a man's life.* New York: Knof.

Liddle, H. (1983). Diagnosis and assessment in family therapy: A comparative analysis of six schools of thought. In J. Hansen & B. Keeney (Eds.), *Diagnosis and assessment in family therapy* (pp. 1–33). Rockville, MD: Aspen Systems Corp.

Luepnitz, D. (1988). *The family interpreted: Feminist theory in clinical practice.* New York: Basic Books.

Luker, K. (1994). Motherhood and morality in America. In A. Skolnick & J. Skolnick (Eds.), *Family in transition* (8th ed.) (pp. 503–520). New York: HarperCollins.

Lyddon, W. (1993). Developmental constructivism: An integrative framework for psychotherapy practice. *Journal of Cognitive Psychotherapy: An International Quarterly, 7,* 217–224.

Macfarlane, J. W. (1964). Perspectives on personality consistency and change from the guidance study. *Vita Humana, 7,* 115–126.

Martin, J. (1994). *The construction and understanding of psychotherapeutic change: Conversations, memories, and theories.* New York: Teachers College Press.

Masnick, G., & Bane, M. J. (1980). *The nation's families: 1960–1990.* Boston: Auburn House.

Mattessick, P., & Hill, R. (1987). Life cycle and family development. In M. B. Sussman & S. K. Steinmetz (Eds.), *Handbook of marriage and the family* (pp. 427–469). New York: Plenum Press.

McWilliams, S. (1993). Construct no idols. *International Journal of Personal Construct Psychology, 6,* 269–280.

Mead, G. H. (1934). *Mind, self, and society.* Chicago: University of Chicago Press.

Neimeyer, G. J., & Hudson, J. E. (1985). Couples' constructs: Personal systems in marital satisfaction. In D. Bannister (Ed.), *Issues and approaches in personal construct theory* (pp. 204–261). London: Wiley.

Neimeyer, R. A. (1985). *The development of personal construct psychology*. Lincoln: University of Nebraska Press.

Neugarten, B. L. (1976). Adaptation and the life cycle. *The Counseling Psychologist, 6*(1), 16–21.

Parry, T. (1993). Without a net: Preparations for postmodern living. In S. Friedman (Ed.), *The new language of change: Constructive collaboration in psychotherapy* (pp. 428–459). New York: Guilford Press.

Pedersen, P. B. (Ed.). (1994). Multiculturalism as a fourth force in counseling [Special issue]. *Journal of Counseling and Development, 70* (1).

Piaget, J. (1955). *The language and thought of the child*. New York: New American Library. (Original work published 1923)

Prawat, R., & Floden, R. (1994). Philosophical perspectives on constructivist views of learning. *Educational Psychology, 29*, 37–48.

Procter, H. (1978). Personal construct theory and the family: A theoretical and methodological study. Unpublished doctoral dissertation, University of Bristol.

Procter, H. (1981). Family construct psychology: An approach to understanding and treating families. In S. Walrond-Skinner (Ed.), *Developments in family therapy* (pp. 47–92). London: Routledge.

Procter, H. (1985). A construct approach to family therapy and systems intervention. In E. Button (Ed.), *Personal construct theory and mental health* (pp. 327–350). Cambridge, MA: Brookline Books.

Reiss, D. (1981). *The family's construction of reality*. Cambridge: Harvard University Press.

Rigazio-DiGilio, S. A. (1994a). A co-constructive developmental approach to ecosystemic treatment. *Journal of Mental Health Counseling, 16*, 43–74.

Rigazio-DiGilio, S. A. (1994b). Beyond paradigms: The multiple implications of a co-constructive-developmental model. *Journal of Mental Health Counseling, 16*, 205–211.

Rigazio-DiGilio, S. A. (1996). *Systemic cognitive-developmental therapy for partner and family development: Directions in clinical and counseling psychology*. New York: Hatherleigh.

Rigazio-DiGilio, S. A., & Ivey, A. E. (1990). Developmental therapy and depressive disorders: Measuring cognitive levels through patient natural language. *Professional Psychology: Research and Practice, 21*, 470–475.

Rigazio-DiGilio, S. A., & Ivey, A. E. (1991). Developmental counseling and therapy: A framework for individual and family treatment. *Counseling and Human Development, 24*, 1–20.

Rigazio-DiGilio, S. A., & Ivey, A. E. (1993). Systemic cognitive-developmental therapy: An integrative framework. *The Family Journal: Counseling and Therapy for Couples and Families, 1*, 208–219.

Rigazio-DiGilio, S. A., & Ivey, A. E. (1995). Individual and family issues in intercultural counselling and therapy: A culturally-centered perspective. *Canadian Journal of Counselling, 29*, 244–261.

Rigazio-DiGilio, S. A., Ivey, A. E., Ivey, M. B., & Simek-Morgan, L. (in press). Developmental counseling and therapy: Integrating individual and family perspectives. In A. Ivey, M. Ivey, & L. Simek-Morgan (Eds.), *Counseling and psychotherapy: A multicultural perspective* (4th ed.). Needham Heights, MA: Allyn and Bacon.

Riley, M. W. (1994). The family in an aging society: A matrix of latent relationships. In A. Skolnick & J. Skolnick (Eds.), *Family in transition* (8th ed.) (pp. 491–502). New York: HarperCollins.

Rosen, D. (1994). What is a family? Nature, culture and the law. In A. Skolnick & J. Skolnick (Eds.), *Family in transition* (8th ed.) (pp. 526–536). New York: HarperCollins.

Ryff, C. (1986). The subjective construction of self and society: An agenda for life-span research. In V. W. Marshall (Ed.), *Later life: The social psychology of aging*. Beverly Hills, CA: Sage.

Sarbin, T. R. (Ed.). (1986). *Narrative psychology: The storied nature of human conduct*. New York: Praeger.

Selman, R. L. (1980). *The growth of interpersonal understanding*. New York: Academic Press.

Sheehy, G. (1976). *Passages: Predictable crises of adult life*. New York: Dutton.

Skolnick, A. (1994). The life course revolution. In A. Skolnick & J. Skolnick (Eds.), *Family in transition* (8th ed.)(pp. 62–70). New York: HarperCollins.

Skolnick, A. & Skolnick, J. (Eds.). (1994). *Family in transition* (8th ed.). New York: HarperCollins.

Solomon, M. A. (1973). A developmental, conceptual premise for family therapy. *Family Process, 12,* 179–196.

Stratton, P. (1988). Spirals and circles: Potential contributions of developmental psychology to family therapy. *Journal of Family Therapy, 101,* 207–231.

Sue, D. W., Ivey, A. E., & Pedersen, P. B. (1996). *A theory of multicultural counseling and therapy*. Pacific Grove, CA: Brooks/Cole.

Taylor, C. (1989). *Sources of the self*. Cambridge: Harvard University Press.

Thomas, M. B. (Ed.). (1992). *An introduction to marital and family therapy: Counseling toward healthier systems across the life-span*. New York: Macmillan.

U.S. Bureau of the Census. (1991). *Population profile of the United States: 1991*. (Current Population Reports, Series P–23, No. 173). Washington, DC: U.S. Government Printing Office.

Veroff, J., Douvan, E., & Kulka, R. A. (1981). *The inner American*. New York: Basic Books.

Vygotsky, L. (1962). *Thought and language*. Cambridge: MIT Press.

Vygotsky, L. (1986). *Thought and language*. Cambridge: MIT Press. (Original work published 1934)

Watzlawick, P. (1978). *The language of change*. New York: Basic Books.

Watzlawick, P. (Ed.). (1984). *The invented reality*. New York: Norton.

Watzlawick, P., Beavin, J., & Jackson, D. (1967). *Pragmatics of human communication*. New York: Norton.

Weikel, W., & Palmo, A. (1989). The evolution and practice of mental health counseling. *Journal of Mental Health Counseling, 11,* 7–25.

Werner, H. (1948). *Comparative psychology of mental development*. New York: Harper and Row.

PART II

Applications of Constructivist Thinking in Counseling Practice

CHAPTER 6

Therapy and the Dance of Language

Don E. Gordon and Jay S. Efran

The influence of language on our existence is largely invisible. We are like fish who, having never broken the surface of the ocean, are unable to appreciate the centrality of water in their lives. We are so thoroughly and continuously immersed in language that it becomes impossible to step back and comprehend what life would be like without it. Except perhaps for the newborn, everything we see, believe, experience, or do is filtered through language. By the time we are old enough to ponder its functions, we are already completely enveloped by it. Moreover, any consideration of language influences must take place in language, creating one of those self-referential "strange loops" (Hofstadter, 1979) that philosophers dread.

Nevertheless, in this chapter, we undertake just such a task of examining language in order to elucidate the crucial interplay between the linguistic and psychotherapy domains. Following the model proposed by biologists Humberto Maturana and Francisco Varela (1987), we define language in biological terms of the human equivalent of grooming in apes and similar, in some respects, to the mating rituals of ring doves. Language is a dance of words and symbols, body and mind. It allows the creation and sustenance of human communities that, in turn, enable people to define themselves and their connection to the elements of their world.

Because of the intrinsically recursive nature of linguistic processes, people are able for better and worse to evaluate and comment on their activities and relationships. Each of these evaluations is automatically woven into the fabric of events that collectively determine what follows. Life, lived in language, is a complex flow of causes and effects without definitive boundaries between the world and our constructions of it. In this chapter, we demonstrate how therapists, through a better understanding of linguistic processes, can help individuals free themselves from their partially self-constructed predicaments.

LANGUAGE CHOREOGRAPHY

From the time of the ancient Greeks, people in Western societies have erroneously split human functioning into cognition, action, and emotion. This tripartite division artificially separates language (construed as a form of mental activity) from behaving and feeling (Neimeyer, 1995). However, speaking, listening, understanding, and behaving are linked communal performances, not individual, isolated mechanisms. As Maturana (1988) notes, the "higher cortical functions" take place not in the space between the ears but in the sphere of the community. Even though linguistic participation requires a sophisticated nervous system, language itself is a communal endeavor. We traditionally think of words, symbols, and meanings as housed in the minds of individuals, but the complex social arrangements that generate meanings are higher-order coordinations of action between and among groupings of people. Language is never a solo performance. We always speak to others, even when we are physically isolated and have to temporarily supply all the voices of the chorus (Varela, 1979). For example, the social act of reminding oneself that it is time to head for home relies on concepts that evolved in the community.

This view of language stands in stark contrast to the notion of thinking as passive, solitary, or preliminary, perhaps as portrayed in Rodin's *The Thinker.* Meaning-making is, in itself, a specialized form of action — it can have powerful effects even if only one's mouth is moving. In our culture, images of generals astride their horses, giving orders, brandishing rifles, and riding into battle seem to represent events in which actions speak louder than words. However, the image is incomplete and misleading. We forget that the affairs of generals are fully dependent on linguistically established meanings. They give orders to their troops using words and symbols, and only through such signifiers does each soldier apprehend his role in the military enterprise. Disputed territory is defined in conceptual terms, and victories and defeats ultimately hinge on verbal negotiation, linguistic ritual, and the placement of symbolic markers. It is rarely noticed that warfare relies as much on language as on gunpowder.

An important characteristic of language is that it permits a recursive layering of levels of abstraction. Unlike other species, we have evolved ways to comment on our actions and then to comment on those comments, progressively ascending the ladder of abstraction. Because of recursion, we can disqualify our own utterances and those of others with phrases such as "I didn't mean it," "I was only kidding," and "he doesn't know what he is talking about." As clinicians know, therapy is often a mind-boggling series of such disqualifications, analyses, and meta-analyses. Similarly, most conflicts consist of strings of piggy-backed interpretations: "Why do you always say that?" "Because it's true!" "That is only your opinion." "It's not just my opinion, everyone knows it!" And so on.

Emotioning and Languaging

Emotion, the third component of the traditional trichotomy, adds an additional level of complexity to language activity. When we speak of emotion we refer to the bodily settings and physical support equipment needed to enact particular behavioral programs, such as fighting, eating, copulating, and resting (Efran & Blumberg, 1994). Every action requires specific hormonal levels, skeletal postures, facial expressions, and so on. When the physical calibrations are in tune with our intentions, we feel ready to proceed. Otherwise, we are not "in the mood" and sense a need to get "psyched up" for the task at hand. In any event, support from the physical structures is required to fully implement language-dependent goals.

Sometimes, when our aims shift rapidly or unexpectedly, our systems need time to recalibrate. It is difficult to immediately kiss and make up, even though both parties agree that the fight is over. Similarly, we often experience periods of emotional contradiction (Mendez, Coddou, & Maturana, 1988) in which competing goals require incompatible bodily states. For instance, insomnia can result from simultaneously mulling over a vexing problem and trying to get some sleep. It feels like we are being pulled in two directions at once. Many client complaints can be understood as situations of chronic emotional contradiction, such as when a couple who want to remain together find themselves locked in frequent turf wars. Being closed and being open imply opposing objectives.

"Languaging" and "emotioning" are intimately intertwined. The impossibility of achieving a sharp demarcation between these processes is underscored by the training exercises sometimes used by actors. They will emulate in exacting detail the physical stance of a particular emotional state, such as grief, attempting to suppress the accompanying thought patterns. However, they usually report that as they adopt the demeanor of a particular emotion, the relevant meanings flood in, seemingly of their own accord. Similarly, when melancholy thoughts are deliberately entertained, actors find themselves automatically sinking into the dejected mien of a depressed individual. In sum, cognition, emotion, and action are not separate processes located respectively in the head, the heart, and the limbs. Every human event beyond infancy has linguistic facets, and each must be supported by appropriate fine-tunings of the bodily machinery.

The Ongoing Dialogue

The advanced forms of social coordination we call language force us to carve the flux of the world into discrete objects and events. We can only "talk" about entities that have been given boundaries and labels. Moreover, it is language divisions that permit us to conceptualize a past, a present, and a future, as well as to discern patterns of causality. They make possible the discrimination of an "us" and a "them" and give rise to the various forms of self-awareness and self-evaluation that, more than any other trait, distinguish our species.

Contrary to the commonsense view, happiness is a language event, a sociolinguistic appraisal rather than a particular sensation, composite of feelings, or standard set of identifiable experiences (Efran, Lukens, & Lukens, 1990). It should therefore come as no surprise that many are disappointed by circumstances they or others had assumed would make them happy. For instance, having won a long-sought job promotion, a woman finds herself pondering whether the accomplishment was worth the effort. She already worries that she will fail to meet expectations in her new position, and the joy she had hoped to experience on promotion was either frustratingly fleeting or absent entirely. On such occasions, many people find themselves muttering "So what?"

Life lived in language requires that each of us formulate at least rudimentary answers to the bigger questions about life's meaning. Furthermore, the very fact that we operate in language obliges us to keep up a running tally about how we look and feel and how well we are doing. Having once eaten of the tree of knowledge, we have lost the option of living in the moment and must continually reevaluate our goals and performances in light of our understanding of life's purpose.

THE THERAPEUTIC CONTRACT

Regardless of specific complaints, clients come to therapy because they are dissatisfied with how this evaluative self-discussion is progressing. Circumstances alone do not constitute problems, but they become problems when they appear to violate an individual's personal theory about how life should be lived. In this sense, psychotherapy is always a conversation about values in which there are no neutral parties. As Richard Rabkin (1970) writes, meetings between a client and a therapist represent an interface between two competing subcultures—a clash of value structures. It is these clashes that propel the therapeutic engine. In fact, little would be accomplished if a client's and a therapist's belief systems meshed completely. Points of disparity enable assumptions to be challenged and progress to be achieved.

Some therapists, misunderstanding the fundamental nature of conversation, assume that they can operate without bringing their own biases into the picture (Efran & Fauber, 1995). For example, some cognitive therapists like to think that they are simply correcting cognitive schemata that are objectively identifiable as defective. A more careful analysis suggests that they are simply cajoling or persuading the client to give up one set of cultural prescriptions in favor of another. Each set of rules has its constituents and opponents, benefits and disadvantages, yet no scheme can claim exclusive rights to objective truth or infallible logic. For example, literature on the "sadder but wiser" phenomenon among depressives has demonstrated that the pattern usually considered pathological is, by certain criteria, more realistic (Alloy & Abramson, 1979). Likewise, the presumably objective interpretations of psychodynamic approaches mask the social pressures that therapists exert on their clients. For instance, interpreting a client's conflicts with the boss as a manifestation of displaced oedipal feelings implicitly urges the client to avoid further confrontations with authority figures at work. Even if clients would be"better off" switching to a more accepted logic system, the interaction between client and therapist remains a process of value-laden social influence rather than one of objective assessment and correction.

THE NATURE OF CONVERSATION

To converse literally means to "turn together" (vers=turn, con=with). Once a conversation gets under way, it becomes virtually impossible to sort out individual contributions (Varela, 1979). Meanings arise and are revised in nonlineal fashion. Each person's responses trigger reactions from others, creating a complex chain of transformations. In reflecting on therapeutic successes, counselors are often puzzled about whether a favorable outcome was attributable to how the client presented his concerns, how the counselor responded to those concerns, or how the client, in turn, reacted to the counselor's interventions. Even a client's silence or apparent passivity can become a powerful aspect of the ongoing conversation. Needless to say, it is difficult to predict in advance which suggestions, interventions, or interpretations will prove fruitful. Just as many of us, sitting in a lecture hall, have had a sudden inspiration with no apparent connection to the speaker's point, the meanings that arise in psychotherapy tend to have a life of their own. Shifts in meaning cannot be fully predicted or controlled by either client or therapist.

Clients, too, frequently have no idea what aspect of the therapy process actually made a difference for them. Often, that which was most meaningful for the client was trivial or unplanned from the therapist's perspective. Many years after the fact, one of the authors ran into a former client who gratefully acknowledged the value she derived from therapy. Asked about the active ingredient in the process, she recalled a somewhat rambling session in which she had become acutely aware that her statements were more platitudinous than heartfelt — she spoke mostly "for effect." Thus, a discussion that the therapist might have considered unfocused was, for the client, highly significant.

This type of phenomenon, so characteristic of the psychotherapy conversation, calls into question the utility of manual-driven therapy protocols. In an unfolding conversation, how does one program the "correct" responses for one of the participants? The danger is that therapy manuals, by attempting to reduce human conversation to a series of standardized techniques, miss the core of the process. Therapists forced to use such manuals often "cheat" — that is, they pay lip service to the script while actually adjusting their responses to the developing interpersonal context. Unfortunately, people reading reports of codified treatments often falsely assume that the essence of the method can be gleaned from the pages of the published protocol.

ORTHOGONAL INTERACTION

Although therapy as conversation cannot be totally scripted, there are some basic guidelines that can help therapists better perform their role. One such operating principle is Maturana's (1990) notion of orthogonal interaction. To make use of orthogonality, clinicians must first recognize that people are members of multiple social "clubs," such as families, political groups, work and friendship cliques, ethnic and religious affiliations, and professional organizations. Moreover, people are capable of numerous behavioral patterns that are not elicited in their usual club settings. Orthogonal interaction involves relating to a system component — in this case, the member of a group — in ways that diverge from what he or she typically experiences. The changes such orthogonality introduces alter the fit between the person and other group members. A common example of this process is the young woman who gets her own apartment and then later attempts to move back home, forcing her parents to adjust to her heightened sense of independence.

Who we are, and how content we are to remain that way, is strongly affected by our ability to move smoothly between club affiliations. Since every club speaks its own language, clashes are unavoidable. When club allegiances conflict, the person attempts to honor several different behavioral codes at once, placing him or her in a condition of emotional contradiction. For example, college students are often mortified by the prospect of a parental visit to their dormitory. The "cool" persona their friends expect clashes with the studious image that parents are anticipating. Parent visiting day usually sets off a frenzy of cleaning activity to bring dormitory living standards closer to what parents might envision. Language, too, is sanitized, and roommates are likely to be coached about which conversational topics are "safe" to broach. Fortunately, parental visits are time-limited.

However, when people feel perennially trapped between competing club expectations they are apt to seek therapeutic assistance. The therapeutic milieu provides an opportunity to reevaluate the basic assumptions that imprison the person in emotional contradictions. To be effective, the therapist must be able to operate outside major club rules — to have the freedom to generate orthogonal interaction. Since they are not constrained by the vocabulary of the client's clubs, therapists can help generate conceptual/behavioral options that are unavailable within club parameters. The person can see that limitations that had formerly seemed immutable are, in actuality, the product of local club ordinances.

Even though therapists like to differentiate themselves as "cognitivists," "behaviorists," and so on, the techniques they employ all involve conversation and reevaluation. When a behavior therapist instructs an ophidiophobic to gradually approach a garden snake, assumptions are being scrutinized and a dialogue is being developed. All forms of action in which therapists have an interest involve language, and it is therefore misleading to classify rhetorical devices as primarily cognitive or behavioral, real or hypothetical. Meanings are always potentially consequential and invariably lead to the rearrangement of actual life circumstances. Life is never lived hypothetically.

Therapy is an ideal arena for generating orthogonal interaction because the therapist specifically avoids reinforcing the client's preexisting belief system. However, orthogonality can also occur unintentionally and in other settings. We are reminded of a gay male with no immediate plans to disclose his sexual orientation to family members. However, his younger sister, on meeting his "friend," realized immediately that he was her brother's lover. Without giving much thought to the matter, she freely shared her observations with her parents. Within the week the brother found himself out of the closet, not because he had planned to come out but because his sister had left him no alternative. In this instance, she was not playing by the implicit club rules. Luckily, the "orthogonality" she introduced worked out well. Once the secret was out, the family accommodated successfully to the new reality. The irreversible conversational shift had profound but positive impact on family relationships as well as on interactions with neighbors, friends, and co-workers. One could say that the sister had unwittingly served as therapist to the family system. The process in formal therapy is much the same, except that therapists are usually more deliberate about which assumptions to question. And, of course, they operate within the boundaries of an agreed-upon contract.

Human beings, operating in language, are conservative systems. Despite their good intentions and professed desire to change, clients will inevitably attempt to keep the therapeutic conversation in familiar terrain, seeking to minimize any discrepancies between their original linguistic framework and the vocabulary the therapist seeks to introduce. In that sense, therapy is always a battle between an existing set of propositions and purviews that have yet to be entertained.

Research suggests that early therapy sessions are more effective than later meetings (Sharma, 1986). From our perspective, this is because as client and therapist become increasingly structurally coupled, the therapist loses the ability to introduce linguistic novelty. As they become more comfortable with each other they tend to buy into common assumptions, eventually compromising the therapist's position as "outsider." Ironically, the therapist comes to understand the client too well and the conversational cutting edge is lost. Although a certain amount of empathy fosters the therapeutic alliance, too much agreement decreases the overall potential of the enterprise. This is no different from the need of corporations to hire outside consultants to help executives reexamine fundamental assumptions—perspectives that, for members of the firm, are already taken for granted. In fact, it would not be inappropriate to think of therapists as "conversational consultants." By closely examining the language of clients they are able to ferret out and challenge unexamined points of view.

AN ILLUSTRATIVE CASE

A salesman recently sought therapy, complaining that he lacked self-esteem and that his job performance was lackluster. He dreaded the "cold calls" his supervisors insisted he make. He had also been drinking too much, heading directly to the bar to "relax" after a frustrating day at the office. From his perspective, self-confidence was a commodity he needed in greater quantity if he was to be more productive and happy. In our view, positive self-evaluations are more often the result than the cause of effective performance. Paradoxically, being locked in the language of self-esteem is usually unproductive and self-defeating. A person who has never skied can hardly expect to descend the slopes with high levels of self-confidence. It is sufficient to follow the ski instructor's directions and be prepared to take some initial falls. After enough time on the trails, confidence in one's abilities presumably rises.

Another linguistic liability confronted this man — his tendency to conflate "doing his job" and "keeping his job." Just as it is easy to interview for a job one does not need, it can be difficult to do well at a job one is desperate to keep. By viewing each day as a struggle to avoid being fired, this client became handicapped by feelings of insecurity that drained him of energy and made him a less effective salesman. He annoyed his supervisor by continually apologizing for his flat sales record and making a public display of his efforts to generate new accounts.

Clearly, it is difficult to be flexible, relaxed, and creative when one is operating primarily out of fear and aversive motivation. To do better, one has to gain some distance from the corporate culture, which continually urges dogged effort at the cost of job satisfaction, ingenuity, and efficiency. Actually, in his anxious state, this client failed to realize that his colleagues felt the same way about cold-calling that he did. He viewed the outcomes of these calls in personal terms, and the language of his sales pitch reflected the adversarial attitude he adopted toward potential clients. Role-playing in session readily revealed the excessive self-focus of his calls. He knew he should chat a bit with customers, but his attempts to do so came across as forced and insincere. In truth, his thoughts were more about closing the deal than finding out about the person at the other end of the line.

To overcome these pitfalls, orthogonal exercises were jointly devised, such as taking a half-hour out of each workday to get to know co-workers. Different phone approaches were rehearsed and, during role-plays, he was stopped when he seemed to be granting precedence to his own needs over those of his customers. Words and phrases indicating defensiveness and impatience were identified. Most of all, he was urged to consider his current job ultimately "expendable," so that he could approach work in terms of sufficiency rather than survival. As he became more friendly with his peers, he learned that they, too, were receiving threats from the supervisor about flagging sales, although few of them took the saber-rattling very seriously. A turning point in therapy was his report of genuinely enjoying a phone interaction with a customer even though he soon realized that no immediate sale would result. In the past, such a call would have been followed by cursing and self-recrimination.

CONCLUSION

As this example illustrates, therapy is an unfolding dialogue during which, ideally, linguistic orthogonality enables the client (and often the therapist as well) to explore new avenues for being. The therapeutic setting and contract allow at least a temporary respite from the strictures imposed by the lexicon of meanings available in the person's ordinary social settings. A new way of languaging permits new ways of experiencing life.

REFERENCES

Alloy, L. B., & Abramson, L. Y. (1979). Judgment of contingency in depressed and nondepressed students: Sadder but wiser? *Journal of Experimental Psychology: General, 108,* 441–485.

Efran, J. S., & Blumberg, M. J. (1994). Emotion and family living: The perspective of structure determinism. In S. M. Johnson-Douglas & L. S. Greenberg (Eds.), *The heart of the matter: Perspectives in marital therapy* (pp. 172–204). New York: Brunner/Mazel.

Efran, J. S., & Fauber, R. L. (1995). Radical constructivism: questions and answers. In R. A. Neimeyer & M. J. Mahoney (Eds.), *Constructivism in psychotherapy* (pp. 275–304). Washington, DC: American Psychological Association.

Efran, J. S., Lukens, M. D., & Lukens, R. J. (1990). *Language, structure, and change: Frameworks of meaning in psychotherapy.* New York: Norton.

Hofstadter, D. R. (1979). *Gödel, Escher, Bach: An eternal golden braid.* New York: Basic Books.

Maturana, H. R. (1988). Reality: The search for objectivity or the quest for a compelling argument. *Irish Journal of Psychology, 9,* 25–82.

Maturana, H. R. (1990). Science and daily life: The ontology of scientific explanations. In W. Krohn, G. Kuppers, & H. Nowotny (Eds.), *Self organization: Portrait of a scientific revolution* (pp. 12–35). Boston: Kluwer.

Maturana, H. R., & Varela, F. J. (1987). *The tree of knowledge: The biological roots of human understanding.* Boston: Shambhala.

Mendez, C. L., Coddou, F., & Maturana, H. R. (1988). The bringing forth of pathology. *Irish Journal of Psychology, 9,* 144–172.

Neimeyer, R. A. (1995). Limits and lessons of constructivism: Some critical reflections. *Journal of Constructivist Psychology, 8,* 339–361.

Rabkin, R. (1970). *Inner and outer space: Introduction to a theory of social psychiatry.* New York: Norton.

Sharma, S. L. (1986). *The therapeutic dialogue: A theoretical and practical guide to psychotherapy.* Albuquerque: University of New Mexico Press.

Varela, F. J. (1979). *Principles of biological autonomy.* New York: Elsevier-North Holland.

CHAPTER 7

Constructivist Foundations for Multicultural Counseling: Assessment and Intervention

Brett N. Steenbarger and Laurie C. Pels

Multicultural counseling has been described as a fourth force in the counseling field (Pedersen, 1994), akin in influence to psychoanalytic, behavioral, and humanistic approaches. Several influential works articulate the counseling skills that are distinctive to multicultural practitioners (Pedersen, 1994; Sue, Arredondo, & McDavis, 1992). Sue and Sue (1990) identify "some important principles of cross-cultural counseling that may predict its effectiveness" (p. 160), including counselors' awareness of their own culture and biases, comfort level with differences between themselves and clients, and sensitivity to factors that might dictate a referral to a counselor of the client's own culture.

A growing body of literature suggests that counselor-client similarity on attitudinal, racial, and ethnic dimensions might be facilitative of positive outcome (Atkinson & Lowe, 1995; Atkinson & Thompson, 1992). Nonetheless, a literature review conducted by the authors has uncovered no controlled studies of counseling outcome to date that have documented the unique efficacy of multicultural skills or approaches. This raises an interesting question concerning the multicultural paradigm: Is it effective because of its distinctiveness as a "fourth force" or is its observed efficacy in practice attributable to features that are shared with other counseling modalities?

This issue is a matter of considerable debate in recent literature. Despite consistent findings that "common factors" account for a larger variance in treatment outcomes than elements specific to individual counseling approaches (Orlinsky & Howard, 1986), an interesting body of research does suggest that particular modalities may be distinctively helpful to individual persons or problems (Steenbarger, 1994). Within the multicultural school, there is a similar tension between "emic" conceptualizations of helping (emphasizing specificity of culture) and "etic" views (stressing universality among cultures) (Pedersen, 1994). Patterson (1996), for example, notes that "the current overemphasis on cultural diversity and culture specific counseling" (p. 230) produces a narrow technique–orientation that loses the common humanity of the participants. McFadden (1996), however, points out that a melting-pot view of culture blurs important distinctions between groups. How this debate is resolved has important implications for the training of mental health professionals.

Following Pedersen (1996), we suggest that the choice between "diversity" and "universality" is a false dichotomy, masking the complex ways in which general and particular influences help to shape the helping process. Drawing on constructivist theory, we assert that the *process* of change is universal, even as its thematic *content* is derived from diverse individual, social, and cultural sources. We illustrate this interplay of process and content with specific examples of constructivist assessment and intervention within multicultural counseling.

CONSTRUCTING CHANGE IN MULTICULTURAL COUNSELING

Investigations such as the National Institute for Mental Health's Collaborative Study of Depression support the notion that, across clients and helping approaches, outcomes are quite similar (Imber et al., 1990). In that study, cognitive, psychopharmacological, and interpersonal approaches did not produce unique changes with respect to thinking, vegetative symptomotology, or social functioning. Indeed, considerable evidence suggests that therapeutic change follows a predictable trajectory regardless of the specific school of intervention (Steenbarger, 1992, 1994). Below, we suggest that this is because there is a general process uniting all of these approaches, best described as one of social construction.

Constructivism, Counseling, and Context

Summarizing the common factors that account for success across therapies, Garfield (1992) stresses the quality of the helping relationship and the role of the counselor in providing explanations for clients' problems. As Frank (1973) notes, clients tend to enter counseling in a demoralized state; they have experienced difficulties, have been unable to alleviate these themselves, and often do not understand the source of their problems. An understanding counselor, offering an interpersonal, behavioral, or cognitive explanation for presenting complaints and a novel set of change strategies, assists the demoralized client in feeling a degree of hopefulness. Summarizing the landmark outcome study of Sloane, Staples, Cristol, Yorkston, and Whipple (1975), Garfield (1992) identifies five factors that accounted for success in behavioral and analytic therapies: the counselor's personality, helping the client understand problems, encouraging practice in facing problems, being able to talk to an understanding party, and self-understanding. The ability of a therapist to offer support, facilitate emotional expression, and encourage understanding was more important to outcome than the intervention techniques specific to the helping approaches.

Interestingly, Garfield (1992) proposes that the counselor's ability to provide a plausible rationale for problems may be more important than the accuracy of any single explanatory framework: "The *particular* explanations or interpretations offered by the therapist do not seem to be of primary importance," he notes. "Rather, the critical factor appears to be whether the patient finds them to be credible and acceptable" (p. 188, emphasis added). A good explanation must be sufficiently discrepant from the client's own to offer new understandings and new action alternatives (Steenbarger, 1992). It cannot stray too far from the schemata of clients, however, or it will be implausible. Successful counseling is thus a building process, in which counselors and clients co-construct problems in ways that are both novel and usable. The various approaches to counseling might be viewed as prefabricated structures in this process: systems of beliefs and meanings that assist in reframing presenting concerns and defining new alternatives for action.

Clients enter counseling with presenting concerns, which are constructed from prior experience and exist within nested biological, social, cultural, and historical contexts (Steenbarger, 1991). In Western culture, with its distinctive emphasis on individualism, these concerns are typically decontextualized (Germer, 1989) and presented in quasi-medical terms: "There is something wrong with me." The client rarely states that he or she experiences depression, anxiety, or anger. Rather, as linguistic convention would have it: "I *am* depressed (anxious/angry)." A large part of the demoralization experienced by the client is the persistent sense of *being* one's problems: trapped within a negative self-definition.

The co-construction of problems inevitably entails a recontextualization (Steenbarger, 1993). Viable co-constructions shift the locus of both problem responsibility and problem resolution, such that the client is simultaneously (and somewhat paradoxically) relieved of blame and opprobrium and invested with responsibility for change. For example, the alcoholic is introduced to the notion that alcoholism is a disease and not a matter of will-power, but is reminded that the disease can be faced and controlled through concerted group intervention. Similarly, the depressed patient is instructed in the construct of "biochemical imbalances" and encouraged to adhere to a regimen of medications and supportive therapy. "The problem isn't you," the counselor says in so many words. "The problem is your _____" ("habitual irrational cognitions," "internalized past interpersonal conflicts," "environmentally conditioned behaviors," "negative identity, acquired from a culture of prejudice," etc.).

In recontextualizing problems, counselors accomplish two important tasks. First, they relieve the client of feelings of inferiority and blame, undercutting negative self-definitions and demoralization and offering a fresh view of presenting concerns. Second, they reinforce the notion that the client is responsible for his future development, underscoring the idea that change is indeed possible from the newly offered vantage point. The client's presenting definition of the problem is limited, constraining solutions. Successful coconstructions empower the client, opening new vistas of understanding and action.

We are far from knowing all of the factors that determine which clients will benefit from intrapsychic, interpersonal, or behavioral constructions. What is clear, however, is that problems will be most readily reconstructed if they are framed in contexts that are salient and relevant to the client. Pastoral counseling will not work for the atheist; transpersonal counseling is not apt to meet the needs of a hard-headed businessperson. If counseling is to coconstruct an alternative meaning system, client and counselor need to share the component building blocks. Successful counseling does not seek to overhaul a client's belief structure. Rather, it elaborates latent meaning structures.

Multicultural Counseling as Constructivist Modality

What makes a meaning structure salient and relevant? Contexts are often transparent to individuals, simply because they are ubiquitous. We are unaware of the temporal bounds of our ideas until we study history and experience different epochs. Similarly, many two-legged, heterosexual Caucasians do not define themselves as such, since almost everyone they interact with also has two legs, a partner of a different gender, and white skin. If, however, we lose a leg, experience attractions to members of the same sex, or belong to a visible racial or ethnic minority group, those dimensions suddenly become quite meaningful. In such instances, the context is made salient by *difference,* and relevant by the fact that people identified as different tend to be viewed and treated differently (Sue & Sue, 1990). Race, culture, and gender are defining contexts for those experiencing minority status. Multicultural counseling is a framework that allows counselors to use this fact to their advantage, recasting problems in terms of those contexts.

While multicultural counseling, like other change approaches, is a coconstructive process (Pedersen, 1994) that allows clients to reshape their self-understandings (Steenbarger, 1993), it significantly differs from other counseling modalities at the level of content. Rather than recontextualize problems in terms of couples, families, past interpersonal interactions, or individual learning, multicultural approaches view them through the wide-angle lens of *social systems*. The problem is not simply within the client, according to the multicultural view; it is a residue of internalized messages from a dominant, and often hostile, culture. Consequently, multicultural approaches cannot affect any stance of therapist neutrality. Indeed, there is a very important sense in which advocacy is more explicitly built into multicultural modalities than other approaches: If the dominant culture devalues and disempowers the individual, therapy must entail a measure of affirmation and empowerment (Steenbarger, 1993). This means that multicultural counselors avoid repeating destructive patterns of social bias and discrimination and, instead, understand, value, and work within the indigenous frameworks of clients (Pedersen, 1994).

The multicultural counselor thus straddles an interesting fence, employing universal principles of constructivist change, even as he or she flexibly adapts the content of constructions to the individual cultural contexts of clients. Because clients possess very different cultural backgrounds, it is not surprising that multicultural counseling is itself becoming diverse, with interesting "cross-cultural" variants that apply modes of helping specific to the client's own culture (Brislin, 1990).

ASSESSMENT AND INTERVENTION IN MULTICULTURAL COUNSELING

From the very earliest phases of assessment to the implementation of specific change strategies, universality and diversity are interwoven in multicultural counseling. In the remainder of this chapter, we illustrate this interplay with specific techniques for assessment and intervention.

Assessment

At the start of counseling, the client typically presents one or more complaints. The counselor establishes an empathic, welcoming environment for the ventilation of these problems, while searching for underlying or overlying patterns. Specifically, counselor and client construct a catalog of specific incidents in which the complaint has occurred and explore the individual (biological, behavioral, and cognitive); social (family-of-origin, dyadic, current family); and cultural (ethnic, racial, gender) contexts surrounding these incidents. The assessment is not simply based on the counselor's own perceptions. Rather, the search is for contexts that are distinctive to the client and that might plausibly serve as a framework for new understandings and actions.

An important early step in multicultural counseling, therefore, is an assessment of the degree to which cultural contexts truly are meaningful to the client. This is *not* the same as simply identifying a client as a member of a different culture or race. Indeed, we have been struck by the number of times in which international clients or clients of color resent the assumption that their problems are cultural in origin. Similarly, we have worked with many white male clients who have internalized a sense of being different because of *their* cultural experiences — growing up in a rural community, a strict religious home, and so forth. Assuming that culture is relevant to one group of clients and not to others is the antithesis of constructivism's joint meaning-making.

A simple technique for such an assessment is a homework assignment generally given at the initial intake session. We ask the client to create a chart, based on the presenting problems. The chart is drawn in the shape of sine waves, with the peaks corresponding to positive emotional experiences (well-being, contentment, happiness) and the valleys to negative experiences (distress, anxiety, depression). We place no expectations on the client concerning the number of peaks and valleys drawn or the time frame captured by the chart. At each peak and valley, the client writes down (a) what was happening in his or her life; (b) who was involved; and (c) what the client thought and felt about the events. To the extent possible, the client helps the counselor vicariously experience the positive and negative events that are relevant to the client's request for assistance.

The resulting chart is diagnostic, though not in the sense of detecting illness. Rather, it reveals important facets of clients' constructions. For example, clients describe problems of varying degrees of complexity and duration. Some clients describe very narrow problem patterns (e.g., test anxiety) that have occurred over a brief time frame (e.g., the chart begins 3 months ago). Other clients frame multiple, broad complaints (e.g., low self-esteem) that have occurred over most of their lives. This can be quite helpful in determining the degree to which the subsequent counseling might be brief and focused versus longer-term and exploratory.

Clients also produce diagrams that vary in their degree of elaboration. Some individuals have numerous peaks and valleys, suggesting that they identify many significant events in their life. Others chart few highs and lows, describing life events in comparatively nonemotive ways. The relative number of peaks and valleys also differs for clients, with some labeling very few of their experiences as positive. Over time, counselors can become quite sensitive to the shapes and sizes of the charts produced and the ways in which the structure of charts are suggestive of clients' processing of life events. The charts thus capture universal aspects of meaning-making, even as they describe the diverse, unique, culturally grounded events of clients' lives.

During the subsequent session, we co-construct the chart. We encourage the client to look for patterns in the highs and lows, based on individual, social, and cultural factors. Our role is one of Socratic questioner, assisting the client in focusing on those factors: "What about your thinking or behaving might have led you to feel the way you did?"; "Is there something about your relationships that leads you to experience your problems?"; "Do you think the fact that you are an African-American woman in a workplace dominated by white men has any bearing upon the way you're feeling?" In elaborating responses to these questions, clients invariably reveal the contexts most salient and relevant to themselves. These will be viable candidates for reconstructions. Our experience is that a client is most apt to make use of a recontextualization if he or she actively participates in the constructive process.

Clients who respond quite favorably to inquiries directed at broad societal and cultural facets of problems are often excellent candidates for multicultural counseling. Only rarely in our experience will a client enter counseling and immediately identify race, gender, or sexual orientation as a relevant issue. Because of previous experiences of discrimination, there is often a distrust of others, including counselors. Once the counselor sensitively initiates inquiries about race, gender, or sexual orientation vis-à-vis the chart, however, it is as if a floor of safety is established, allowing clients to speak safely about such themes. The resulting response can be a bit like opening the floodgates: Once safety is established, the client is eager to share important elements of his or her life and offers rich elaborations of the charted events. In our experience, this is perhaps the single best indicator that multicultural counseling is apt to be well received and effective.

A good example from the senior author's counseling center practice concerns a young man who entered counseling complaining of depression and a series of failed relationships. When he presented his sine-wave chart, his low points corresponded to incidents of rejection in relationships, but they were described in such a manner as to assiduously avoid mentioning the partner's gender. The counselor pointed this out and noted that, in his experience, students often found it difficult to maintain stable gay relationships in the midst of the turmoil of keeping those relationships secret. The student, surprised that his secret was detected but pleased at the outcome, immediately revised some of his chart entries, adding rich detail concerning the intolerance he had experienced from friends and family. As a result, counseling did not focus on the biological, cognitive, or purely interpersonal aspects of his depression. Rather, it framed his feelings in broad, multicultural terms, exploring his identity as a gay-male-yet-to-come-out-in-a-straight-world.

Many other tools are available to counselors for the purpose of multicultural assessment (Grieger & Ponterotto, 1995). Even standardized pencil-and-paper personality measures can be completed and interpreted interactively, allowing for a co-construction of problem patterns. By asking probing questions regarding the client's socioeconomic status, race, religion, gender, and ethnicity, the counselor may be surprised to find that a large number of clients never thought of in terms of cultural background can best frame issues and solutions within this framework. In the senior author's practice, located in upstate New York, this has been especially true of bright, high-achieving white clients who have been raised in lower- and lower-middle income rural areas. The pervasive sense of being different from one's peers and resented for this difference is strikingly similar to the racial identity issues encountered by "minority" clients (Helms, 1995).

Intervention

A good co-construction of a problem is one that not only speaks to the client, but also allows for novel and adaptive solutions. Psychodynamic, cognitive, client-centered, and other therapies are distinctive because they offer ways of changing problem patterns, as well as understanding them.

Here, at the content level, multicultural counseling is quite different from other modalities. If the therapy is going to be culture-affirmative, it cannot simply introduce solutions drawn from the counselor's own culture. Instead, multicultural counseling must be capable of defining and selecting from a universe of possible solutions that are acceptable within the client's culture. This requires a measure of culture-specific knowledge and sensitivity.

A good example can be drawn from one of our recent counselor education classes. An Asian student raised the dilemma of a client who fell in love with someone who was not favored by her family. This led her to feel depressed and hopeless. What should she do?

It was instructive to hear the range of potential solutions offered by the class. Euro-American students were apt to encourage the client to assert herself and challenge her parents. Asian students, alternatively, sought ways in which the client could happily adapt to her parents' wishes. Clearly, imposing a solution from an American counselor's own vantage point would have been risky. Solutions, no less than problems, are co-constructed, with culture playing an important role in defining the universe of acceptable alternatives.

A simple exercise that can be useful in the construction of novel and adaptive action patterns requires clients to identify culturally relevant role models from their life experience. These may be well-known public figures, family members, teachers, or even individuals from history or the client's religion. Ideally, clients can identify more than one such exemplar. We then ask clients to engage in a fantasy involving guided imagery. In the fantasy, clients imagine themselves as the chosen role model, facing a dilemma similar to their own. How would you view the problem if you were this revered person?

What might you be feeling? How would you handle your feelings? How would you deal with others?

Like the sine-wave chart, the above exercise helps the counselor enter clients' worlds and read their maps. The exercise also defines and elaborates the universe of culturally defined solutions acceptable to the client, often opening the door to a mode of thought and action not yet explored. An explicit message underlying the exercise is that the counselor is a student, needing to learn from the client, the cultural expert. This reversal of roles is, in itself, affirming and empowering.

During the session, the counselor and client may role-play some of the fantasied responses, allowing the client to act out his or her ideal. Tasks assigned between sessions can extend this role-playing. Much as children acquire role-constructs through creative play, clients are encouraged to try on different identities and live their ideals. Undertaken in a supportive, encouraging counseling relationship, this work can then extend to other settings and relationships.

In a recent student counseling case, an African-American woman sought help for academic problems. It quickly became clear that her academics were suffering due to the stress of relationship difficulties. Specifically, she had experienced a breakup with a black man, who found her to be too "aggressive," despite the fact that she saw herself as shy. Despairing that she would ever meet a compatible African-American man in her small-town, largely white academic environment, she began to question herself and her ability to "hold onto a man." Adding further to her pressure was the fact that all her friends from her urban neighborhood had either already married or were engaged to be married.

Interestingly, when the author initiated the "ideal persons" exercise, the student could not think of a single role model! Though she loved her parents and relatives, she did not identify them as people that she wanted to emulate in relationships. Nor could she identify with her white friends, most of whom could not understand the angst of a professional black woman. She did, however, read a considerable amount of fiction and autobiography, often written by black authors. These books became an explicit topic within counseling and several were assigned by the client to the therapist as readings. Over the course of the discussions, several female characters stood out and became the focus of counseling exercises. The client eagerly entered into structured role-plays, in and out of session, in which she explored ways of viewing and responding to challenging life situations. Despite her self-described shyness, she used the role-plays to become more involved in campus activities, derive feelings of confidence, and meet new people. For example, she drew on one of the women in an autobiography to become successfully involved in campus political action. Over time, this became her culturally valid response to her isolation: a completely unique manifestation of a general change process.

CONCLUSION

Constructivism offers a useful framework for conceptualizing the facets of multicultural counseling that are both universal and diverse. At a process level, multicultural modalities assist clients in reconceptualizing their problems and discovering solutions. With respect to content, multicultural counseling offers a set of tools for operationalizing constructivist processes in user-friendly ways. By elaborating their meaning systems, counselors and clients can co-construct a wealth of novel problem framings and solutions, moving beyond prefabricated counseling schools to customized approaches with significant individual and cultural validity.

REFERENCES

Atkinson, D. R., & Lowe, S. M. (1995). The role of ethnicity, cultural knowledge, and conventional techniques in counseling and psychotherapy. In J. G. Ponterotto, J. M. Casas, L. A. Suzuki, & C. M. Alexander (Eds.), *Handbook of multicultural counseling* (pp. 387–414). Thousand Oaks, CA: Sage.

Atkinson, D. R., & Thompson, C. E. (1992). Racial, ethnic, and cultural variables in counseling. In S. D. Brown & R. W. Lent (Eds.), *Handbook of counseling psychology* (2nd ed., pp. 349–382). New York: Wiley.

Brislin, R. W. (Ed.). (1990). *Applied cross-cultural psychology.* Newbury Park, CA: Sage.

Frank, J. D. (1973). *Persuasion and healing* (2nd ed.). Baltimore: Johns Hopkins University Press.

Garfield, S. L. (1992). Eclectic psychotherapy: A common factors approach. In J. C. Norcross & M. R. Goldfried (Eds.), *Handbook of psychotherapy integration* (pp. 169–201). New York: Basic Books.

Germer, C. K. (1989). The contextual-epistemic approach to psychotherapy. In D. A. Kramer & M. J. Bopp (Eds.), *Transformation in clinical and developmental psychology* (pp. 115–135). New York: Springer-Verlag.

Grieger, I., & Ponterotto, J. G. (1995). A framework for assessment in multicultural counseling. In J. G. Ponterotto, J. M. Casas, L. A. Suzuki, & C. M. Alexander (Eds.), *Handbook of multicultural counseling* (pp. 357–374). Thousand Oaks, CA: Sage.

Helms, J. E. (1995). An update of Helms's white and people of color racial identity models. In J. G. Ponterotto, J. M. Casas, L. A. Suzuki, & C. M. Alexander (Eds.), *Handbook of multicultural counseling* (pp. 181–198). Thousand Oaks, CA: Sage.

Imber, S. D., Pilkonis, P. A., Sotsky, S. M., Elkin, I., Watkins, J. T., Collins, J. F., Shea, M. T., Leber, W. R., & Glass, D. R. (1990). Mode-specific effects among three treatments for depression. *Journal of Consulting and Clinical Psychology, 58,* 352–359.

McFadden, J. (1996). A transcultural perspective: Reaction to C. H. Patterson's "Multicultural counseling: From diversity to universality." *Journal of Counseling and Development, 74,* 232–235.

Orlinsky, D. E., & Howard, K. I. (1986). Process and outcome in psychotherapy. In S. L. Garfield & A. E. Bergin (Eds.), *Handbook of psychotherapy and behavioral change* (3rd ed., pp. 311–381). New York: Wiley.

Patterson, C. H. (1996). Multicultural counseling: From diversity to universality. *Journal of Counseling and Development, 74,* 227–231.

Pedersen, P. (1994). *A handbook for developing multicultural awareness* (2nd ed.). Alexandria, VA: American Counseling Association.

Pedersen, P. (1996). The importance of both similarities and differences in multicultural counseling: Reaction to C. H. Patterson. *Journal of Counseling and Development, 74,* 236–237.

Sloane, R. B., Staples, F. R., Cristol, A. H., Yorkston, N.J., & Whipple, K. (1975). *Psychotherapy versus behavior therapy.* Cambridge: Harvard University Press.

Steenbarger, B. N. (1991). All the world is not a stage: Emerging contextualist themes in counseling and development. *Journal of Counseling and Development, 70,* 288–296.

Steenbarger, B. N. (1992). Toward science-practice integration in brief counseling and therapy. *The Counseling Psychologist, 20,* 403–450.

Steenbarger, B. N. (1993). A multicontextual model of counseling: Bridging brevity and diversity. *Journal of Counseling and Development, 72,* 8–15.

Steenbarger, B. N. (1994). Duration and outcome in psychotherapy: An integrative review. *Professional Psychology: Research and Practice, 25,* 111–119.

Sue, D. W., Arredondo, P., & McDavis, R. J. (1992). Multicultural counseling competencies and standards: A call to the profession. *Journal of Counseling and Development, 70,* 477–486.

Sue, D. W., & Sue, D. (1990). *Counseling the culturally different: Theory and practice* (2nd ed.). New York: Wiley.

CHAPTER 8

A Constructive Framework for Career Counseling

R. Vance Peavy

In the last decade there have been several important shifts within social science generally (Kvale, 1992; Polkinghorne, 1988) and to a lesser extent, in counseling and therapy (Peavy, 1996a, c; Schaef, 1992). As Maturana (1988) makes clear, we now understand that we exist as a plurality of possible worlds, personal realities, and voices created by our own perceived distinctions. The concepts of external reality and objectivity are being replaced by self-referentiality (Giddens, 1991) and by the notion that human reality is constructed and participatory.

Along with this shift to constructivism, there has been an increasing attention to the importance of "relationships" in self-construction (Gergen, 1994) and the rise of social constructionism. The penetrating insights of G. H. Mead (1934) and Harold Garfinkel (1967), together with Berger and Luckmann's *The Social Construction of Reality* (1966), Erving Goffman's (1959) many writings, and Kenneth Gergen's (1994) works, have resulted in serious study and consideration of social constructionism in sociology and beyond. McNamee and Gergen (1992) have made an initial attempt to define therapy as "social construction."

In this chapter, I use the term *constructive* to refer to both constructivist and constructionist concepts. Constructivists and constructionists are both committed to a project of attempting to understand and document the realities that inform and organize the everyday meanings and actions of individuals as agents. This commitment is accompanied by a suspension of realist ontology that adheres to external, nonagentic explanations of human action.

In marking out their territory, constructivists utilize a variety of terms: *narrative, possibility, constructive alternative, postmodern, collaborative,* and *co-constitution,* for example. In spite of differences, the full range of constructivism as a modern psychological movement advocates common features: a cooperative, respectful relationship between therapist and client; an emphasis on client strengths and personal resources; a valuing of everyday meaning, experience, and action; and a "hopeful eye toward the future" (Hoyt, 1994). I also use the terms *counseling* and *therapy* (counselor and therapist) interchangeably on the assumption that both refer to processes of personalized change that have more in common than they have that differentiates them.

A "NEW LOOK" FOR CAREER COUNSELING

In their book *Career Choice and Development,* Brown, Brooks and Associates (1990) point out that even now, in the final decade of this century, most models of career development and counseling remain based on logical positivism. While it is widely accepted among philosophers of science that logical positivism as a philosophical position has been dead since the 1970s, Brown and colleagues assert that logical positivism is not dead in career development and counseling. This strange state of affairs manifests itself most clearly in such aspects of career counseling as trait and factor theories of self, step-by-step theories of career development, testing, expert status of the counselor/therapist, and the very concept of career as a rational, linear, one-in-a-lifetime phenomenon (Peavy, 1992c). It is a better assessment of the present philosophical foundation of career counseling to say that logical positivism with its linear logic and reductionism is dead, yet remains dominant.

A life-affirming revision of career counseling, both philosophically and practically, is needed in order to enable it to respond capably and proactively to the counseling needs of labor force members and potential members, as we move into the 21st century. In the following sections I will briefly examine some aspects of a constructive framework that constitutes part of the "new look" in career counseling. I am obviously interested in promoting constructive concepts and practices. However, I refrain from comparing and contrasting them with other existing career counseling and therapy approaches. I do not think that debates about "my counseling is better than your counseling" are likely to result in the perfection of career counseling practice. Instead I introduce a new vocabulary of counseling, and present explanations of why a constructive career counseling approach is useful.

The Workplace Isn't What it Used to Be

As career counselors and vocational psychologists, we must recognize the many ways in which work and workplaces are being transformed as we move into the postmodern, postindustrial era. As Giddens (1991) has observed, the emerging conditions of postindustrial society—globalization, deskilling, commodification, rapidly changing market conditions, and corporatism—produce change in workplaces that is rapid, unpredictable, and risky to virtually all people who work.

In this flux of workplace doubt, uncertainty, and conflict, the concept of career loses much of its meaning. Most individuals can look forward to holding many jobs and work positions in their lifetime as well as to being unpredictably unemployed from time to time. The idea that most people join a company and advance "up a career ladder" seems irrelevant and gratuitous in postmodern work life. More and more work will be defined in terms of symbolic skills, interactional skills, creativity, and role flexibility (Hage & Powers, 1992). The distinctions between work and personal life are blurring, and the only relevant meaning of "career" is that one's life is one's career.

In other papers, I have reviewed some of the needed changes in career development and counseling that postmodern and postindustrial transformations are calling forth (Peavy, 1992c, 1993a, 1994, 1996b). Many changes are needed, including: (1) reducing the gap between "life" and "career," (2) updating our conceptions of self, and (3) placing increased attention on the "social" aspects of self and career. All three revisions have far-reaching implications for career counseling.

Reducing the Gap Between "Life" and "Career." One of the unfortunate results steming from counseling's adoption of an instrumental, reductionist way of thinking—which was itself derived from logical positivist philosophy and behavioral psychology—is fragmentation. Reductionist thinking produces classifications of counseling and the development of various "types" of counseling, the burgeoning of diagnostic categories and personality classifications, and the separation of life into parts such as private and public, personal and career, work and play.

In order to get into a more viable way of thinking about career counseling, the "gap" (both conceptual and practical) between personal life and work life must be eliminated. More and more, social scientists are recognizing that the human individual is cut from whole cloth. One attempt to bridge the gap is illustrated by the concept of "lifecareer" as put forward by Miller-Tiedeman (1988). Other holistic approaches have been put forward by Bolles (1982); Shepard (1965); and Zunker (1994). Holistically, each individual organizes and lives a single life—a whole way of being—within which there may be many careers, within which there are various "jobs," and throughout all of which is woven the individual's evolving consciousness of the meaning of work (Ginsburg, 1972, 1984). A new look in career theory and counseling should recognize that "lifecareer histories" are constructed (or authored) by the individual out of an ongoing dialectic between context and self—and that this is a holistic phenomenon. Tyler recognized this very point in 1978 when she wrote:

> An individual is not limited to one way of dealing with any of life's demands. Through encounters with a very large number of situations and persons exemplifying different possibilities for structuring reality, one puts together one's own repertoire of possibility processing structures. (p. 9)

In everyday living, self-references of individuals typically fall within four possibility structures — references about health, personal relations, work/education, or spirituality (Peavy, 1992a). What is perhaps even more important is that a concern about work almost always implicates, to some degree, each of the other three domains of self-reference. The four structures are interwoven so that in most instances of self-referential concern, the individual is experiencing self as a gestalt or whole. The individual who is concerned about losing a job will nearly always also find that this concern implicates personal, relational, health, and spiritual aspects of self. Life is lived holistically.

In Search of Postmodern Conceptions of Self. A second aspect of a new look in career counseling is the need for revised models of self on which vocational psychologists and career counselors can base counseling and therapeutic interventions that make sense in the postmodern era. For more than half a century, the dominant model of self that career counselors have used for purposes of assessment, testing, and therapy has been what I call the "psychometric self." By this I mean the conception that a self is a matrix of intersecting lines (traits, factors, dimensions, variables). In the long-standing behavioral paradigm, the self has the status of "object" — real and empirical, but not agentic. In Skinner's (1974) words, "A person is not an originating agent; he is a locus, a point at which many genetic and environmental conditions come together in a joint effect" (p. 185).

From such a model of the self as a set of fixed, determined variables are derived personality profiles, interest clusters, and various ways of measuring dimensions of the self for use in the predictive and diagnostic efforts of career counselors and vocational psychologists. It is on this psychometric theory of self that a multimillion dollar industry of testing has been built. Arguably, the "testing industry" now represents economic enterprise more than psychological astuteness.

New-Look Selves. Of course, the behavioral conception of self has already been under revision since the so-called cognitive revolution, in which "mind" or "subjectivity" has once again been given a valid place in the vocabulary of self (Fancher, 1995). For example, Martin (1988) has suggested that cognitive researchers pay more attention to the relationships between counselors' and clients' theories of self—clinical practice can benefit from a detailed epistemic account of what is going on in the heads of both clients and counselors. Martin is indicating the desirability of a shift from the information-processing model of self, which has dominated cognitive theorizing, to an epistemic model of the self as embodied knower, which is congruent with constructive theory. This is a step in the direction of constructivist versions of self that offer valuable practical guidance to career counselors and vocational psychologists.

As social science has taken a postlogical positivist turn and has begun to recognize the influence of postmodern thinking, a flood of new self-conceptions has appeared. The dialogical self, the possible self, the quantum self, the saturated self, the distributed self, the process self, the self-as-story, and others have begun to find their place in self-theory discussions. A recent article by Hoskins and Leseho (1996) discusses the advent of postmodern conceptions of self and the resultant implications for counselors. How the self is construed has serious implications for the conduct of research and practice of therapy, assessment (Peavy, 1996b), career decision making, guidance, and the professional education of counselors. Gonçalves (1995) has recently reviewed the constructive self literature and has identified four central, common assumptions underlying most of the new paradigm self-conceptions:

1. Human knowledge processes are anticipatory. As proactors, individuals project reality. Human knowledge is constructed through processes of embodied understanding. The self is neither objective nor subjective—it becomes a "project"; the notion of "self-as-project" is also advanced by Giddens (1991).
2. Individuals are self-organizing and entropic. Entropy has structure and human projects originate a hierarchical structural organization coupled to more explicit and tacit ways of knowing. The concept of conditioning is being replaced by those of evolving hierarchical meaning systems and narrative structures.
3. Humans are metaphors of the environment. Humans do not have theories of their environment—they are those theories. Conjoint motor and emotional activity enables individuals to "author" an immediate and global apprehension of reality. In this process the individual is more an artist than scientist.
4. The self is evolving (Kegan, 1982, 1994) and is characterized developmentally by increasingly more complex, integrated, and viable structures. Neither the self nor its aspects or structures are fixed.

Under the influence of constructivist versions of the self, both the participants and the process of counseling and therapy become teleonomic and metaphorical. The object of therapy is to "throw clients forward" into processes of movement and evolution opening them to more and more change and reorientation. In the counseling process (which is itself metaphorical), "the best metaphors are those that find their own way of construction and deconstruction inside our clients, like a kaleidoscope assuming new and ever growing meanings" (Gonçalves & Craine, 1990, p. 149).

To Act Is to Become

The concept of action is central to the constructivist career counseling paradigm. As I sit here at my computer, I am engaged in the act of writing. I certainly am not just engaged in narcissistic self-reflection, nor am I just the intersect of a matrix of variables, nor am I merely an information processor. I am creating, changing, and developing/evolving. I am doing so through my act of writing, which is itself an action project and a way of initiating new ways of understanding both for myself and for others. Writing as an act enables me to throw myself forward into the future and to do so visibly. This insight should lie at the heart of a new look in career counseling.

When doing career counseling, the client and I are engaged in a particular type of conversation — one that embodies the principles of dialogue. That is, this is communication in which acts of listening have status equal to acts of speaking and each participant remains open to the possibility of being changed by what the other says (Levin, 1989). In counseling, by acts of speaking, writing, and mapping we are continuously projecting new understandings and trying out new versions of voice and self.

In constructive counseling it is essential not to encourage clients to guide their lives solely or excessively by external criteria and guidelines (for example, as represented by psychometric devices and grids using imposed constructs) but to encourage clients to see themselves as projects — dynamic and self-organizing. Further, clients should come to understand that they are engaged in construction and co-construction of their selves through acts, both behavioral and mental. As Guidano (1991) has pointed out, life projects are dynamically constructed or deconstructed, hour by hour, day by day, and year by year. The self is an authoring system. What is written today is a building block that constitutes part of tomorrow's self-as-project. The self is always in transitional states, some of which are seemingly stable, others turbulent, and others even chaotic. Yet the story goes on. Human life is linguistic life and humans are narrators. Counseling/therapy is a kind of rehearsal studio in which narratives are co-constructed and deconstructed — a setting in which we live out our stories and our stories live us out. Whatever understandings are achieved are ontological projections of the landscapes of consciousness of client and counselor.

Because we are human our cognitive-emotional apparatus condemns us "to see something as something else." This makes us metaphorical creatures. Through our use of metaphor we are able to act as if, to throw ourselves into the future, to pose counterfactual scenarios, to consider analogue conditions, and to use empathy. According to Vahamottonen, Keskinen, and Parilla (1994), "metaphors can be used as tools to enhance the client's innovativeness in finding answers to career questions" (p. 26). Accordingly, the purpose of career counseling as a metaphorical process or reality is to enhance the client's plasticity in reference to work life and to "illustrate the non-normative nature of post-modern worklife" (p. 26).

Habitus and Lifecareer Construction

North American psychology has developed as an ideology of the individual — a "cowboy" psychology. This has strongly influenced the applications of psychology in areas such as career counseling and therapy, generally making them both individualistic and decontextualized. Some career and vocational theorists (Gottfredson, 1981; Nurmi, 1991; Osipow, 1983) have attempted to integrate sociological considerations into their psychological theories. Perhaps the most sophisticated attempts to show the importance of the social (in contrast to the individual) is occurring in France (Bordieu, 1992; Guichard, 1994) and in Finland (Sinisalo, 1991; Vahamottonen, Keskinen, & Parilla 1994).

One of Bordieu's (1992) key concepts is that of "habitus." Habitus is from the Latin verb *habere,* meaning to be in condition. The word *habit* generally implies a mechanistic or deterministic structure, and is a psychological construct. Habitus implies creativity and inventiveness and is a social term. Habitus is a structuring mechanism that operates within an agent, binding the agent, as it were, to his or her micro-culture. It is construed as a strategy-generating principle enabling agents to handle uncertainty, risk, and ever-changing circumstances. As a concept, habitus is both individualistic and de-terminative — in Bordieu's terms, it also designates a way of being — and implies disposition, tendency, propensity, or inclination. Most of all it is an eco-logical term — much like the existential term *being-in-the-world.*

According to Bordieu (1992), habitus changes through two processes. One is social trajectory — leading to living differently, or in different conditions, than those initially. For example, a lower-class student placed in a prestigious school will be accorded the opportunity to change preferences in clothing, art, music, cultural behavior, and other habits. Habitus can also be changed or controlled through an awakening of consciousness — a consciousness that gazes inward to the subject and outward to connectedness.

Habitus is necessarily a social field or space. Every society is made up of a number of such social spaces — each different and at the same time interrelated to all other social spaces. Habitus transforms the meaning of individual from that of "cowboy" into an eco-being, at once connected on many levels to the surrounding world and at the same time having a creative potential capacity for plasticizing self and surrounding.

Education plays a fundamental role in the theory of habitus. For the most part it is education that produces an interiorization of habitus, that is, schemes of thought, perception, and action that make up habitus. At the same time, it is education that attempts to impose the legitimacy of the dominant habitus. People making vocational and career choices do not do so in full comprehension of all the relevant considerations nor do they do so blindly and completely under the influence of external considerations. People make decisions according to a practical, commonsense, best-guess prehension. This "sense of the game" enables people to act, react, and interpret what is going on in reference to the state of the social space that they inhabit and that has colonized them. Habitus implies neither rationality nor irrationality. It operates preconceptually as a cultural sense of "what is the best thing to do here" and signifies a connecting link between interior representations and contextual presentations. Habitus brought under the gaze of consciousness enables people to decide and act in a "sound" way without either over-reliance on rational, instrumental logic or excessive compliance with social regularities.

If we apply the notion of habitus to interpret such concepts as career "interests" and "choice," the emphasis changes from interests' being defined as "measured responses to defined occupations" to interests as a reflection of the dominant habitus of a society; thus interests are more correctly defined as a type of stereotype. Further, interests and their meaning vary depending on the particular social space the individual occupies in society. The same interest or choice made by different people in different social contexts and occupying different social statuses necessarily conveys different meanings. Averaging procedures used in psychometrics and tests obscure the very differentiations habitus implies. In conventional career counseling, interests are defined by responses to a test. In constructive counseling, interests are located by exploration and differentiation of the client's life experience and social space — that is, through habitus brought under the gaze of consciousness.

CONSTRUCTIVIST CAREER COUNSELING PRACTICE

In light of the forgoing discussion, what can be said about practical aspects of career counseling from a constructive perspective? First, it should be acknowledged that the constructive perspective is a conceptual framework to guide the work of the counselor. It is at once philosophical, psychological, sociological, and cultural. Counseling has unfortunately either remained rather naive philosophically, or else has hitched its wagon to a reductionistic and now bankrupt philosophy — logical positivism. Over the centuries philosophy has provided wisdom and practical guidance to people in the conduct of their lives. In one sense, the aims of counseling and philosophy are identical: to assist people to lead better lives. For most counselors, the need for a psychological component to counseling is obvious, albeit overdone in most models. As existentialists have it, we are always situated, we never exist out of relationship to ourselves, others, and the world. We inhabit social space. In order to adjust counseling to better take the social into account, we need to bring more of the social constructionist perspective to bear in our career counseling work. Finally, counseling has largely failed to take cultural embeddedness or habitus into account in its various forms of practice. No matter how a person acts, thinks, or feels, the influence of habitus is ever present.

Attempts to promote the concept and practice of multiculturalism indicate an awareness of habitus or cultural factors bearing on the counseling situation. However, the attempt to sensitize counselors to a range of possible cultural factors produces a rather murky stew. Most so-called multicultural counseling situations are in fact bicultural. They usually involve a member of the dominant culture and a member or members of a single minority culture. A constructive approach to career counseling is interdisciplinary (social, psychological, philosophical, and cultural) since the task of co-construction requires working with the "whole" of the individual, not just fragments or dimensions (Zunker, 1994). As a one-to-one process of personal reality co-construction, however, it is almost always monocultural or bicultural and seldom, if ever, multicultural.

Perhaps a good definition of constructive career counseling is "general methodology for life planning" (Peavy, 1994). Activity is an important aspect of the constructive approach. In fact, Vahamottonen and colleagues (1994) refer to their innovation in career counseling as "activity-based." It uses the client's practical activity as an essential part of the career counseling process. This approach aims to "combine the clients' external practical activity with their internal psychological processes" (p. 19). Theoretically, this form of career counseling aims to increase plasticity in individual workers. This is very important in postmodern workplaces, which are themselves plastic (Keskinen & Vahamottonen, 1991). The concept of plasticity in careers and counseling is not entirely new (see Lerner, 1984). It was used in the 1960s by Puranen and Harms (1964) to denote an individual's ability to shape a job or occupation to suit his or her own goals. More recent usage of the term (Vondracek, Lerner, & Schulenberg, 1986) emphasizes the capacity of the individual to shape work environments and themselves — as well as others in the work environment, and at the same time indicates the embeddedness of the individual in the environment and the ways in which the environment influences the individual. Plasticity implies dialectical, dynamical processes at work by means of which both individuals and environments are simultaneously transformed.

What are some practical procedures that will enable the career counselor to implement the constructive perspective? In another paper I indicated that I believe the main functions of counseling are the provision of hope, support, and clarification (Peavy, 1996a). The term *clarification* includes a wide range of counseling and therapeutic procedures, many of that are used in other forms of counseling. Important considerations in using counseling and therapy clarification procedures that convey and implement a constructive perspective include the following:

1. Do the procedures enable the counselor and client to construct a cooperative relationship within which the client is the "expert" on his or her life experience, and the counselor is an expert on the process of planning (Peavy, 1996b), the language of change (Efran, Lukens, & Lukens, 1990), and the generation of personal meaning (Carlsen, 1988)?

2. Do the procedures support an increased openness in the career counseling process? This openness is essential in equipping the client to meet the demands of work life, which are increasingly complex, plastic, unpredictable, non-normative, and changeable (Vahamottonen et al., 1994).

3. Do the procedures support a reflective counseling process that is more sensitive to questions than to answers (White & Epston, 1990) and that helps the client to develop maps and plans to follow in coping with and understanding "fuzzy" work-life experiences (Peavy, 1996b)?

4. Do the procedures support a counseling process that often proceeds in a nonlinear, transformational manner, where continuous, step-by-step progress is not the rule (Huteau, 1988), but innovative actions, the opening of new horizons, and the development of ad hoc, unique individual learning projects are the rule (Peavy, 1996b)?

5. Does the counseling process validate the use of metaphors by means of which the client can both express and understand increasingly germane and complex relationships between self and work, self and counselor, and self and others? Metaphors are more flexible than verbal reasoning alone; they can be used as tools for understanding fuzzy situations, and they

are the "germs" of system formation (Walgenbach, 1990). In this sense metaphors can be the foundation on which clients can initiate new concepts and meanings, and innovative questions and solutions to career dilemmas (Angus & Rennie, 1988).

6. Are the procedures resonant with a fluid, evolving concept of self continuously under construction and reconstruction? Is the self construed in terms of authorship and agency (Parry & Doan, 1993) and constituted by means of dialogical processes (Hermans & Kempen, 1993)?

7. Do the procedures focus the counseling process on plasticity and changeable aspects of self and context including role redefinition and empathy (Hage & Powers, 1992), which is deemed ever more necessary for success in postmodern workplaces?

8. In addition to the usual activity of discourse in the interview, do the procedures allow the client to make himself or herself visible? Procedures such as clustering, diagramming, mapping, using objects to physicalize concepts, and letter writing are examples of in-therapy activities that can be used to metaphorize, construct, and visualize self and situation (Peavy, 1995b).

9. Do the procedures help the client to understand how he is already living some aspects of life in a sensible and culturally sound way? ("You faced this situation once before—how were you able to cope with it then?") (White & Epston, 1990).

10. Do the procedures promote "as if" thinking, the use of counterfactual scenarios, and the generation of alternate possibilities? Clients who have stereotyped images or who are entrenched in disempowering assumptions about themselves, or their careers or constraints, often need assistance in lifting themselves out of habituated patterns of assuming, perceiving, and thinking so that the future can open to new possibilities and projects for them and so that they can increase their capacity for mindfulness.

11. Finally, do the counseling procedures or project help the counselor and client to construct and implement decisions and plans of action that are personally meaningful and that bolster the individual's existential robustness in the face of economic unpredictability, commodification, and consumerism? As we increasingly realize, the postmodern self must be reflexively achieved in environments that are complex and that demand various technical and linguistic competencies, but at the same time must be achieved in conditions of moral aridity and absence of traditional guidance and models. The lack of tradition in late modern society has placed us in a moral vacuum as we enter the postmodern period. Underlying questions of career and life direction, and the ceaseless doubt and

uneasiness that large numbers of people experience on a daily basis, comprise the looming threat of personal meaninglessness. (Giddens, 1991)

Questions such as these may seem to place an inordinate amount of responsibility on the shoulders of the constructive career counselor — and indeed they do! Yet, we must remember, if counseling is to be lifted out of its more-or-less dysfunctional rut and reinvigorated with new thinking and practice consonant with the 21st century, then the work of the career counselor will have to take on more sophisticated and system-sensitive components. The narcissism with which Lasch (1979) claims North American society to be redolent seems to be magnified by a highly individualistic, cowboy type of career counseling. Yes, indeed "times are a changing." Clients need help in investigating how and why they are, or are not, connected to other people and to various aspects of society, both micro and macro. Postmodern happenings — both local and global — radically alter the daily social life of individuals and affect the most personal aspects of day-to-day experience. Mahoney (1995) points out that in therapy, and especially for the constructive therapist,

> never before has the act of balancing individual rights and social responsibilities required such a comprehensive appreciation for the dynamic complexities of life on this planet. (p. 394)

A Paradigmatic Case Example of Constructive Counseling

In order to illustrate some constructive concepts and guidelines, I will present the example of "Maggy," who responded to an advertisement for free career counseling in return for permission to use the resulting videotapes with professional audiences. Thirty years old, Maggy lives with a partner and a 5-year-old stepson. She has returned to university study after some years working as a free-lance writer. In accordance with the tasks of the constructive interview (Peavy, 1993b) the first 10 minutes of the interview are spent establishing rapport, setting the stage for co-operation, and establishing that the client probably knows much more about her own life than does the therapist, although she may lack clarification of important issues and aspects of her life that she is currently trying to deal with.

The client presents her central concern as "Should I or should I not have a child?" She is filled with doubt and uncertainty about this decision and believes that it is very much tied to her future work-life plans. Of course this decision is also intricately intertwined with her role as life partner and as "stepmother" to her partner's son. The counselor then asks the client if she is willing to cooperatively develop a life space map as a therapeutic "experiment." She agrees to take part.

Life Space Map. The counselor asks the client if she would like to investigate her life space by making a map on blank paper — the task is to be carried out cooperatively. The client agrees and the following dialogue ensues.

> COUNSELOR: On this blank page, which can represent what you are thinking about, feeling, and doing at present in relation to your concern and we can call your "life space," draw a small circle somewhere to represent your self.
> CLIENT: Where should I draw it?
> COUNSELOR: Anywhere you like — do you feel in the center of your space today?
> [Client draws a circle about the size of a quarter in the center of the blank page and labels it "self."]
> COUNSELOR: Who are the important people in your world, especially in relation to your concern about whether or not to have a child?
> CLIENT: My partner and my stepson — shall I put them in my space?
> COUNSELOR: Yes, put them where they are in relation to you. [The client draws a circle representing her partner. The circle overlaps her own circle. She then draws another circle representing her stepson more distant from herself and on the far side of her partner.]

In this fashion, the counselor and client, working together, construct a map of (1) the client's relationships, (2) recurring emotional references to the concern, and (3) other voices (internal meaning systems) and life experiences that the client interprets as somehow related to her concern. In this life space map, we — counselor and client — are examining the social habitus of the client.

A Metaphor Crystallizes. At one point Maggy remarks that she has a feeling of sacrifice and then draws a black clump of squiggly lines that are outside the circle representing her self, but that she nonetheless describes as very much a part of herself. She tries to describe what this dark blob is, but she has difficulty finding the right words. The counselor remarks that it seems like a "dark cloud" and the client responds "Yes, that is what it is like, like a dark cloud." The client is able to partially describe the dark cloud as holding her feelings of sacrifice. In turn these feelings seem to be related to her observation of the life of sacrifice and self-denial she believes her own mother had lived. The client is dimly aware of the ambiguity with which she apprehends the dark blob: "Is this part of myself, am I being colonized by my mother's biography, or is this an external force I am resisting?"

The self is fluid, voiced, and multifaceted. The counselor and client then explore, identify, and name the various "voices" (of possible selves) of which the client is aware and which constitute her internal subself system and which are engaging in internal dialogues. She identifies such voices as "freedom," "sacrifice," "selfishness," "guilt," "fear," "mistake," and the voice of being wrong. All of these voices are placed in the life space by the client.

Writing Makes Me Visible: A Project in Self-Construction. After further discussion about the meaning of the stories that each voice is expressing, the counselor suggests that the client consider doing a personal project that might help her gain fuller understanding and meaning from one of her voices, and thus shed light on the ambiguity surrounding her stalled decision about having a child. The counselor suggests that the client select one of the voices with which she would like to have a focused, in-depth conversation. This would constitute a project for the client to do prior to another session with the counselor and would take the form of a letter that the client, as "I," would write to one of her voices. Perhaps this will provide her an opportunity to make meaning out of what the voice has been saying to her and at the same time make visible an important aspect of herself that is being dealt with as a metaphor.

The client responds enthusiastically and chooses to write to the voice of sacrifice—which also has the metaphorical status as a "dark cloud." This interview ends with the counselor and client agreeing that a decision on the client's part does not seem any closer, but they have been able to open up several possibilities for meaning-generation and the client is clearly in control of a personal project by means of which she can further investigate her concern.

Nearly a year passes before a second interview is conducted in which the client speaks of the letter she has written, events in her life that have transpired since the first meeting, and where she now stands in relation to her original concern. The counselor and client again construct a life space map and discussed the various issues raised by the client.

An Act of Writing Readies the Client for Change. The client begins by reading the rather poetic letter she has written to "sacrifice." She described sacrifice as a gooey, molten lava-like phenomenon that, much to her surprise, is not immutably fixed, but plastic and potentially changeable. She writes of digging into the black lava material with her hands and, in doing so, realizing that she might be able to work with it. Somewhat like sculpting, she might be able to shape and influence sacrifice. This metaphoric style of writing indicates that the thinking and writing about the black cloud of sacrifice is preparing the client for possible changes to come.

Nonlinear and Unpredictable Life Experiences. The client then relates how, shortly after the first interview, she had learned that her father, who lived in a distant city, was believed to be terminally ill with cancer. She arranged to go to her parents' home and spent several weeks with her father, having many deep and spiritual conversations with him. She recounts how her father wanted to, and was, dying with dignity and composure. He also told her in detail many thoughts and feelings that he had about her as his daughter, and about himself as her father — conversations of a nature they had never had before.

During these conversations she observed how wonderful it seemed to be for her father that he was able to confide in her his feelings of love and acceptance of his own life. She says, "I began to realize that he was able to speak this way, and express these deep feelings because he had me as a daughter. If he and my mother had not had me [as a child] then he would have been deprived of the final fulfilment of being able to confide these deep thoughts to his own offspring. This made me think of what I would be missing by not having a child of my own — I could not have the same kind of experience as I neared the end of my own life. I would not be able to pass on my own deepest reflections to my successor(s). As the days passed I began to see in my father a model of how I would like to approach the end of my own life. I realized that I could only have this incredible rewarding, spiritual, human experience if I too had a child or children."

This experience of being with her dying father, completely unpredicted, and outside of the course of therapy, had a profound influence on the client and changed the very nature of her concern. However, her transparency to this experience was, in part, made possible by the therapeutic work with the black blob.

Agency and the Empowerment of "I." The remainder of the second therapy session consists in fleshing out understandings of the client's "decision" in the context of her dark cloud and her conversations with her father. It becomes clear for both Maggy and her counselor that the focus of her concern has shifted. Originally, the question for her was whether to have a child and around this question there was a large amount of ambiguity. Now the question is changed to an empowering existential understanding: "I realize that I have the power of choice. I now see the grounds for my decision much more clearly and I feel that I can make a decision and live with it without all the doubt I felt before." The concern is no longer a question surrounded by ambiguity and anxious feelings of sacrifice. The concern was transformed into an agentic voice: "I am the one who can decide." It has now become a voice of the "I" as "self-critical subject and creativity with enough strength to resist forces to the contrary" (Touraine, 1995, p. 205).

CONCLUSION

In this chapter I have attempted to open up the possibility of building a new look in career counseling from the conceptualizations of constructivist and constructionist thinking. I am convinced that such a rebuilding is sorely needed — not only because career theory is largely based on assumptions and philosophy long since abandoned by nearly everyone else, but also because as we move into the 21st century, counseling must awaken to the fact that humans are being thrust into a new ball game. This task of rebuilding is large and complicated and I have only been able to touch on a few issues and make certain suggestions. I will end by saying that I have been using and teaching others how to use constructive career counseling since 1989. It is a joy to teach; graduate students find it enormously inspiring and empowering — a far cry from the reception usually given to seminars and courses in career counseling. As far as work with clients is concerned, as a therapist I have experienced more gratification and feelings of doing valuable work in the past 7 years of working as a constructive therapist than I did in the previous 30 years as a behaviorist, then a humanist, and finally an eclectic before I read *Order Out of Chaos* (Prigognine & Stengers, 1984). In this book, Ilya Prigognine, a Nobel laureate in chemistry, presents a very strong argument for the validity of the constructivist perspective. In essence, Prigognine's claim is that whatever it is we call reality is revealed to us only through active construction in which we participate. This understanding helped thrust me into a new, postmodern career as a constructivist.

REFERENCES

Angus, L., & Rennie, D. (1988). Therapist participation in metaphor generation: Collaborative and non-collaborative styles. *Psychotherapy, 25,* 552–560.

Berger, P., & Luckmann, T. (1966). *The social construction of reality.* New York: Doubleday.

Bolles, R. (1982). *The three boxes of life and how to get out of them.* Berkeley: Ten Speed Press.

Bordieu, P. (1992). *An invitation to reflexive sociology.* Chicago: University of Chicago Press.

Brown, D., Brooks, L., & Associates. (Eds.). (1990). *Career choice and development* (2nd ed.). San Francisco: Jossey-Bass.

Carlsen, M. B. (1988). *Meaning-making: Therapeutic processes in adult development.* New York: Norton.

Efran, J., Lukens, M., & Lukens, R. (1990). *Language structure and change: Frameworks of meaning in psychotherapy.* New York: Norton.

Fancher, R. (1995). *Cultures of healing.* New York: W. H. Freeman.

Garfinkel, H. (1967). *Studies in ethnomethodology.* Englewood Cliffs, NJ: Prentice-Hall.

Gergen, K. (1994). *Realities and relationships.* Cambridge: Harvard University Press.

Giddens, A. (1991). *Modernity and self-identity.* Stanford: Stanford University Press.

Ginsburg, E. (1972). Toward a theory of vocational choice: A restatement. *The Vocational Guidance Quarterly, 20,* 169–176.

Ginsburg, E. (1984). *Career development.* San Francisco: Jossey-Bass.

Goffman, E. (1959). *The presentation of self in everyday life.* New York: Doubleday.

Gonçalves, O. (1995). Hermeneutics, constructivsm and cognitive-behavioral therapies: From the object to the project. In R. Neimeyer & M. Mahoney (Eds.), *Constructivism in psychotherapy* (pp. 195–230). Washington, DC: American Psychological Association.

Gonçalves, O., & Craine, M. (1990). The use of metaphors in cognitive therapy. *Journal of Cognitive Psychotherapy, 4,* 135–150.

Gottfredson, L. (1981). Circumscription and compromise: A developmental theory of occupational aspiration. *Journal of Counseling Psychology, 28,* 545–579.

Guichard, J. (1994, June). *Social and cultural experiences of adolescents and the categorization of occupations.* Paper presented at the Eighth Biennial Meetings of the International Society of Behavioral Development, Amsterdam.

Guidano, V. (1991). *The self in process: Toward a post-rationalist cognitive therapy.* New York: Guidford Press.

Hage, J., & Powers, C. (1992). *Post-industrial lives: Roles and relationships in the 21st century.* Newbury Park, CA: Sage.

Hermans, H., & Kempen, H. (1993). *The dialogical self: Meaning as movement.* San Diego: Academic Press.

Hoskins, M., & Leseho, J. (1996). Changing metaphors of the self: Implications for counseling. *Journal of Counseling and Development. 74,* 243–252.

Hoyt, M. (1994). Introduction: Competency-based future-oriented therapy. In M. Hoyt (Ed.), *Constructive therapies* (pp. 1–10). New York: Guilford Press.

Huteau, M. (1988). Comment analyser et evaluer les interventions educatives afin d'ameliorer leur efficacite? *Orientation Scholaire et Professionnelle, 17,* 125–141.

Kegan, R. (1982). *The evolving self.* Cambridge: Harvard University Press.

Kegan, R. (1994). *In over our heads: The mental demands of modern life.* Cambridge: Harvard University Press.

Keskinen, A., & Vahamottonen, T. (1991, September 13). An activity-based approach to career counseling. *Proceedings,* AIOSP Conference, Lisbon.

Kvale, S. (Ed.). (1992). *Psychology and postmodernism.* Newbury Park, CA: Sage.

Lasch, C. (1979). *The culture of narcissism.* New York: Norton.

Lerner, R. (1984). *On the nature of human plasticity.* Cambridge: Cambridge University Press.

Levin, D. (1989). *The listening self.* London: Routledge.

Mahoney, M. (1995). The psychological demands of being a constructive psychotherapist. In R. Neimeyer, & M. Mahoney (Eds.), *Constructivism in psychotherapy.* (pp. 57–400). Washington, DC: American Psychological Association.

Martin, J. (1988). A proposal for researching possible relationships between scientific theories and personal theories of counselors and clients. *Journal of Counseling and Development, 66,* 261–265.

Maturana, H. (1988). The search for objectivity, or the search for a compelling argument. *Irish Journal of Psychology, 9,* 25–82.

McNamee, S., & Gergen, K. (1992). *Therapy as social construction.* Newbury Park, CA: Sage.

Mead, G. H. (1934). *Mind, self, and society.* Chicago: University of Chicago Press.

Miller-Tiedeman, A. (1988). *LifeCareer: The quantum leap into a process theory of career.* Vista, CA: LIFECAREER Foundation.

Nurmi, J.-E. (1991). How do adolescents see their future? A review of the development of future orientation and planning. *Developmental Review, 11,* 1–59.

Osipow, H. S. (1983). *Theories of career development.* Englewood Cliffs, NJ: Prentice-Hall.

Parry, A., & Doan, R. (1993). *Story re-visions: Narrative therapy in the postmodern world.* New York: Guilford Press.

Peavy, R. V. (1992a). A constructivist model of training for career counselors. *Journal of Career Development, 18,* 215–228.

Peavy, R. V. (1992b). *Four domains of self-referentiality.* Unpublished manuscript, NorthStar Research, Victoria, BC, Canada.

Peavy, R. V. (1992c, January). *New concepts and practice in career counseling: A research and development project.* Paper presented at the National Consultation on Career and Vocational Counseling, Ottawa.

Peavy, R. V. (1993a). Constructivist counseling: A prospectus. *Guidance and Counseling, 9,* 3–12.

Peavy, R. V. (1993b). Envisioning the future: Worklife and counseling. *Canadian Journal of Counseling, 27,* 123–139.

Peavy, R. V. (1994). *Constructivist career counseling: Two Video Instructional Package.* University of Victoria, Victoria, BC, Canada.

Peavy, R. V. (1995a). *Constructivist counseling: "Maggy"* [Videotape]. University of Victoria, Victoria, BC, Canada.

Peavy, R. V. (1995b, August). *Paradigmatic transformations in society and history: Re-thinking counseling and therapy.* Paper presented at the XVth Congress of the International Association for Vocational Education and Guidance, Stockholm.

Peavy, R. V. (1996a). Assessment in constructivist career counseling. *Guidance and Counselling, 11,* 8–14.

Peavy, R. V. (1996b, May). *Constructing personal plans in constructive counseling.* Paper presented at the 1996 International Round Table for The Advancement of Counseling, Vancouver, Canada.

Peavy, R. V. (1996c). Counseling as a culture of healing. *British Journal of Guidance and Counseling, 24,* 141–150.

Polkinghorne, D. (1988). *Narrative knowing and the human sciences.* Albany, NY: State University of New York Press.

Prigogine, I., & Stengers, I. (1984). *Order out of chaos.* New York: Bantam.

Puranen, E., & Harms, W. (1964). *Ammanatinvalinnanohjauksen validiteetin selvittamisen periatteista.* Helsinki: Kulkulaitosten ja yleisten toiden ministerio.

Schaef, A. (1992). *Beyond therapy, beyond science: A new model for healing the whole person.* San Francisco: HarperCollins.

Shepard, H. (1965). Planning for living workshop. Unpublished manuscript.

Sinisalo, P. (1991). Conceptions of vocational interests: From personality constructs to representations. In H. Perho, H. Raty, & P. Sinisalo (Eds.), *Crossroads between mind, society and culture.* Joensuu, Finland: Joensuu University Press.

Skinner, B. F. (1974). *About behaviorism.* New York: Vintage Books.

Touraine, A. (1995). *Critique of modernity.* London: Basil Blackwell.

Tyler, L. (1978). *Individuality, human possibilities, personal choice in the psychological development of men and women.* San Francisco: Jossey-Bass.

Vahamottonen T., Keskinen, A., & Parilla, R. (1994). A conceptual framework for developing an activity-based approach to career counseling. *International Journal for the Advancement of Counseling, 17,* 19–34.

Vondracek, F., Lerner, R., & Schulenberg, J. (1986). *Career development: A life-span developmental approach.* London: Lawrence Erlbaum.

Walgenbach, W. (1990, May). *Self-system formation through interdisciplinary system formation.* Paper presented at the Second International Congress for Research on Activity Theory, Lahti, Finland.

White, M, & Epston, D. (1990). *Narrative means to therapeutic ends.* New York: Norton.

Zunker, V. (1994). *Career counseling: Applied concepts of life planning* (4th ed.). Pacific Grove, CA: Brooks/Cole.

CHAPTER 9

Reframing Guidance and Counseling in the Schools with a Constructivist Perspective

Jerald R. Forster

The counseling profession was born in the first decade of the 20th century and has changed during each succeeding decade. These changes, although inevitable, caused friction, pressure, and the need for continual negotiation and adaptation on the part of practitioners. During the second half of the century, these changes created special pressures for counselors working in schools. They have faced conflicting forces from movements in the counseling profession that contrasted with those in the school work setting. This conflict is highlighted by each movement's position regarding the usefulness of the term *guidance* to describe the counselor's role. While the counseling profession called for discontinuing the use of guidance, school communities found the term useful for designating the practices of counselors in the schools. The thesis of this chapter is that a guidance model can be retained if a *constructivist* perspective is used to reframe the guidelines and practices of both counseling and guidance.

In subsequent sections of this chapter, I will briefly illustrate the conflicting positions of the counseling profession and school setting regarding guidance and propose a rationale for reframing counseling and guidance with a constructivist perspective. Later sections will describe counseling and guidance practices that flow from the constructivist perspective and suggest the implications that such a perspective might have on the future.

THE COUNSELING PROFESSION MOVES TO ELIMINATE GUIDANCE

Although the roots of counseling and supervision are firmly planted in the ground of the guidance movement, there have been subsequent attempts to lop these guidance roots. In a comprehensive textbook, *Introduction to Counseling and Guidance,* Gibson and Mitchell (1995) state, "The term *guidance* was the popular designation for the counseling movement in schools for well over 50 years. However, in recent generations *guidance* has been sometimes viewed as an outdated label" (p. 8).

Evidence that the profession views guidance as outdated can be found in the sequence of names chosen for the primary professional organization of American counselors. In 1913, the forerunner of the professional organization that currently represents counselors and other guidance workers was established under the title National Vocational Guidance Association (NVGA). In 1952 the organization was expanded and named the American Personnel and Guidance Association (APGA). The name of this organization was changed to the American Association for Counseling and Development (AACD) in 1983, and then to the American Counseling Association (ACA) in 1991.

The demise of the guidance label was forecast by Wrenn (1962) in his trend-setting report titled *The Counselor in a Changing World.* In 1986, Tyler wrote the epitaph in an article titled "Farewell to Guidance."

Guidance Thrives in the Schools

The counseling profession's move to eliminate guidance has not been successful in the schools. Hoyt's (1993) article "Guidance Is Not a Dirty Word" in *The School Counselor* argues that the guidance label is still viable. Activities in the schools support this assertion. State plans for guidance and counseling in the schools continue to be developed in various parts of the United States. Gysbers and Henderson's (1993) second edition of *Developing and Managing Your School Guidance Program* has become one of the best sellers in the ACA Press. School-to-work transition programs have been legislated and funded by federal and state governments, creating new guidance activities in the schools. School counselors, feeling the pressure of declining financial support and vulnerability to *building-based management,* have looked for ways to broaden their role and functions. Guidance functions, such as facilitating career development and mental health by preventive programs, broaden the role of the school counselor.

It has been useful to differentiate guidance practices from the general instructional practices carried out by teachers. Guidance activities facilitate the development of the individual by focusing on the individual's uniqueness and special qualities. This *individualizing* theme of guidance is an important contribution to American education, where individualism is valued.

Guidance functions in the schools include many activities that do not fit the meaning of counseling. Counseling is usually defined as an interactive process in which one person facilitates the development of the other. The relationship between the counselor and the client is an important factor in the facilitation process. The range of use typically applied to counseling is too specific to cover many of the guidance practices. Guidance is a broad concept that includes counseling, but also includes a number of noncounseling activities that aid students in their development. Examples of these activities are exercises facilitated by teachers and specialists as well as counselors; the use of guidance materials, including computer-assisted searches for educational and career information; career days; diversity workshops; and so forth.

Why Did the Disparity Come About?

The primary problem addressed in this chapter is the disparity of opinion about the usefulness of the guidance model. This disparity has led to serious role confusion for the school counselor. This confusion is particularly dangerous during a period of school reform, when roles and structures are in a state of flux. School counselors need a coherent and adaptable model to guide their practices and they are not ready to give up the guidance theme that has characterized the model during the past 50 years.

Why has there been a disparity of opinions about guidance? One explanation, pointing to a paradigm shift in Western thought, is offered below.

A PARADIGM SHIFT FROM MODERNISM TO POSTMODERNISM

Gergen (1991, 1994) and others (Geertz, 1983; Rorty, 1979) have described a paradigm shift in Western culture during the second half of the 20th century. This shift, from *modernism* to *postmodernism,* is characterized by an erosion of the foundations for objective knowledge, and an increasing awareness of multiplicity in perspective. Practices developed in the modernist era became incongruent and outdated in the postmodern era. There are signs that the counseling and guidance profession was influenced by this paradigm shift.

The profession was clearly spawned and developed within a modernist framework grounded in neorealism. Beck (1963), in *Philosophical Foundations of Guidance,* built a solid case for the thesis that counseling and guidance developed with neorealist assumptions. These assumptions posited a "real" world with preexistent truths that could best be discovered by scientific methods and inductive logic. Guidance practices helped students discover their talents and interests and environments compatible with their qualities. Modern practitioners were proud that truth was determined by scientific methods rather than by divine revelation and other "prescientific" ways of knowing. Correspondence with truth was an assumption underlying each goal of guidance practices developed during the modern era.

The *trait-factor* approach, recognized as the dominant framework for counseling and guidance for several decades, exemplifies the neorealist foundation. An important construct of this traditional approach to guidance was the *trait,* a quality characterizing an individual. In keeping with the neorealist framework, traits were considered inherent or genetic in nature. Aptitude tests played a prominent role in the trait-factor approach. Validity studies were conducted to verify that scores on these instruments reflected a person's "true" abilities. Studies involving prediction of outcomes were used to provide evidence that measures of these aptitudes were valid, implying that the aptitudes were real. Guidance counselors applied the trait-factor approach to help clients understand and use their aptitudes to choose jobs and environments where success was predicted. Truths about the person were matched with truths about the world of work. Parsons (1909) described the process of "true reasoning" to show how the truths about the person and the world could be reconciled. This basic approach fueled the portion of the National Defense Education Act (NDEA) that funded the largest expansion of counselor training ever implemented by federal support. The underlying rationale of this extensive government program emphasized the utilization of individual talents by means of counseling and guidance. While these practices were well supported and compatible with the modernist framework of the times, they also created feelings of discomfort in many counselors. For example, Shertzer and Stone (1966), when discussing guidance in their basic textbook, stated: "Critics point out that the term conveys direction, authoritarianism, and paternalism" (p. 49).

Several influential members of the counseling profession recognized the strong association between guidance and the practice of guiding others to preexistent truths about themselves and the real world. These leaders reasoned that it would be easier to separate counseling from the more directive methods associated with guidance by simply declaring that guidance no longer characterized the practices of counseling.

REFRAMING GUIDANCE IN THE POSTMODERN ERA

I have suggested that the counseling profession tried to separate the practices of the profession from *modernist* assumptions by getting rid of *guidance.* If so, the adage "They threw the baby out with the bath" might apply. I propose a different way of dealing with the paradigm shift — that guidance be reframed with a constructivist perspective, which situates it in the *postmodernist* era.

In order to reframe the idea of guidance, it may be useful to start with the definition put forth by Beck (1963):

> Guidance, in the broadest sense of the term, was the aid given by one person to another, or by a group to its members, in seeking what was the "best" course of action in terms of survival of the individual and the group. (p. 10)

The general idea of "giving aid" still seems appropriate, although the ways of giving aid must be carefully considered before we accept this wording for describing what we do. The way we give aid makes a big difference. Bolles (1970) began his popular book *What Color Is Your Parachute?* with the ancient proverb: "Give me a fish, and I will eat for today; teach me to fish and I will eat for the rest of my life." This distinction between ways of giving aid demonstrates that there may be an important difference in the assumptions we have when aiding others. Continuing with the fishing metaphor in the context of the postmodern era, I lend another suggestion for giving aid. Instead of teaching clients to fish, facilitate their self-empowerment and enhanced adaptability. Self-empowered people can learn specific skills like fishing on their own.

As was suggested above, guidance and counseling can become more congruent with the postmodern times by reframing the guidelines and practices in a *constructivist* perspective. Before describing these guidelines and practices, I will identify four bodies of literature contributing to a constructivist perspective: Education-Related Constructivism, Personal Construct Psychology, Social Constructionism, and Narrative Psychology. Since this literature is addressed in the first section of this book, only selected ideas and examples of recent works will be mentioned.

Education-related Constructivism

This body of constructivist literature was written by people such as Piaget (1974), Dewey (1938/1963), Bruner (1966), and Vygotsky (1962). This literature is important to the reframing of guidance in the schools because it reflects the major ideas undergirding the efforts of school reform organized around constructivism. This variety of educational reform has been especially influential in subject matter areas such as mathematics and science. It also underpins much of the work of constructivist leadership in the schools (L. Lambert et al., 1995).

Personal Construct Psychology

This strain of constructivism was originally developed by Kelly (1955). Kelly developed many of his ideas while working as a school psychologist and as an educator of therapists. He provided a solid philosophical base for his practices, which he called *constructive alternativism*. In his theory, people develop personal constructs, which influence and filter their perceptions. The construing and interpreting of these people are more or less determined by their personal constructs. Many of the developments in Personal Construct Psychology have been in the area of psychotherapy. *Constructivism in Psychotherapy*, edited by Neimeyer and Mahoney (1995), reflects these developments quite well.

Social Constructionism

The third body of literature informing this reframing process is *social constructionism* (Gergen, 1981). This strain of constructivism gives more emphasis to the social construction of reality. Early ideas about this topic were presented in Berger and Luckmann's (1966) direction-setting *The Social Construction of Reality*. Like other strains of constructivism, social constructionism assumes that individuals construct their realities. Social constructionism, however, emphasizes the influence of culture and language on the realities constructed by individuals. Social constructionists deny the idea that human nature is transhistorical or transcultural. Humans are considered to be embedded in a culture made up of language, symbols, rules, morals, and so forth. Culture infuses people with daily social practices that strongly influence their behaviors. Humans are shaped by the social frameworks that pervade their cultures. For example, gender identity is very much created by the ways men and women see each other in a given society. Meaning itself is constructed through interactions. Thus, the etiology of meaning is relational. This perspective emphasizes the social construction of meaning and gives import to negotiation skills for the creation of shared realities and agreements. Social constructionism has been useful for elaborating how people construct their realities. Ideas from this strain of constructivism remind us that our constructions are molded from cultural influences, especially the language that has been used to build and communicate the individual's culture.

Narrative Psychology

Ideas about *narrative* were articulated by Bruner (1990) when he suggested that people organize their experiences in a narrative way more often than in logical or categorical ways. A narrative framework emphasizes context in the process of constructing and describing experiences. As in a story or a drama, personal events are framed in a temporal sequence and the context is important for carrying out the plot. Ideas from narrative psychology provide additional insights into the ways that people make sense of their experiences and the ways in which guidance practices can be reframed with a constructivist perspective. Hopkins (1994) presents a comprehensive case for transforming American education by means of narrative schooling. He builds his program around a new root metaphor, "the narrative process." The narrative process fits well with Dewey's (1938/1963) conception of education as the "reconstruction of experience." Hopkins's concept of *reconstructive query* suggests an educational process that could just as easily be framed under the name of constructivism.

The Common Assumption in Constructivist Literature

The common denominator of the four literatures mentioned above is the basic assumption that human realities and meanings are constructed rather than discovered. The profound implication of this assumption is that realities and meanings are open to reinterpretation rather than being accepted as "the way things are." The possibility of reconstruing one's personal realities enhances one's ability to adapt and change. A person approaching the future with openness to alternative constructions has a perspective very different from that of a person who is looking for clues to "real" reality. The latter person, operating with a neorealist assumption, posits a reality that is determined by forces and structures in the world unrelated to how he or she happens to construe the situation. Such people often assume that after they find the "facts" they will have a better grasp on reality. They often define education as the process of obtaining information, which they think of as facts.

GENERAL GUIDELINES FOR CONSTRUCTIVIST GUIDANCE

The following general guidelines provide a frame for specific practices found in constructivist guidance programs:

1. A basic assumption of constructivist guidance is that people create their own meanings. It is hoped that students and other participants in a constructivist guidance program will become aware of their own assumptions about constructing personal realities.
2. School counselors and other constructivist guidance practitioners focus their efforts on facilitating the articulation of their clients' personal meanings, especially those concerning their selves. The focus is on the clients' interpretations of important events in their lives. Their values are explored and clarified. The term *self-articulation* is useful for describing this emphasis.
3. The communication of personal meanings is emphasized in a constructiv-

ist guidance program. The importance of this communication is based on the idea that all communities and societies are based on interpersonal agreements, which depend on shared meanings. The most important interpersonal activity that occurs when two or more people work together toward common goals is the communication of shared meanings. Constructivist guidance programs facilitate negotiation processes.

4. Constructivist counselors try to facilitate their clients' ability to articulate what they need to know and to take responsibility for investigating how those needs could be satisfied. Guidance professionals help students develop their investigative skills. It is understood that learning what is needed and how to find it is far more important than any specific bit of information they might seek.

These guidelines can be better understood by contrasting them with principles of traditional guidance programs developed with neorealist assumptions in the modernist era. Traditional guidance emphasizes the acquisition of information about self and the real world, such as learning about occupations or future educational options. These methods are based on the assumption there is a real world that humans can come to know.

PRACTICES EMPHASIZED IN CONSTRUCTIVIST GUIDANCE

The practices that take place in a constructivist guidance program may look similar to those occurring in traditional guidance programs, in that most educators believe that young people need aid as they develop into adults. Regardless of their philosophical foundations, counselors and other educators recognize that young people need a period of growth and development, during which they are dependent on adults. Young people need to be guided and supported while they are maturing. Constructivist guidance practitioners certainly do aid youngsters, but their philosophical perspective causes them to frame that aid in a different way than those with a neorealist framework. The constructivist's assumptions about how people create meanings lead to practices that emphasize self-awareness and self-reflection. Constructivist educators focus on the interpretations of the youngsters. Youngsters are encouraged to communicate what they mean, especially when they are dealing with topics that involve others. These youngsters are also encouraged to inquire and listen to others as common areas of interest are explored. Constructivist practitioners strive to be aware of their own meanings and they are willing to communicate their meanings to others. They try to serve as models for self-reflection and communication of important values. As they communicate these interpretations they also acknowledge that these are not descriptions of fixed realities. The practices of constructivist counselors emphasize the articulation of personal meanings and the negotiation of shared meanings.

One important practice of guidance counselors operating within a constructivist perspective is *active listening,* a well-known practice of nondirective counselors (Gordon, 1970). The essence of active listening is facilitating the client's articulation of thoughts and feelings. This practice emphasizes the personal meanings of the client, and clearly respects the reality constructed by the individual. A client who has experienced active listening gets the idea that his or her constructions or personal meanings are attended to by the counselor.

Active listening is a practice that exemplifies a wider range of guidance practices that can be categorized under the label *self-articulation.* Practices that facilitate self-articulation include the identification and communication of the personal constructs (Kelly, 1955) used by a person to construe self-identity. In keeping with this goal, I have developed and described two standardized exercises that facilitate the articulation of a person's strengths and goals (Forster, 1991, 1992). These self-articulation processes serve purposes similar to those of standardized tests in traditional guidance programs. The primary difference can be found in the assumptions underlying these different methods of describing the self. In the constructivist approach, the constructs elicited to articulate self-identity features come from the mind of the person who is describing the self, while in the more traditional psychometric approach, the dimensions are specified by others. The dimensions specified by others were more than likely developed or "discovered" after statistical analyses designed to find traits or "real" qualities.

The Dependable Strengths Articulation Process (Haldane, 1989) is one example of how personally constructed strengths can be articulated. When people articulate their strengths using this process, they increase the likelihood that their self-identities will be based on their self-identified strengths. This process demonstrates how people can change their self-constructions and become more positive in their self-evaluations (Forster, 1991).

A common practice in a constructivist guidance program is to focus on the articulation of personal goals and possible life-styles. Plans and personal viewpoints are evaluated in terms of the client's estimation of the likelihood that these plans would be useful for achieving personal goals. Clients are encouraged to develop a variety of plans and viewpoints, which can be explored during counseling sessions. One standardized exercise developed to facilitate this process is the *Goals Review & Organizing Workbook* described by Forster (1992). Constructivist guidance counselors may facilitate the articulation of personal meanings during individual sessions, in classroom activities, in pairs, and in small groups.

Other standardized exercises have been developed and used to help indi-

viduals extend and define their system of constructions for career and life planning. Neimeyer (1992) described two techniques that have been useful for
these purposes. One is called The Vocational Reptest, a technique that is modeled on the Role Construct Repertory Test (reptest), a classic instrument developed by Kelly (1955). Neimeyer (1992) also described a laddering technique that can help clients clarify their personal priorities, an important
process in self-articulation.

The development of a *personal portfolio* is another constructivist guidance
practice that helps the individual organize and assemble results of self-
articulation efforts. A portfolio allows a student to put together a set of docu-
ments and other products that express his most valued abilities, interests, and
self-identities. Hopkins (1994) describes an example of this approach, calling
it a "narrative portfolio" to demonstrate one of his ideas about implementing
narrative schooling. He wrote, "The portfolio effectuates the self and drives
the process of the narrative school" (p. 145).

Cochran (1992) also provides a format for helping clients articulate their
personal perspectives in his descriptions of *career projects*. This approach uses
the organizing idea of narrative meaning-making, as is indicated by Cochran
when he writes:

> In helping a person to construct and perform actions of a career project, a coun-
> selor functions somewhat like a co-author of a novel in progress, focusing upon
> the immediate action while emplotting its role in a larger story. (p. 195)

Other practices found in constructivist guidance programs facilitate the
articulation of shared meanings and the negotiation of agreements. Facilitated
activities that teach communication skills help students improve their ability
to articulate personal meanings and their willingness to listen to another's
personal meanings. Similarly, students improve their negotiation skills as they
co-construct shared realities during interactive sessions designed to facilitate
compromises and agreements. Techniques such as *conflict resolution* teach students how negotiation skills can be used to resolve disagreements in schools
and other settings. An important principle of conflict resolution is the exchange of viewpoints by conflicting parties. This exchange will be hindered if
either party believes in the absolute certainty of his or her viewpoint. People
who assume that their view of a situation is the real truth are unwilling to
negotiate a new way of interpreting the situation. These people assume that
truth cannot be negotiated. Conflict resolution programs in a constructivist
guidance program encourage participants who are in conflict with one another to reflect on the different ways people construe their realities before
they give their interpretation of the situation at issue. When conflicting par-

ties are asked to give their interpretations of what happened, they are reminded that they are not necessarily telling everyone how it "really was," but are expressing their "side" or "version" of the story.

The *class meeting*, as conceived by Dreikus (1957) and Glasser (1969) and described by Dinkmeyer, McKay, and Dinkmeyer (1980), is another activity that fits nicely within a constructivist guidance program. During this activity, students learn the skills of establishing group rules and norms. This process allows students to experience the negotiation of agreements and the development of shared realities.

Practices that encourage the articulation of *multicultural perspectives* also fit into a constructivist guidance program. In these programs, students are encouraged to learn about and respect diverse beliefs and practices associated with different ethnic, racial, and religious groups. During explorations of diversity issues, questions often arise as to why certain perspectives seem to be sanctioned more than others. When these questions come up, guidance professionals help students explore the concept of *power* and how it affects the expression of different perspectives. Participants in these discussions can acknowledge multicultural perspectives more easily when they can make sense of how power influences the expression of diverse perspectives in a mixed community. They can explore scenarios wherein groups with more power force their perspective on people who have less power. Constructivist guidance programs can also facilitate discussions of the use of physical force as a means of power. Students are often inarticulate about multicultural viewpoints and the related use of power. Awareness of their own constructing processes and of the ways realities are socially constructed can enhance exchanges among people from different cultural backgrounds.

In summary, constructivist guidance programs include opportunities for group discussions and the generation of multiple perspectives on problems and issues. Self-empowerment is encouraged by emphasizing the personal viewpoint of each individual in a group or class. The viewpoints of all participants are respected and encouraged. Individuals are encouraged to trust their own constructions, and to continually reflect on these constructions.

IMPLICATIONS OF REFRAMING WITH A CONSTRUCTIVIST PERSPECTIVE

The primary implication of reframing counseling and guidance with a constructivist perspective is that it can contribute to improved adaptability and survival. Four personal qualities are suggested as concomitants of a constructivist perspective and are important examples of qualities facilitated by programs based on a constructivist perspective: flexibility, open-mindedness, self-empowerment, and tolerance for diversity. It is suggested that these personal qualities will significantly enhance the adaptability of individuals and the communities created by the individuals.

A constructivist perspective is partially defined by the flexibility of the perceiver. A person with a constructivist perspective is aware of his or her interpretive processes and strives to entertain two or more alternative possibilities for understanding any given situation. Such people are likely to consider more than one possibility and act in accordance with the explanation thought to contribute the most to their goals. In contrast, people operating from a neorealist model are more likely to assume that their understandings of a given situation are fairly close to the way it "really is." Such people are less likely to consider alternative possibilities and are more likely to be rigid about change.

Another personal quality, similar to flexibility but also somewhat different, is open-mindedness. Bruner (1990) suggested that people with constructivist perspectives are likely to be open-minded when he wrote:

> But it is whimsical to suppose that, under present world conditions, a dogged insistence upon the notion of "absolute value" will make the uncertainties go away. All one can hope for is a viable pluralism backed by a willingness to negotiate differences in world-view. . . . It concerns open-mindedness — whether in politics, science, literature, philosophy, or the arts. I take open-mindedness to be a willingness to construe knowledge and values from multiple perspectives without loss of commitment to one's own values. Open-mindedness is the keystone of what we call a democratic culture. (p. 30)

Self-empowerment is another quality implied by a constructivist perspective. People with a constructivist perspective are aware that they are constructing their realities. This awareness helps them recognize that they are determining the meaning of their experiences and this knowledge leads to a sense of control and power, which is another way of defining self-empowerment.

The fourth quality expected to be enhanced by a constructivist guidance program is tolerance for diversity. The connection between a constructivist perspective and tolerance is suggested by logical analysis. People who assume they are constructing and interpreting their own realities can be expected to realize that others are engaged in similar processes. This awareness should help them accept the idea that there are many different beliefs and perspectives, and that no single particular belief or perspective is likely to be the "right" one. Such an awareness suggests that the person will be tolerant of other beliefs or perspectives.

CONCLUSION

In closing, I argue that the goal of facilitating movement toward "a constructivist perspective" is important for the survival of the human species. Adaptation to change is the primary means of survival. The rapidity of change is generally acknowledged in our complex world where populations and technologies are growing at high rates. The four personal qualities described above will be important contributors to adaptability and survival during the next millennium.

The idea that survival might be related to a constructivist perspective was presented with eloquence and support by Anderson (1990) in *Reality Isn't What It Used to Be*. He wrote about the constructivist world view, calling it a story about stories. The following quote from that work summarizes some of the ideas I have been offering in this chapter and provides an appropriate ending:

> We are seeing in our lifetimes the collapse of the objectivist world view that dominated the modern era, the worldview that gave people faith in the absolute and permanent rightness of certain beliefs and values. The worldview emerging in its place is constructivist. If we operate from this worldview we see all information and all stories as human creations that fit, more or less well, with our experience and within a universe that remains always beyond us and always mysterious. . . . Learning about such things, continually reexamining beliefs about beliefs, becomes *the most important learning task of all the others needed for survival in our time.* (p. 268; emphasis added)

REFERENCES

Anderson, W. T. (1990). *Reality isn't what it used to be.* San Francisco: HarperCollins.

Beck, C. E. (1963). *Philosophical foundations of guidance.* Englewood Cliffs, NJ: Prentice-Hall.

Berger, P. L., & Luckmann, T. (1966). *The social construction of reality: A treatise in the sociology of knowledge.* Garden City, NY: Doubleday.

Bolles, R. N. (1970). *What color is your parachute?* Berkeley: Ten Speed Press.

Bruner, J. (1966). *Toward a theory of instruction.* New York: Norton.

Bruner, J. (1990). *Acts of meaning.* Cambridge: Harvard University Press.

Cochran, L. (1992). The career project. *Journal of Career Development, 18*(3), 187–197.

Dewey, J. (1963). *Experience and education.* New York: Collier Books. (Original work published 1938)

Dinkmeyer, D., McKay, G., & Dinkmeyer, D. (1980). *Systematic training for effective teaching.* Circle Pines, MN: American Guidance Service.

Dreikus, R. (1957). *Psychology in the classroom.* New York: Harper & Row.

Forster, J. R. (1991). Facilitating positive changes in self-constructions. *International Journal of Personal Construct Psychology, 4,* 281–292.

Forster, J. R. (1992). Eliciting personal constructs and articulating goals. *Journal of Career Development, 18*(3), 175–185.

Geertz, C. (1983). *Local knowledge: Further essays in interpretive anthropology.* New York: Basic Books.

Gergen, K. J. (1981). The social constructionist movement in modern psychology. *American Psychologist, 40,* 266–275.

Gergen, K. J. (1991). *The saturated self: Dilemmas of identity in contemporary life.* New York: Basic Books.

Gergen, K. J. (1994). *Realities and relationships: Soundings in social construction.* Cambridge: Harvard University Press.

Gibson, R. L., & Mitchell, M. H. (1995). *Introduction to counseling and guidance* (4th ed.). Englewood Cliffs, NJ: Prentice-Hall.

Glasser, W. (1969). *Schools without failure.* New York: Harper & Row.

Gordon, T. (1970). *Parent effectiveness training.* New York: Peter Wyden.

Gysbers, N. C., & Henderson, P. (1993). *Developing and managing your school guidance program* (2nd ed.). Alexander, VA: American Counseling Association.

Haldane, B. (1989). *The dependable strengths articulation process: How it works.* Ann Arbor, MI: ERIC/CAPS Clearinghouse. (ERIC Document ED 305575)

Hopkins, R. L. (1994). *Narrative schooling: Experiential learning and the transformation of American education.* New York: Teachers College Press.

Hoyt, K. B. (1993). Guidance is not a dirty word. *The School Counselor, 40*(4), 267–273.

Kelly, G. A. (1955). *The psychology of personal constructs.* New York: Norton.

Lambert, L., Walker, D., Zimmerman, D. P., Cooper, J. E., Lambert, M. D., Gardner, M. E., & Slack, P. J. (1995). *The constructivist leader.* New York: Teachers College Press.

Neimeyer, G. J. (1992). Personal constructs in career counseling and development. *Journal of Career Development, 18*(3), 163–173.

Neimeyer, R. A., & Mahoney, M. J. (Eds.). (1995). *Constructivism in psychotherapy.* Washington, DC: American Psychological Association.

Parsons, F. (1909). *Choosing a vocation.* Boston: Houghton Mifflin.

Piaget, J. (1974). *The construction of reality in the child.* New York: Ballantine Books.

Rorty, R. (1979). *Philosophy and the mirror of nature.* Princeton, NJ: Princeton University Press.

Shertzer, B., & Stone, S. C. (1966). *Fundamentals of guidance* (3rd ed.). Boston: Houghton Mifflin.

Tyler, L. E. (1986). Farewell to guidance. *Journal of Counseling and Human Service Professionals, 1,* 152–155.

Vygotsky, L. S. (1962). *Thought and language.* Cambridge: MIT Press.

Wrenn, C. G. (1962). *The counselor in a changing world.* Washington, DC: American Personnel and Guidance Association.

PART III

Applications of Constructivist Thinking in Counseling Research

CHAPTER 10

Methods of Constructivist Inquiry

Mary Lee Nelson and Karen Poulin

A major critique of research in counseling and counseling psychology is that most practitioners do not read the research literature, because they do not consider it to be relevant to practice (Howard, 1985, 1986). Clearly, not all counseling research is irrelevant to practice, and most of us can recall particular research findings that have strongly influenced how we conduct our practice. The problem with a great deal of counseling research is that it focuses on such minutiae that one must often read a body of literature on a topic in order to incorporate the data into a useful theoretical or technical position for practice. This type of focused study is demanding and often more work than many practitioners have the time to undertake. Most research in the counseling field comes from the positivist model of science, which reduces human behavior and experience into numbers, which must then be interpreted and rendered meaningful by the researcher (rather than by the subjects themselves). Thus, such a reduction often results in a loss of the meaning of the participants' experience. The investigator and the reader are left with a small piece of a picture that is much more complex than the phenomenon that has been isolated for examination.

Early psychologists, in need of a paradigm for the conduct of inquiry and seeking a respectable niche in the academy, adopted the positivist model of natural science, or the hypothetico-deductive model, often referred to as the received view of science (Giorgi, 1985; Polkinghorne, 1984). Social science research based on the hypothetico-deductive model must conform to the rules of hypothesis formation and disconfirmation. It relies on control of variation and utilizes statistical procedures that express human experience in terms of statistical values that can be used to conduct comparisons and make predictions, which will then be interpreted and generalized to whole populations. The hypothetico-deductive model deemphasizes outliers, exceptions to the rule, or unusual and interesting circumstances. Although some current procedures, such as path analysis, emphasize variation, complexity, and diversity more than traditional procedures like analysis of variance, in general, methods are designed to emphasize the rules rather than the exceptions. They are pointed toward the discovery of lawfulness.

If one adopts the social constructivist perspective that knowledge about human nature is the product of social agreements regarding what constitutes the nature of experience, then the notion that lawfulness governs the domain of human experience is called into question. The positivist paradigm cannot provide an adequate window on human experience, which is abundantly complex and meaningful. Clearly, an epistemology is needed that would better fit the practice of counseling, which is a meaning-making process.

THE QUALITATIVE PARADIGM

Because of its emphasis on understanding experience, qualitative research seems well suited to the task of pursuing the nature of meaning that individuals associate with particular life experiences such as counseling. Ironically, much of counseling research has not focused on individual experiences, such as client experiences in counseling. The absence of such a focus may be traced to positivistic, behavioral, and psychoanalytic influences, which question the validity of verbal accounts of conscious experience (Rennie, 1994).

Perhaps because of the recognition that quantitative research was not providing enough of the kinds of information needed to advance the practice of counseling and psychotherapy, the counseling field in recent years has become more receptive to methods of inquiry that do not adhere tightly to the positivist paradigm. In 1984 the *Journal of Counseling Psychology* published a special issue that addressed the need for methodological diversity in counseling research (Polkinghorne, 1984). Around that time, empirically based case studies and multiple case studies began to appear in counseling journals. Such studies utilized stochastic techniques such as proportional and sequential analysis to analyze the coded content of counseling and supervision processes (e.g., Hill, Carter, & O'Farrell, 1983; Holloway, Freund, Gardner, Nelson, & Walker, 1989; Holloway & Wampold, 1983; Martin, Goodyear, & Newton, 1987; Tracey & Ray, 1984). Such methods represented a step in the direction of qualitative research in that they examined individual cases, albeit in a numerical fashion. More recently, a special issue of the *Journal of Counseling Psychology* ("Qualitative Research," 1994) included several articles focusing on qualitative research in counseling process and outcome. Many of these investigations relied on personal narrative as a source of individuals' expressions of their perceived experience.

Clearly, we are entering a new era of inquiry in the counseling field. The researcher's assumption of an "experience near" posture vis-à-vis clients and counselors will allow us to ask questions that will challenge our theoretical assumptions about what happens in counseling and supervision. The study of personal narratives permits the researcher and the subject to mutually construct and report the essences of the subject's experiences at given points in time in particular contexts.

A qualitative approach to investigation embraces the concept of emergence, which suggests that as a culture evolves, old structures no longer apply, and new, more complex structures emerge (Polkinghorne, 1988). Thus, we cannot assume that new processes can always be predicted from old ones. As counseling practitioners, we cannot help but be aware of social change and its effects on people, just as we are aware of changes in counseling theory and application of theory as it evolves over time. We need a research methodology that allows us to be receptive to change and to identify the characteristics of change as it occurs. Because it does not pretend to uncover universal, immutable truths, qualitative research allows for chronicling emerging processes, such as individual and cultural growth and the development and evolution of the systems we use to understand and facilitate those phenomena. In addition, qualitative research allows us to include the examination of the contexts that frame and thus influence personal events.

The purpose of this chapter is to discuss the fundamentals of qualitative research approaches that are most applicable to counseling at this time: the phenomenological psychological paradigm and the grounded theory paradigm. First, we will provide a background for understanding the development of these qualitative models—the intellectual traditions from which each has emerged. Second, we will outline general guidelines for conducting constructivist inquiry, including methods of gathering and processing data. Third, we will provide guidelines for the conduct of grounded theory and phenomenological psychological research. And finally, we will discuss implications for the counseling field of constructivist approaches to inquiry.

THE PHENOMENOLOGICAL PSYCHOLOGICAL PARADIGM

The notion that reductionistic science is not adequate to represent the richness of human experience is not new. In the late 19th century Franz Brentano, a professor at the University of Vienna, proposed "act" psychology, which, in sharp contrast to the reductionistic psychology of structuralism proposed by Wundt, defined a psychological event as directed, intentional, and purposive. After an experience of pure experiential representation, which may be influenced by biology, a judgment is made about the perception; the individual then personalizes the experience by making sense of it through existing mental structures. According to Brentano, this meaning-making process was the essence of psychology (Brennan, 1994). Among Brentano's students were Sigmund Freud and Edmund Husserl, who became Brentano's protégé and who provided much of the original thinking behind the later development of a phenomenological psychology.

Husserl attempted to develop a system for examining the structure of intentionality, or the structure of experience itself without attending to the connection between the experience and the actual world. He described a procedure for "bracketing," or putting out of one's mind all judgments about connections between experience and worldly events, thus freeing the mind to examine its own pure experience, independent of everyday biases. He believed that human agreement about reality is a result of how humans impose the structure of their consciousness on the world. The originality of this hypothesis is represented in the notion that culture is a function of fundamental human mental structures, a notion that approaches social constructivist ideas.

Heidegger, a student of Husserl, incorporated a consensual component by suggesting that true phenomenology must account for a person's experience of being in the world, with both "being" and "in the world" being important components of experience (Brennan, 1994). According to Heidegger, the subject of phenomenological investigation is a person's sense of being and the social/contextual influences that affect that being.

Merleau-Ponty (1945/1962) criticized Husserl for his dichotomization of pure experience and language. Whereas Husserl saw language and experience as separate, Merleau-Ponty viewed them as inextricable. He saw humans as maintaining culturally constructed linguistic structures that guide our interpretation of all experience and that this experience is framed in language. According to Merleau-Ponty, science can never arrive at pure truth. It can only describe and interpret experience after the fact, as it is processed through the basic mental structures (Varela, Thompson, & Rosch, 1993).

Merleau-Ponty (1945/1962) suggested a method for inquiry based on his definition of phenomenology. That method involves four components: (1) description of the experience, free of interpretation; (2) reduction, or summary of the process being examined without including the point of view of the researcher; (3) a search for essences, or essential structures through the process of imaginative variation or considering a range of possible categories; and (4) use of intentionality. Intentionality refers to the process of assuming a psychological attitude toward an event, or considering the psychological meaning of it. Merleau-Ponty's method has served as the foundation for current approaches to conducting phenomenological psychological research, which will be described in a later section.

SYMBOLIC INTERACTIONISM AND GROUNDED THEORY

The roots of grounded theory as an intellectual tradition are directly embedded in the Chicago School of Sociology (Bowers, 1990). "The Chicago School," as it has come to be known, refers specifically to symbolic interactionism, a branch of sociology that was the zeitgeist between 1920 and 1950 in the Department of Sociology at the University of Chicago. Interactionist theory evolved during an era of scholarship characterized by the oral tradition, in which ideas germinated, developed, and were passed around by word of mouth (Kuhn, 1970). Particularly significant during this period was the work of George Herbert Mead, a University of Chicago professor from 1893 to 1931. Mead's most important contribution to symbolic interactionism was his philosophical foundation in pragmatism (Charon, 1992).

Interactionist theory was in part a response to functionalism, a sociological paradigm that characterizes individuals as "'empty vessels,' ready to receive and internalize the expectations [norms] of the larger social system" (Bowers, 1990, p. 36). This view restricts a person to the activities defined by his or her role functions within a static social structure that is assumed to exist prior to and apart from individuals. Accordingly, individuals cannot act; they can only be acted on. Functionalism is unable to account theoretically for the thinking, feeling individual who in part determines, rather than is wholly determined by, the structure of society.

Symbolic interactionists challenged functionalism by seeking to understand society not only as a structure, but as a process of becoming — driven by self-aware, acting individuals. Interactionists criticized rationalist epistemology for assuming that inquiry must and can separate the knower from that which is to be known. Drawing from pragmatism, they rejected the practice of approaching the phenomenon under inquiry by removing it from its rich context and reducing it to a single, disembodied concept. This focus, then, necessitated a methodology that would pragmatically reveal the complex processes through which society is constructed.

To address the foregoing problem, Glaser and Strauss (1967) developed and explicated the process of grounded theory, which was presented in their seminal work *The Discovery of Grounded Theory: Strategies for Qualitative Research*. It describes a process of data collection that defines the researcher as a participant-observer and places him or her in direct relationship to individuals within their situated contexts. Data analysis, which is loosely described in their original book, is more clearly articulated in later works (Schatzman & Strauss, 1973; Strauss & Corbin, 1990) and will be presented in the following section.

CONSTRUCTIVIST INQUIRY

The task of many of the aforementioned thinkers has been to translate the notion that phenomenological meaning and related experiential dimensions are knowable and identifiable into modes of inquiry that can produce those types of information. Schwandt (1995) suggests that the term *method* is traditionally associated with positivistic forms of inquiry and implies an abstract formal process that is independent of the subject under investigation. In positivistic thought, the method, rather than the phenomenon being investigated, guides the inquiry. Schwandt (1995) contrasts the positivistic definition of method with the concept of "normative method" (Madison, 1988). *Normative method* is a term derived from ontological hermeneutics, a field related to symbolic interactionism in that it is concerned with negotiated meanings between investigator and informant. The normative method is driven by the phenomenon under investigation. It is a pragmatic, ethical process of approaching data that may not be entirely specified at the outset of the inquiry process, but that may grow out of the pictures and stories that emerge from the process. It is guided by the investigator's best judgment, often in negotiation with the best judgments of fellow investigators and informants. In general, the types of qualitative approaches undertaken should be selected according to the kinds of questions asked and the types of knowledge sought. There are numerous approaches to data gathering and processing. We will delineate some of those in the following section on research process. Then, in a section on analyzing data, we will present two methods of analysis that are compatible with inquiry into counseling phenomena: grounded theory and phenomenological analysis.

Research Process

Regardless of the type of analysis undertaken, certain guidelines should be observed when planning and carrying out qualitative research (for a thorough discussion of general guidelines for phenomenological research, see Polkinghorne, 1989). This section will identify some important tips to keep in mind when planning and conducting a qualitative project.

1. Depending on the type of study you wish to do and also on the audience you will be writing for, you may or may not choose to conduct a thorough literature search prior to your investigation. Some proponents of a classic grounded theory method would recommend maintaining a naive position with regard to your topic as you enter the field (Schatzman & Strauss, 1973). More recently Strauss and Corbin (1990), in their text on qualitative research basics, recommended conducting a literature

search in order to develop "theoretical sensitivity," or a readiness to recognize pattern and phenomena, prior to approaching the study.

2. Determine what kind of inquiry will provide the desired understanding.
   It is possible that your question would be better addressed in a correla-
   tional or experimental study. This possibility should be considered, because not all questions can be answered through qualitative inquiry. If
   the nature of your question is how individuals experience a given phenomenon, how they live their experience, or how they make meaning out
   of their experience, a qualitative method would be an appropriate choice.

3. Examples of research questions that could be addressed qualitatively:

   • How do ethnic minority students in counseling experience their mi-
     nority status? What strategies do they use to progress through gradu-
     ate school?
   • How do parents of disabled children experience the act of parenting?
     What strategies do they use to cope with their challenges?
   • What is the experienced meaning of a sexual abuse victim in counsel-
     ing? How does the client come to understand and reckon with his or
     her experience?

4. Identify your biases about what you are likely to find, basing them in the
   literature if you can. Include a description of your own prior experiences
   with the phenomenon under investigation along with a description of
   how those experiences would influence your objectivity. Document your
   biases in writing and commit yourself to "bracketing," or openly examining your data for disconfirmation of your hypotheses and for nonantici-
   pated phenomena.

5. Decide what kinds of information you will collect, such as interviews (see
   Kvale, 1983; Seidman, 1991), notes from field observations, and taped
   conversations of dyads or groups. A liberating aspect of qualitative inquiry is that not all methodological decisions have to be prespecified. For
   instance, an investigator may feel that he or she needs to conduct a pilot
   study prior to the primary investigation in order to specify what kinds of
   questions might yield the desired information. After the pilot study is
   conducted, the investigator(s) may stumble on a concept highly relevant
   to the phenomenon under investigation but about which the informants
   were not questioned. Thus a second pilot may be needed to derive appropriate questions that address the emergent concept. Or during the process of analyzing and categorizing the data, the investigator(s) may identify an emergent concept that he or she wishes to develop and may set
   up another round of interviews with participants or with new informants
   who might be more familiar with the emergent concept.

6. Identify the sample you wish to investigate. Van Kaam (cited in Polking-

horne, 1989) proposed that subjects should have several skills related to the ability to provide full and accurate descriptions. First, they should be able to express themselves well verbally. They should be able to address inner feelings without a great deal of inhibition and to identify the experiences that gave rise to the feelings. They should have experienced the phenomenon under study somewhat recently so that their memories are still rich. Finally, they should have an interest in the phenomenon so that their commitment to providing the desired material is high. In addition, subjects should represent a variety of backgrounds to ensure a breadth of perspectives on the phenomenon. Subjects may be individuals or focus groups brought together to discuss a particular type of experience.

7. In his discussion of the qualitative research interview, Kvale (1983) discussed important aspects of the interview that specify the interview's "mode of understanding" (p. 174). He stresses that the interview should be centered on the individual's "life world" and that it should be aimed at understanding the meaning of experiences of the life world. It should be qualitative in that it should emphasize rich narrative description rather than quantifiable answers. The interviewee's analysis of his or her own situation is less important than a detailed and specific description of it, which will provide information for the researcher to reach psychologically based understandings. The interviewee's analysis may also be useful, but it should not be the primary data sought. The interview should be presuppositionless in that its structure should not reflect preidentified categories or themes. It must remain open to the identification of unexpected phenomena. The interview should not, however, be unfocused. It must guide the interviewee toward a continued description of the phenomenon under investigation rather than allowing him or her to wander into other areas. It should also attend to ambiguity in the interviewee's expressions, seeking to clarify what the interviewee means. Contradictions in the interviewee's expressions should be addressed and clarified. If there is real confusion about an experience, that confusion should be documented. The interview should also be open to the possibility that the interviewee could change his or her view of the phenomenon as a result of the clarification process inherent in the interview. This process of change should be noted, along with an inquiry about what led to the change. The phenomenological psychological nature of the interview implies an awareness that the interview situation is an interpersonal one; thus there will be interpersonal dynamics, such as excitement and cooperation, but also defense and resistance. These aspects should be noted, particularly with regard to possible roadblocks to obtaining full descriptions of experience. These observations can contribute to a broader understanding of the phenomenon, from the interviewee's perspective as

well as from the interviewer's. Kvale emphasizes that the interview can often be a highly positive experience for the interviewee, who may seldom have a chance to receive such undivided attention. The interviewee may not wish to end the dialogue, and it is important to address this type of event gracefully.

8. All interviews or sessions should be transcribed. Plan to buy or borrow a transcription machine. Select a machine that will use the size of audiotape (regular or micro) that you use in your tape recorder. Most qualitative researchers believe that one should transcribe one's own data in order to secure a thorough knowledge of it. The process of transcribing will alert you to phenomena that simple reading of transcripts simply cannot provide.

9. Divide your transcripts into units for analysis. This can be done by line, by speaking turn, by topic, or by some other predetermined meaningful division. Unitizing should be guided by the type of paradigm you select for your data analysis. Some modern software programs designed to process qualitative data, such as NU*DIST, do routine unitizing — such as line-by-line — for you. Meaning units, on the other hand, must be determined by the investigator. Giorgi (1985) describes meaning units as "spontaneously perceived discriminations within the subject's description arrived at when the researcher assumes a psychological attitude toward the concrete description, and along with it, the set that the text is an example of the phenomenon [being examined]" (p. 11).

10. Proceed with your analysis according to your selected method of inquiry.

Triangulation. It is important to address the issue of triangulation at this point. Triangulation refers to obtaining more than one perspective on the data. It can take many forms. Using two or more researchers in the data analysis process, which Denzin (1978) terms "investigator triangulation," is a common method. A research team meets together to negotiate the meanings that accrue from the data. Team members are expected to discuss and document their biases in advance of the data analysis and agree to play the role of skeptic with each other, thereby challenging fellow team members' assumptions and conclusions. Negotiated meanings should be reached by consensus. Some journals prefer to see the data analyzed by at least three investigators. Some do not require this but want the data to be triangulated in some other way, such as using more quantitative measures such as valid, reliable, pencil-and-paper questionnaires.

Another method recommended by Denzin (1978) is "methodological triangulation," or using two or more approaches to investigate the same phenomenon. In counseling research, two such approaches might be to interview counseling dyads about their experience of their interactions and to observe the actual interactions, documenting certain types of phenomena such as critical incidents.

It might be helpful before deciding on your method of triangulation to decide what population you wish to address with your findings and identify what journals reach that population. Then you can inquire about particular editorial policies for those journals. A thorough examination of methods of triangulation can be found in Denzin's (1978) *The Research Act.*

Methods of Analyzing Data

Both grounded theory and phenomenological psychological schools have developed methods of analyzing data that provide understanding about the selected participants' experience and the meanings that participants have constructed about their experience.

Grounded Theory. The grounded theory paradigm emphasizes patterns of meaning. It focuses on understanding the meaning of a particular experience by interviewing a group of informants who have been through the experience and obtaining other pertinent sources of data, such as transcripts of counseling or supervision sessions, then identifying themes and patterns that emerge from the data. It also emphasizes examining unique or individual cases for which the identified patterns do not apply. Through a process of comparing the cases, a theory of the phenomenon is developed.

Glaser and Strauss (1967), in their book *The Discovery of Grounded Theory: Strategies for Qualitative Research,* described their original process of developing a procedure for data organization and coding. Schatzman and Strauss (1973) and Schatzman (1987) further refined Strauss's earlier work with Glaser. Since then numerous investigators have recommended appropriate steps to be taken in the thematic organization of qualitative data (Berg, 1995; Miles & Huberman, 1983). In their book *Basics of Qualitative Research,* Strauss and Corbin (1990) intricately and systematically describe a process of grounded theory analysis. This section will briefly describe their recommended steps for organizing and analyzing qualitative data. However, the reader should approach Strauss and Corbin's recommendations with caution. Because they are presented in linear fashion and seem, in a sense, "operationalized," it would be tempting to impose the structure on one's data, using it in the same way one might apply an experimental method: as a template designed to reduce data and to produce objective results. The systematic presentation is intended only to suggest a way of organizing, comparing, and extracting meaning from data. It is not intended to suggest a rigid, controlled process leading to proof or justification.

Essential to approaching qualitative data analysis is what Strauss and Corbin describe as theoretical sensitivity. The researcher needs to have an understanding of the context within which the phenomenon is being investigated. Such understanding comes in part from knowing the literature in the field, the extant theory or theories and research findings that currently guide and influence inquiry in the researcher's area. Professional and personal experiences also inform the scientific attitude. In counseling, our experiences with our clients and resulting phenomenological understanding of human nature based on our observations are important sources of theoretical sensitivity. Our own personal experiences as human beings interacting with others in our families and extended social contexts are also important sources of understanding, in that they provide us with commonsense hunches that can guide our focus in examining our data.

Just as it is important to be theoretically informed, it is also important to maintain an attitude of skepticism. In the same stroke that one may see a connection between observed data an prior personal experience, one must ask, "Am I acting on a bias?" One of the most demanding requirements of conducting qualitative research is to be aware of one's biases and of how they may be shaping an interpretation. Strauss and Corbin emphasize that all interpretations must be regarded as provisional, not as fact, and that they should be subjected to triangulation, tested again and again against the data.

The first step in the analysis of the data is called open coding. It consists of examining each unit of data and assigning it to a category. Thus it is a highly laborious process of labeling phenomena, creating categories to accommodate the data, and naming the categories. It consists of asking such questions as "What is this event or phenomenon?"

Janko (1994) used a grounded theory procedure to create a highly readable and moving account of how abusive families move through the social service system. In her book *Vulnerable Children, Vulnerable Families: The Social Construction of Child Abuse,* she described how she began to openly code her data, which included extensive interviews with families that had entered the system because of a child abuse incident. One phenomenon that continually came up in her data was "dental problems." Over and over, she found meaning units that included this phenomenon. Thus, as a part of her open coding process, she created a category called "dental problems." This is an excellent example of the kind of banality categories can represent at the open coding stage! In open coding, the categories should exhaust the data, meaning that categories should be created to accommodate all of the data.

The next type of coding is called axial coding. In axial coding, connections are made between categories. In this process, contexts and causal conditions of the phenomena are considered, as well as strategies used by the subjects to manage or cope with the phenomenon and outcomes of those strategies. For instance, the phenomenon of dental problems in Janko's

(1994) study eventually began to take on greater meaning for her, as she realized that dental problems were one facet of poverty. To impoverished families, dental care is an often unobtainable luxury. Thus the category of dental problems was incorporated into the broader category of stress related to families' inability to meet basic needs such as housing and health care.

The final coding process is called selective coding. It involves identifying a core category around which all other categories organize. It involves exhausting the realm of possible categories at the axial level and then examining the resulting gestalt to identify the primary dimension or central phenomenon being observed. Part of this process is explicating the story line that emerges from the data. The importance of temporality is emphasized here in that a process is described. The process might be a developmental one, for example the development of professional identity as a therapist, as identified in Skovholt and Rønnestad's *The Evolving Professional Self* (1992). Or the process might describe movement through a sequence of coping strategies as Janko (1994) elucidated in her work on child abuse. She described how families, trying to cope with inadequate resources, enter and move through the social services system. In their *Basics of Qualitative Research,* Strauss and Corbin (1990) describe an investigation that examined how women cope with high-risk pregnancies. The book contains examples of each of the types of coding as they apply to the examination of that process. Though selective coding has been criticized for suggesting a reductionistic methodology for examining qualitative data, it is currently widely used in the social sciences as a process that can lead to publication because of its clarity.

The Phenomenological Method. In *Phenomenology and Psychological Research,* Giorgi (1985) adapts the process of the philosophical phenomenological method to psychology. Giorgi, who was strongly influenced by Merleau-Ponty, emphasizes that the process of analysis must adhere as closely as possible to the original phenomenon, attempting to capture it in its pure and complex form, including social context of the phenomenon and influencing factors. Like Merleau-Ponty, Giorgi stresses the importance of thorough description. The phenomenological approach is very experience-near, providing a close examination of an individual's experience. Because of its strong emphasis on understanding the meaning of experience, the phenomenological approach is particularly well suited to counseling research.

Whereas traditional phenomenological method involved describing one's own personal experience, the psychological phenomenological method entails recording another's description of experience and then applying a psychological "lens" to the experience, describing it in psychological terms. Thus the psychological description is once-removed from an individual's description of his or her experience. It is a psychological analog of the experience provided by the psychologist-researcher.

Giorgi (1985) outlines four essential steps to the process of a phenomenological analysis. The first step involves reading an entire description or transcript in order to obtain a sense of the whole. One reading might not be sufficient; in certain situations several readings might be necessary for the investigator to feel familiar with the phenomenon.

The second step involves reading the transcript again to divide it into "meaning units." Meaning units are described as, "spontaneously perceived discriminations within the subject's description arrived at when the researcher assumes a psychological attitude toward the concrete description, and along with it, the set that the text is an example of the phenomenon" (Giorgi, 1985, p. 11). The divisions into meaning units are noted directly on the transcript (possibly by slashes in between the units) whenever the researcher becomes aware of a shift in meaning. Giorgi points out that meaning shifts could also be interpreted as perceived shifts in the emotional quality of the description. The purpose of dividing the transcript into meaning units is to allow the researcher to psychologically examine and describe meaningful constituents of the experience, staying as close to the data as possible. Giorgi discriminates between elements and constituents of experience, stressing that an element is independent of context, whereas a constituent is context-laden. Therefore, the meaning units are seen not as independent, but rather as expressions of aspects of the whole phenomenon, or the gestalt.

The third step involves examining each constituent for its psychological meaning and translating the described experience into psychological language, emphasizing the phenomenon under investigation — in other words, highlighting the psychological characteristics of the phenomenon. This process is necessary in order to bring psychological meaning to the naive descriptions of the person whose experience is being examined. This task involves Merleau-Ponty's process of imaginative variation, or consideration of the constituent for possible relevant meanings, using theoretical understanding, and selecting the meanings that make the most sense, given the situated context of the experience.

The final step involves synthesizing the meanings into a general statement about the subject's experience. It is a summary that attempts to describe the total gestalt of the experience in psychological terms. Giorgi (1985) emphasizes that the more subjects one has, the better one is able to summarize the essence of an experience, drawing from multiple descriptions. Thus this final step is not unlike the final step in grounded theory analysis. It searches for the essence of an experience, examining several accounts of the experience for common features, as well as exceptions to commonality.

IMPLICATIONS OF A QUALITATIVE PARADIGM FOR
COUNSELING RESEARCH

The future of counseling and the mental health field in general lies in our ability to be reflective about our practice — our capacity to examine and critique our work and to be open to innovation (Neufeldt, Karno, & Nelson, 1996). That ability will be facilitated by the types of knowledge we produce. Positivistic research has brought the mental health field to a crossroads. Outcome research on psychotherapy has pointed out that our particular theories and techniques are perhaps less related to outcome than our more personal qualities, particularly genuine empathy (Dawes, 1994; Weinberger, 1995; Whiston & Sexton, 1993). The "humanness" of the counseling relationship is of profound importance to a client's improvement. That humanness, however, has managed in many respects to elude quantification. Qualitative methods that allow us to apprehend as closely as possible the meanings people construct about their painful experiences and the meanings they construct about their healing experiences will bring us closer to understanding not only how clients construe their worlds but also how what we do impacts them. For instance, recent qualitative investigations of counseling process have provided insights about how clients experience and handle problems with their therapists (Rennie, 1994; Rhodes, Hill, Thompson, & Elliott, 1994; Watson & Rennie, 1994). Other investigators have focused on elucidating the properties of change in counseling and therapy (Cummings, Hallberg, & Slemon, 1994; Elliott et al., 1994; Friedlander, Heatherington, Johnson, & Skowron, 1994), client experiences of the working alliance in counseling (Bachelor, 1995), interracial vs. intraracial counseling interactions (Thompson & Jenal, 1994), and other process phenomena.

Similarly, training and supervision research that allows us to better understand how trainees and trainers alike experience their relationships will give us insight into how to be better counselor trainers. Qualitative investigations of supervision and training issues have focused on identifying the characteristics of reflective supervision (Neufeldt et al., 1996), aspects of trainee nondisclosure in supervision (Ladany, Hill, Corbett, & Nutt, 1996), the characteristics of good supervision (Worthen & McNeill, 1996), and trainee experiences in gender awareness training (Good & Heppner, 1995).

The addition of qualitative forms of inquiry to the counseling research field will provide another powerful means of understanding what we do as professionals. Quantitative methods can continue to provide us with understanding about the size of differences between groups; the size of relationships between constructs; and the predictive capacities of person, environmental, and intervention-related variables. Quantitative inquiry can demonstrate how theories of personality, treatment, and training apply in a probabilistic sense. Qualitative inquiry can provide understanding about the experienced meanings of individual and family development, learning phenomena, social problems, and process and outcome in counseling and training. It can contribute to theory generation and testing from an experiential perspective. What matters is advancing our knowledge about our practice. As Hoshmand and Martin (1995), in *Research as Praxis,* conclude:

> [T]he increasing pluralism in the use of quasi-experimental and hermeneutic paradigms (in addition to the experimental), the flexible or combined use of discovery and verification strategies, as well as the new attention given to criteria and methods of validation in the discovery context — all point toward a gradual evolution of the praxis. (p. 239)

The addition of qualitative approaches to our repertoire of research strategies can only advance our expertise. It will provide us with greater understandings about the feelings that counselors, clients, counselor trainees, and counselor trainers and supervisors experience in their work and the meanings that they make of their experiences. It will allow us to construct a more completely articulated discipline of counseling, from both training and practice perspectives.

REFERENCES

Bachelor, A. (1995). Clients' perception of the therapeutic alliance: A qualitative analysis. *Journal of Counseling Psychology, 42,* 323–337.

Berg, B. L. (1995). *Qualitative research methods for the social sciences* (2nd ed.). Boston: Allyn and Bacon.

Bowers, B. (1990). Grounded theory. In B. Sarter (Ed.), *Paths to knowledge* (pp. 33–58). New York: National League for Nursing.

Brennan, J. F. (1994). *History and systems of psychology.* Englewood Cliffs, NJ: Prentice-Hall.

Charon, J. M. (1992). *Symbolic interactionism: An introduction, an interpretation, an integration.* Englewood Cliffs, NJ: Prentice-Hall.

Cummings, A. L., Hallberg, E. T., & Slemon, A. G. (1994). Templates of client change in short-term counseling. *Journal of Counseling Psychology, 41,* 464–472.

Dawes, R. M. (1994). *House of cards: Psychology and psychotherapy built on myth.* New York: Macmillan.

Denzin, N. K. (1978). *The research act.* New York: McGraw-Hill.

Elliott, R., Shapiro, D. A., Firth-Cozens, J., Stiles, W. B., Hardy, G. E., Llewelyn, S. P., & Margison, F. R. (1994). Comprehensive process analysis of insight events in cognitive-behavioral and psychodynamic psychotherapies. *Journal of Counseling Psychology, 41,* 449–463.

Friedlander, M. L., Heatherington, L., Johnson, B., & Skowron, E. A. (1994). Sustaining engagement: A change event in family therapy. *Journal of Counseling Psychology, 41,* 438–448.

Giorgi, A. (1985). *Phenomenology and psychological research.* Pittsburgh: Duquesne University Press.

Glaser, B., & Strauss, A. (1967). *The discovery of grounded theory: Strategies for qualitative research.* Chicago: Aldine.

Good, G. E., & Heppner, M. J. (1995). Students' perceptions of a gender issues course: A qualitative and quantitative examination. *Counselor Education and Supervision, 34,* 308–320.

Hill, C. E., Carter, J. A., & O'Farrell, M. K. (1983). A case study of process and outcome of time-limited counseling. *Journal of Counseling Psychology, 30,* 3–18.

Holloway, E. L., Freund, R. D., Gardner, S. L., Nelson, M. L., & Walker, B. R. (1989). Relation of power and involvement to theoretical orientation in supervision: An analysis of discourse. *Journal of Counseling Psychology, 36,* 88–102.

Holloway, E. L., & Wampold, B. E. (1983). Patterns of verbal behavior and judgments of satisfaction in the supervision interview. *Journal of Counseling Psychology, 30,* 227–234.

Hoshmand, L. T., & Martin, J. (1995). Concluding comments on therapeutic psychology and the science of practice. In L. T. Hoshmand & J. Martin (Eds.), *Research as praxis* (pp. 235–241). New York: Teachers College Press.

Howard, G. S. (1985). Can research in the human sciences become more relevant to practice? *Journal of Counseling and Development, 63,* 539–544.

Howard, G. S. (1986). The scientist-practitioner in counseling psychology: Toward a deeper integration of theory, research, and practice. *The Counseling Psychologist, 14*(1), 61–105.

Janko, S. (1994). *Vulnerable children, vulnerable families: The social construction of child abuse.* New York: Teachers College Press.

Kuhn, T. S. (1970). *Structure of scientific revolutions.* Chicago: University of Chicago Press.

Kvale, S. (1983). The qualitative research interview: A phenomenological and a hermeneutical mode of understanding. *Journal of Phenomenological Psychology, 14*(2), 171–196.

Ladany, N., Hill, C. E., Corbett, M. M., & Nutt, E. A. (1996). Nature, extent, and importance of what psychotherapy trainees do not disclose to their supervisors. *Journal of Counseling Psychology, 43,* 10–24.

Madison, G. B. (1988). *The hermeneutics of postmodernity.* Bloomington: Indiana University Press.

Martin, J. S., Goodyear, R. K., & Newton, F. B. (1987). Clinical supervision: An intensive case study. *Professional Psychology: Research and Practice, 18,* 225–235.

Merleau-Ponty, M. (1962). *Phenomenology of perception* (L. Smith, Trans.). New York: Humanities Press. (Original work published 1945)

Miles, M. B., & Huberman, M. A. (1983). *Qualitative data analysis.* Beverly Hills, CA: Sage.

Neufeldt, S. A., Karno, M. P., & Nelson, M. L. (1996). A qualitative study of experts' conceptualization of supervisee reflectivity. *Journal of Counseling Psychology, 43,* 3–9.

Polkinghorne, D. E. (1984). Further extensions of methodological diversity for counseling psychology. *Journal of Counseling Psychology, 31,* 416–429.

Polkinghorne, D. E. (1988). *Narrative knowing and the human sciences.* Albany: State University of New York Press.

Polkinghorne, D. E. (1989). Phenomenological research methods. In R. S. Valle & S. Halling (Eds.), *Existential-phenomenological perspectives in psychology* (pp. 1–43). New York: Plenum Press.

Qualitative research in counseling process and outcome [Special issue]. (1994). *Journal of Counseling Psychology, 41* (4).

Rennie, D. L. (1994). Clients' deference in psychotherapy. *Journal of Counseling Psychology, 41,* 427–437.

Rhodes, R. H., Hill, C. E., Thompson, B. J., & Elliott, R. (1994). Client retrospective recall of resolved and unresolved misunderstanding events. *Journal of Counseling Psychology, 41,* 473–483.

Schatzman, L. (1987). Dimensional analysis: Notes on an alternative approach to the grounding of theory in qualitative research. In D. R. Maines (Ed.), *Social organization and social processes: Essays in honor of Anselm Strauss* (pp. 303–313). New York: Aldine DeGruyter.

Schatzman, L., & Strauss, A. L. (1973). *Field research: Strategies for a natural sociology.* Englewood Cliffs, NJ: Prentice-Hall.

Schwandt, T. A. (1995). Constructivist, interpretivist approaches to human inquiry. In N. K. Denzin and Y. S. Lincoln (Eds.), *Handbook of qualitative research* (pp. 118–137). Thousand Oaks, CA: Sage.

Seidman, I. E. (1991). *Interviewing as qualitative research: A guide for researchers in education and the social sciences.* New York: Teachers College Press.

Skovholt, T. M., & Rønnestad, M. H. (1992). *The evolving professional self.* New York: Wiley.

Strauss, A., & Corbin, J. (1990). *Basics of qualitative research.* Newbury Park, CA: Sage.

Thompson, C. E., & Jenal, S. T. (1994). Interracial and intraracial quasi-counseling interactions when counselors avoid discussing race. *Journal of Counseling Psychology, 41,* 484–491.

Tracey, T. J., & Ray, P. B. (1984). Stages of successful time-limited counseling: An interactional examination. *Journal of Counseling Psychology, 31,* 13–27.

Varela, F. J., Thompson, E., & Rosch, E. (1993). *The embodied mind.* Cambridge: MIT Press.

Watson, J. C., & Rennie, D. L. (1994). Qualitative analysis of clients' subjective experience of significant moments during the exploration of problematic reactions. *Journal of Counseling Psychology, 41,* 500–509.

Weinberger, J. (1995). Common factors aren't so common: The common factors dilemma. *Clinical Psychology: Science and Practice, 2,* 45–69.

Whiston, S. C., & Sexton, T. L. (1993). An overview of psychotherapy outcome research: Implications for practice. *Professional Psychology: Research and Practice, 24,* 43–51.

Worthen, V., & McNeill, B. W. (1996). A phenomenological investigation of "good" supervision events. *Journal of Counseling Psychology, 43,* 25–34.

CHAPTER 11

Applying Second-Generation Cognitive Science Toward Assessing Therapeutic Change

M. Harry Daniels and Lyle J. White

> Ordinary words convey only what we know already; it is from metaphor that we can best get hold of something fresh.
>
> —Aristotle, *Rhetoric*

People enter into counseling because they want their lives to be better, that is, to change. Thus the concept of "change" is basic to any counseling practice or theoretical discussion. The significance of change leads to the question "What are the defining qualities of change?" This question is critical to the practice of counseling, although it connotes different meanings to different parties. To the clinician this question becomes "How will I and my client(s) know when the goals established for this counseling endeavor have been met and this individual, couple, or family are better ready to lead more satisfying lives?" To the supervisor or trainer the question becomes "How can I instruct counselors-in-training so that they develop clinical skills that will promote client change?" To the researcher the question becomes "How can I establish or argue that change occurred that was, at least in part, related to the counseling provided?" In order to frame a response to these questions, it first is necessary to specify the focus of the assessment and then to designate a unit of change, a concept or notion whereby change can be discussed.

Identifying an appropriate focus and unit of change is a task that is fraught with difficulty, not to mention differences of opinion. Two difficulties are significant for our purposes. One has to do with the difficulty of defining change in a complex social system. For example, whose perspective, and at what point in time, forms the basis of the evaluation? The second has to do with the difficulty of constructing assessment procedures that are psychometrically sound, yet sufficiently sensitive to the idiosyncratic nature of the problems presented by clients. Clearly, different writers have offered differing responses to these difficulties, resulting in the formation of two opposing points of view (i.e., quantitative versus qualitative) about how best to assess change. Despite the fact that both perspectives enjoy a well-established history within the field of psychological inquiry, they have almost always been portrayed as being in opposing, mutually exclusive domains. Unfortunately, the distinction may have hindered, rather than helped, the profession develop evaluation methods that (a) fit the practice of counseling, (b) are consistent with theory-based notions about causality, experience, and meaning, and (c) emphasize empirical rigor.

In Chapter 10, Nelson and Poulin have provided a review of the rich history of constructivism within qualitative psychological research and inquiry. They summarized and echoed previous calls for specific research and evaluation methods that "allow us to be receptive to change and to identify the characteristics of change as it occurs." In this chapter we introduce an experientialist research and evaluation method that is consistent with criteria for social constructivists research and inquiry methods and responds to the challenge posed by Nelson and Poulin. In so doing we address the aforementioned perennial question — "What are the defining qualities of change?" — with methods that are rooted in second-generation cognitive science.

COGNITIVE SCIENCE AND THE NATURE OF THE MIND

Elsewhere (Daniels, Johnson, White, & Hedinger, 1993), we have argued that cognitive science embraces a number of related fields (such as philosophy, psychology, linguistics, anthropology, neurosciences, computer science, and even legal theory) that are producing interdisciplinary research on the nature of the mind, knowledge, and language. There are two major orientations within the cognitive sciences. First-generation cognitive science traditionally has regarded the mind as a set of functional relations that are to be represented by formal symbol systems, especially formal logics (Putnam, 1981). In this view, which underlies generative linguistics, information processing psychology, and classical artificial intelligence, the fact that human beings are embodied plays no essential role in the account that is given of the functioning of the mind. Moreover, concepts are thought to be fundamentally literal and capable of mapping directly onto the world to give us knowledge (Lakoff & Johnson, 1980).

A number of authors have argued that the objectivist, literalist view of the mind is inadequate because it overlooks the embodied and imaginative nature of human concepts and reasoning (Johnson, 1987; Varela, Thompson, & Rosch, 1991). Second-generation cognitive science has shown why the objectivist picture will not work, and it has provided an alternative view of concepts and reasoning as grounded in structures of our embodied experience that are elaborated through various imaginative devices (Lakoff, 1987). For instance, there is a large body of converging empirical evidence from various disciplines that many of our most basic concepts are defined by multiple, often inconsistent, metaphors, and that these systematic metaphors are grounded in the nature of our bodily experience (Damasio, 1994; Lakoff & Johnson, 1980; Turner, 1991). Johnson (1987) has used the term *embodied knowledge* to represent the basis of second-generation cognitive science. Therefore, throughout the remainder of this chapter the terms second-order cognitive science and embodied knowledge will be used interchangeably. This suggests that all of our fundamental concepts are metaphoric, and that our lives are organized around these metaphors — who we are, how we understand situations, the way we relate to others, and what we see as possible courses of action open to us all depend on the metaphors that make up the fabric of our experience.

The notion of 'conceptual' metaphor that we are employing is quite different from standard objectivist and literalist accounts (Lakoff, 1993). Those first-generation accounts treated metaphor as a derivative function performed on core literal concepts, and therefore as not being cognitively basic (Johnson, 1981). To the contrary, Johnson and Lakoff (Johnson, 1981; Lakoff, 1993; Lakoff & Johnson, 1980) and others (Quinn, 1987; Turner, 1987) have discovered that *metaphor is a basic, irreducible cognitive scheme that is in no sense derivative.* Rather, metaphor and other structures of imagination determine the nature of our conceptual systems, our inferential patterns, and our language. Research shows that human beings understand their basic spatial experiences by means of lived, embodied experiences that are abstracted into image structures (called "image schemata") that recur over and over again in their mundane bodily interactions with their environment (Damasio, 1994; Johnson, 1987; Stern, 1985). Image schemata include cognitive structures such as containment, balance, compulsive force, attraction, source-path-goal, center-periphery, up-down, and other types of basic bodily and spatial relations (Johnson, 1987).

One of the most remarkable things second-generation cognitive scientists have discovered about human cognition is that people use these *concrete, bodily based* image schemata to structure their *abstract* concepts (such as love, marriage, life, relationships, causation, change). The result is a conceptual mapping of structure from a source domain (e.g., some bodily experience) onto a more abstract, or less well-articulated, target domain (e.g., love, change, ideas, relationships). People then project the "logic" of the bodily source domain to structure the logic of the abstract domain. In this way, our knowledge of the source domain can be carried over into the target domain. These bodily based cross-domain reflexive projections are called *conceptual metaphors* (Johnson, 1987; Lakoff, 1993; Lakoff & Johnson, 1980). The extent to which bodily based language serves as a way for individuals and couples to understand and express their thoughts and feelings about their lives and relationships is just beginning to be recognized.

For example, Quinn (1987) has analyzed the conceptual metaphors by which couples understand their marriage. She found a recurring set of basic metaphors (such as MARRIAGE IS A BUSINESS PARTNERSHIP, MARRIAGE IS A JOURNEY, MARRIAGE IS A SAFE HAVEN, MARRIAGE IS A CONSTRUCTED OBJECT, etc.), and she found that the partners in the marriage typically operate by one or more *different* metaphors. The key point here is that people do not merely *talk* about their marriages metaphorically. Rather, their very understanding and experience of their marriage is determined by one or more of these metaphor systems. Moreover, they *act* on the basis of these metaphors. Quinn found that all sorts of marital difficulties arise when one spouse has a particular metaphor (e.g., MARRIAGE IS A BUSINESS PARTNERSHIP) that conflicts with the expectations generated by the other spouse's dominant metaphor (e.g., MARRIAGE IS A SAFE HAVEN).

Meichenbaum (1994), an important contributor to the theory and practice of cognitive therapy, has recently acknowledged the fundamental nature of metaphor in human expression. After reviewing the language used by his clients to express their thoughts and feelings about the trauma they have experienced, he concluded, "I would propose that our clients, as well as you the reader, cannot describe intense emotional experiences to others without using metaphors" (p. 109).

COGNITIVE SCIENCE AND THE NATURE OF CHANGE

It is our position that if counselors want to understand therapeutic change, they must understand what "change" means *to the actual people who are undergoing counseling*, rather than looking at the nature of change merely through the perspectival lens of a particular psychological theory. Because humans are fundamentally and irreducibly metaphoric animals, counselors must understand the basic metaphors for change that people project. Only then will it be possible to determine when and how therapeutic change is likely to occur, and what directions it might take. Second-generation cognitive science provides a way to discover the imaginative and embodied nature of concepts (such as change) that differ dramatically from traditional quantitative and qualitative approaches.

The emergence of second-order cognitive science points to an essential fact for social scientists and practitioners of the mental health arts. Namely, we are not limited to the "either/or dualism" imposed by many philosophers and research methodologists when we seek to examine and understand human behavior. There *are* alternatives to the philosophies of objectivism and subjectivism, and the methods of quantitative and qualitative research (cf. Firestone, 1987; Garrison, 1986; Lakoff & Johnson, 1980). To illustrate the opportunities that are available through the use of second-order cognitive science, Table 11.1 compares three methods for assessing therapeutic change: quantitative, qualitative, and embodied knowledge. Each of these methods uses different criteria to define change because the criteria are based on different assumptions about the nature of human experience. Because of space limitations, we have chosen to focus on seven criteria only, the nature of: reality, the person-environment relationships, meaning, truth, knowledge of objects, change, and a meaningful unit of change. Rather than providing a recapitulation of the philosophical and theoretical arguments for and against each of the methods illustrated in Table 11.1, we offer three pragmatic reasons why counselors should consider using conceptual metaphor as a basis for assessing change:

1. This assessment of change allows for data collection without stopping the counseling process, generating fatigue, and inducing reactivity while providing a high degree of sensitivity to change (Gurman, Kniskern, & Pinsof, 1986).
2. This evaluation method fits the practice of counseling; is consistent with social constructivist notions about causality, experience, and meaning; and emphasizes empirical rigor.
3. The client's conceptual reference is the source for defining change.

A METHOD FOR DEMONSTRATING AND EVALUATING COUNSELING CHANGE USING CONCEPTUAL METAPHOR

One notable example of how researchers have addressed the dilemma of providing psychometrically sound yet sensitive evaluation data can be found in the work of John Gottman at the University of Washington. In his recent books, *What Predicts Divorce?* and *Why Marriages Succeed or Fail,* Gottman (1994a, 1994b) has reviewed 20 some years of research involving the measure of physiological responses to marital conflicts and problem solving. His methodology has allowed immediate measures of behavioral responses during the course of counseling. In a parallel manner, we are developing a research method using conceptual metaphors that allows for an immediate appraisal of cognitive processes — that is, how couples understand their rela-

TABLE 11.1. Comparison of Three Methods for Assessing Therapeutic Change

QUESTION: What is the/a...	Response Set		
	Quantitative Knowledge	*Qualitative Knowledge*	*Embodied Knowledge*
Nature of reality?	Reality is ontological relativity without human understanding.	The context of reality is unstructured and dependent on individual imagination.	Metaphor unites reason and imagination; new and conventional metaphors have the power to define reality.
Nature of the person-environment relationship?	Persons are separate from their environment.	Persons are separate from their environment.	Persons are embedded in their environment.
Nature of meaning?	Meaning is objectivist, disembodied, compositional, independent of use, and based on a theory of truth.	Meaning is subjectivist and private.	New metaphors can give new meaning to our pasts, our daily activity, and what we know and believe.
Nature of truth?	Truth is absolute and can be known, but sometimes only in successive approximation.	Truth cannot be known and may only exist in the human mind.	Truth is not absolute, but relative to understanding and to our conceptual system. Different conceptual systems produce different truths.
Nature of the knowledge of objects?	Knowledge is gained by experience with objects.	Knowledge is gained by relying on senses and developing intuition; experience is holistic.	Objects are only entities relative to our interactions with the world and our projections onto it.
Nature of change?	Change can be operationalized and assessed as separate from the observer.	The observer and observation cannot be separated; all change is relative.	Changes in conceptual systems change what is real and how we perceive the world and act upon those perceptions.
Meaningful unit of change?	Units are operationalized prior to measurement, and authenticated with estimates of validity and reliability.	Units are developed to represent participants' beliefs about the phenomena under study.	The conceptual metaphors used by clients are the measure of change.

tionships at a specific point and how such understanding colors the quality and amount of their participation in the relationship. Our method, like Gottman's, allows for data collection without stopping the counseling process, generating fatigue, and inducing reactivity while providing a high degree of sensitivity to change. It also provides an evaluation method that fits the practice of counseling; is consistent with social constructivist notions about causality, experience, and meaning; emphasizes empirical rigor; and uses the client's conceptual reference as the basis for defining change.

AN ILLUSTRATION

Our systematic analysis of experiential metaphor has focused on the assessment of change in couples counseling. This initial analysis of the transcripts (from audio/video tapes) suggests that (1) couples in counseling use conceptual metaphors to express abstract notions about their relationships and the changes they wish to make in their lives; (2) metaphors, and the use of particular conceptual metaphors, change over the course of counseling; (3) counselors frequently, intentionally or not, enter into couples' metaphor usage in ways that seem to enhance the counseling process; and (4) it is methodologically possible to categorize and tabulate specific metaphoric usage and to trace that usage over the course of counseling.

Mapping conceptual metaphor requires a process that is in many ways similar to those processes already used by researchers and supervisors, that is, listening closely to the language used by clients and counselors. The major difference is that a significant focus of the evaluator's attention is on the conceptual language used, not the counseling techniques (e.g., paraphrasing, reflection, etc.).

The intent of the initial analysis is to identify the metaphoric expressions from the source domain (the concrete, bodily based image) that are used to express an abstract notion (the target domain). The schemata used to reveal the ontological correspondences of these two domains are referred to as cognitive maps. In the following example, the ontological correspondence links vehicle with relationship, and obstacles to motion to problems in the relationship. These ontological correspondences project a variety of epistemic correspondences. The overall mapping system is labeled the mnemonic.

Identification of Metaphoric Expressions

"We're *stuck* and feel like this relationship *isn't going anywhere*." "We're just *spinning our wheels*." "We got *off to a rocky start*." "This relationship is *at a dead end*."

Cognitive Mapping of Metaphor

ONTOLOGICAL CORRESPONDENCES

Source Domain	*Target Domain*
Vehicle	Relationship
Obstacles to motion	Problems in the relationship

EPISTEMIC CORRESPONDENCES

• Vehicles can get stuck, stall, and meet obstacles in the road. In a like manner, relationships can get stuck, stall, and encounter obstacles. Vehicles can carry passengers, cargo, dead weight; relationships can do the same.

• Motion can be stopped or blocked when something gets in the way; progress in a relationship can be stopped or blocked when something — or someone — gets in the way. Obstacles can be maneuvered around, overcome, or damage or stall the vehicle and its passengers. Likewise, problems in a relationship can be worked out, overcome, or damage the relationship and the people in it. If obstacles are insurmountable, they can put an end to the journey; if problems in a relationship are insurmountable, they can put an end to the relationship.

Mnemonic: Mapping

The mapping of LOVE RELATIONSHIP IS A JOURNEY from an actual transcription of a counseling session (noted by counseling session, transcript page, and line) is illustrated below. For example, the first statement below was made by the wife in this couple during the seventh session, page 7, line 13 of the transcript.

TRAVELERS ON A JOURNEY AS MARRIAGE
PARTNERS IN A FAMILY SYSTEM

7(7:13)	WIFE: So I think *you finally need to realize that I'm with you,* and I married you, and I am faithful to you and take it to heart, you know, it means something.
7(12:3)	WIFE: I mean there's been some rough times, *and I thought we were not going to make it* and that scared the shit out of me, and *I don't want to go through that.*
7(13:7–8)	HUSBAND: It kind of shows you *where you are.*
7(14:7–10)	HUSBAND: I think it made her look at herself and see *that the way I was,* you know, and *if I stay that way, it's going to work.*

And by the same token, *she's made progress,* and *I've come along, too.*

Obstacles to Motion (Adversaries)—Problems in Relationship

7(12:2–5)   WIFE: I don't, I just really believe that *we've made it over some kind of hump here.*

7(12:19–21) HUSBAND: We was in Florida and got into it, and I decided this is — *we're going to get through this Christmas* if I have anything to say about this. *We're going to get through this Christmas,* and I'm going to enjoy it.

Common Destination—Goals for Marriage

7(12:3)   WIFE: I mean there's been some rough times, *and I thought we were not going to make it* and that scared the shit out of me, and I don't want to go through that.

Path of Motion—Course of Relationship

7(2:17)   WIFE: (Name), I really appreciate what you did, because *it makes it so much easier for us to get along.*

8(12:17–18) WIFE: *He doesn't think I go out of my way,* but I do.

8(25:8)   WIFE: It was a period where *things were going smooth.*

In order to follow the mappings across counseling sessions, we charted the metaphoric usage with the following format. This format was repeated for other metaphor mnemonics, such as ANGER AS HEAT OF FLUID IN A CONTAINER and RESPECT IN RELATIONSHIPS AS PHYSICAL POSITION. The procedure for identifying and counting statements is identical to the one described above. The map is shown in Table 11.2.

IMPLICATIONS

Given the three defining features of this method of assessment (as mentioned earlier), we believe the method has significant implications for practitioners, trainers, and researchers who have an interest in applying social construction to counseling.

Practitioners

The practice of counseling is guided by counselors' training and experience. As Parloff, Waskow, and Wolfe (cited in Alberts & Edelstein, 1990) observed,

TABLE 11.2. RELATIONSHIP AS A JOURNEY Map

Source: Journey	Target: Relationship	Session 7	Session 8
Travelers	Marriage partners in family system	7:13 12:3 13:7 14:8-9,17-18	
Common designation	Goals for marriage	12:3	
Path of motion	Course of relationship	2:17 6:17 7:17 12:19 13:8 14:8-9,10,17	4:19 12:17-18 24:23-25 25:8,14 33:10
Motion toward destination (markers)	Progress in relationship	2:17 5:8 6:6-7,16-18 9:24 10:16 12:11 13:2,7-8 14:8-9	11:22-25 15:17
Obstacles to motion (adversaries)	Problems in relationship	12:2,3,5,11,14, 19,20-21	2:12-14
Aids to motion (allies)	Facilitation of relationship	2:15-17 4:17 12:12-13	
Absence of hindrances to motion	Freedom	5:21-22,24 9:10-15 14:17	33:3-4
Navigational decisions	Who determines marital goals?	6:7-8 14:17-18	12:17-18 15:15-17,19 21:13-14 23:5-7 30:11-13, 17-18 33:19-20 36:12-17
Recklessness/out of control	Endangering the security of the relationship/family	15:21-23	

An entire generation of psychologists has been influenced by the idea that the necessary and sufficient conditions for effective psychotherapy are simply these: that the patient perceives the therapist to be "genuine," and that the patient believes the therapist to be experiencing some minimal degree of empathy and warmth toward him/her over a sustained but unspecified period of time. (p. 499)

If genuineness, warmth, and emotional sharing are considered metaphoric explanations of the counseling process, then the counseling profession has created its own metaphorical language, and has imposed it on its consumers. We and others (cf. Meichenbaum, 1994) believe great caution is warranted before counselors impose their metaphors on clients. Support for this assertion is found in Sexton's (1994) observation that clients' compliance with treatment interventions increases when counselors use the clients' language. Consequently, it is preferable to help clients dismantle and discover the entailments (i.e., meanings) of their own metaphors rather than impose ones that were conceived by the counselor prior to the onset of counseling (Meichenbaum, 1994; Ryder, 1988). By paying attention to the conceptual metaphors used by their clients, counselors are more likely to be perceived by their clients as using their (the clients') language. We have found that training counselors to attend and respond to conceptual metaphor can be accomplished through the use of proven training practices.

Trainers

The purpose of counselor training is to move the novice counselor toward the status of expert. There is evidence that expert practitioners employ cognitive processes that are somehow different from those of novices (Dreyfus & Dreyfus, 1986; cited in Polkinghorne, 1992). Little is known, however, about how the cognitive processes employed by expert counselors are learned or evidenced in counseling sessions (Alberts & Edelstein, 1990). Despite this void in understanding, counselor educators have declared that it is critical to train the novice in those processes. In this regard Etringler, Hillerbrand, and Claiborn (1995) have suggested that "an important focus in counselor preparation is the acquisition of new, more complex, and comprehensive schemas for understanding human interaction" (p. 7). Conceptual metaphor may provide a practical response to this need identified by Etringler and colleagues. That is, conceptual metaphor represents a resource that trainers can use to equip trainees with new, comprehensive, and effective ways for understanding and communicating with clientele.

With the aid of audio/video tape, conceptual metaphor provides a technique for tracking the conceptualization of issues by counselor trainees, as well as clients. This particular attribute of conceptual metaphor (i.e., that it allows for data collection without stopping the counseling process, generating fatigue, and inducing reactivity while providing a high degree of sensitivity to change) may provide a means for trainees to monitor their own counseling sessions and enhance their capacity for the essential skill of self-supervision (N. Colangelo, personal communication, 1978). Considered together, these uses point to the utility of conceptual metaphor as a unit for assessing change in counseling research.

Researchers

As stated above, we believe conceptual metaphor has the potential to contribute to counselors' understanding of the therapeutic process. It also has the potential to expand the focus of family therapy research. Most research on the client's role in the family therapy change process has been concerned with observable behavior (e.g., Gottman, 1994a, 1994b). In contrast, there is a dearth of research about the covert emotions and cognitions of family members in therapy (Pinsof, 1988) and the impact that these phenomena have on the behavior of family members. It is our view that conceptual metaphor will stimulate researchers who are interested in investigating problems of social construction to develop new research paradigms and methods. As we consider the possibilities, the following examples come to mind (the list is not meant to be exhaustive). Conceptual metaphor could be used to study complex skill acquisition, a field of research that is in its infancy (Etringler et al., 1995). It could also be used to conduct research about how changes occur in clients' belief systems (Pinsof, 1988). Similarly, Gurman's (1988) challenge to identify the most potent change-inducing elements within counseling could be addressed through the use of conceptual metaphor.

Gurman's (1988) challenge has particular relevance to the field of family counseling. As noted by Pinsof (1988), there is no empirical or even quasi-scientific foundation for generating hypotheses about the processes or mechanisms of change in family therapy. Clinical researchers are left with family therapy theory as a basis for generating process-outcome hypotheses. The field of family therapy would benefit from a series of investigations of specific hypotheses about change processes in family therapy (cf. Friedlander, Wildman, Heatherington, & Skowron, 1994).

In addition to developing and testing specific hypotheses about change processes, family therapy investigators should conduct research that is responsive to the needs of practitioners. According to research conducted by Beutler, Williams, and Wakefield (1993; cited in Friedlander et al., 1994), practitioners called for "research that focuses on therapist and/or client behaviors leading to important moments of change during psychotherapy" (p. 391).

CONCLUSION

As stated at the beginning of this chapter, people enter into counseling because they want their lives to be better, that is, to change. The clients' goal notwithstanding, counselors have agreed that it is difficult to identify an appropriate focus and unit of change. We identified two critical difficulties: defining change in a complex social system, and constructing assessment procedures that are psychometrically sound, yet sufficiently sensitive to the idiosyncratic nature of the problems presented by clients.

We have argued that conceptual metaphor provides counselors, counselor trainers, and researchers with the opportunity to reexamine the defining qualities of change, the process of counseling, and interpersonal communication. The method of assessing change allows for data collection without stopping the counseling process, generating fatigue, and inducing reactivity while providing a high degree of sensitivity to change. It also provides an evaluation method that fits the practice of counseling; is consistent with social constructivists notions about causality, experience, and meaning; emphasizes empirical rigor; and uses the client's conceptual reference as the basis for defining change.

We have attempted to provide only an introduction to this exciting and vibrant way of considering what we do when we counsel others. It is an approach that is in its infancy. We hope that we have stimulated others to think differently about the nature of client change, evaluation of our efforts, and character of our profession.

REFERENCES

Alberts, G., & Edelstein, B. (1990). Therapist training: A critical review of skill training studies. *Clinical Psychology Review, 10,* 497–511.

Daniels, M. H., Johnson, M., White, L. J., & Hedinger, T. (1993). *Mapping change in family therapy: A study in the applications of second generation cognitive science.* Unpublished manuscript, Southern Illinois University at Carbondale.

Damasio, A. R. (1994). *Descartes' error: Emotion, reason, and the human brain.* New York: Putnam.

Etringler, B. D., Hillerbrand, E., & Claiborn, C. D. (1995). The transition from novice to expert counselor. *Counselor Education and Supervision, 35,* 4–17.

Firestone, W. A. (1987). Meaning in method: The rhetoric of quantitative and qualitative research. *Educational Researcher, 16*(7), 16–21.

Friedlander, M. L., Wildman, J., Heatherington, L., & Skowron, E. A. (1994). What we do and don't know about the process of family therapy. *Journal of Family Psychology, 8,* 390–416.

Garrison, J. W. (1986). Some principles of postpositivistic philosophy of science. *Educational Researcher, 15*(9), 12–18.

Gottman, J. M. (1994a). *What predicts divorce?: The relationship between marital processes and marital outcomes.* Hillsdale, NJ: Lawrence Erlbaum Associates.

Gottman, J. M. (1994b). *Why marriages succeed or fail.* New York: Simon and Schuster.

Gurman, A. S. (1988). Issues in the specification of family therapy interventions. In. L. C. Wynne (Ed.), *The state of the art in family therapy research: Controversies and recommendations* (pp. 125–138). New York: Family Process Press.

Gurman, A. S., Kniskern, D. P., & Pinsof, W. M. (1986). Research on marital and family therapies. In S. L. Garfield & A. E. Bergin (Eds.), *Handbook of psychotherapy and behavior change* (3rd ed.) (pp. 565–624). New York: Wiley.

Johnson, M. (1981). *Philosophical perspectives on metaphor.* Minneapolis: University of Minnesota Press.

Johnson, M. (1987). *The body in the mind: The bodily basis of meaning, imagination, and reason.* Chicago: University of Chicago Press.

Lakoff, G. (1987). *Women, fire, and dangerous things: What categories reveal about the mind.* Chicago: University of Chicago Press.

Lakoff, G. (1993). The contemporary theory of metaphor. In A. Ortony (Ed.), *Metaphor and thought* (2nd ed.) (pp. 202–251). New York: Cambridge University Press.

Lakoff, G., & Johnson, M. (1980). *Metaphors we live by.* Chicago: University of Chicago Press.

Meichenbaum, D. (1994). *A clinical handbook/practical therapist manual for assessing and treating adults with post-traumatic stress disorder (PTSD).* Waterloo, Ontario: Institute Press.

Pinsof, W. M. (1988). Strategies for the study of family therapy process. In L. C. Wynne (Ed.), *The state of the art in family therapy research: Controversies and recommendations* (pp. 159–174). New York: Family Process Press.

Polkinghorne, D. E. (1992). Postmodern epistemology of practice. In S. Kvale (Ed.), *Psychology and postmodernism* (pp. 146–165). London: Sage.

Putnam, H. (1981). *Reason, truth, and history.* Cambridge: Cambridge University Press.

Quinn, N. (1987). Convergent evidence for a cultural model of American marriage. In D. Holland & N. Quinn (Eds.), *Cultural models in language and thought* (pp. 173–192). New York: Cambridge University Press.

Ryder, R. G. (1988). The holy grail: Proven efficacy in family therapy. In L. C. Wynne (Ed.), *The state of the art in family therapy research: Controversies and recommendations* (pp. 47–54). New York: Family Process Press.

Sexton, T. L. (1994). Systemic thinking in a linear world: Issues in the application of interactional counseling. *Journal of Counseling & Development, 72,* 249–258.

Stern, D. (1985). *The interpersonal world of the infant.* New York: Basic Books.

Turner, M. (1987). *Death is the mother of beauty: Mind, metaphor, criticism.* Chicago: University of Chicago Press.

Turner, M. (1991). *Reading minds: The study of English in the age of cognitive science.* Princeton: Princeton University Press.

Varela, F., Thompson, E., & Rosch, E. (1991). *The embodied mind: Cognitive science and human experience.* Cambridge: MIT Press.

PART IV

Applications of Constructivist Thinking in Counseling Training and Supervision

CHAPTER 12

A Social Constructivist Approach to Counseling Supervision

Susan Allstetter Neufeldt

Supervision is defined as an interactive process between two or more individuals that has as its goals the professional development of the supervisee as a therapist and the delivery of effective service to the therapist's client. Except in cases of peer supervision, the supervisor is someone with more training and/or professional experience than the supervisee. The American Counseling Association, the American Psychological Association, and state licensing boards, which require supervision for program accreditation and licensure of counselors and psychologists, accept this definition. Within this framework, however, supervision has developed along two rather distinct paths, consistent with theories of knowledge described by Polkinghorne (1992) in psychology in general.

Polkinghorne (1992) differentiated scientific psychology, knowledge acquired and valued by research psychologists (who are often academics), from practitioner knowledge, acquired and used by counselors and psychotherapists. Scientific psychologists seek knowledge from rigorous, controlled experimentation with large samples in order to explain human behavior. Schön (1983) calls this scientific paradigm "technical rationality" and defines professional activity within this paradigm as consisting of instrumental problem solving made rigorous by the application of scientific theory and technique (p. 21). This approach to problem solving within the professions grows out of a positivist or modernist philosophy that says that through rigorous methodology, scientific solutions can be found to all problems, including human problems. As these answers are found by experts, the solutions can be applied by practitioners in a systematic way. It is a top-down model, whereby scientists dictate to practitioners who practice expertly with the uninformed lay population. In Schön's words, however, "An artful practice of the unique case appears anomalous when professional competence is modelled in terms of application of established techniques to recurrent events" (p. 19). In fact, practitioners read little scientific research and instead apply what they have learned from other practitioners and, most particularly, from their own clinical experience (Beutler, Williams, Wakefield, & Entwistle, 1995; Skovholt & Rønnestad, 1992a).

Practitioners construct knowledge from their experience of counseling and psychotherapy with individuals, families, or small groups. They function within the social constructionist paradigm, with which this book is concerned. Social constructionism, by definition, is a shared construction of mental schemata to view the world and determine behavior (Steenbarger, 1994). As indicated in this volume and other works, a constructivist approach to psychotherapy is anticipatory (Mahoney, 1991; Neimeyer & Mahoney, 1995; Neimeyer & Neimeyer, 1987; Polkinghorne, 1992). It incorporates context (Pepper, 1961), the interaction of client and therapist (Mahoney, 1991), personal experience (Kelly, 1977), theory as a means of understanding (M. H. Rønnestad, personal communication, December 8, 1995) and prediction (Polkinghorne, 1992), hypothesis-making and hypothesis-testing (Kelly, 1955; Neimeyer, 1985), and reflexivity (Hoshmand, 1994). It involves constant revision (Kelly, 1977) because reality is not stagnant; alternative theories are welcomed. It is not a solipsistic view where each individual has a view of reality unrelated to that of others (Neimeyer, 1995); it is social. Knowledge is jointly constructed as a viable means to understand events and act effectively within a context (Feixas, 1995). New knowledge should not ignore previous knowledge; in fact, to some degree it should be consistent with it (Feixas, 1995).

Like psychology in general, supervision has developed along two lines. In the following sections, I will identify the development of both modernist and constructivist approaches to supervision. Following that, I will suggest principles of constructivist supervision as a basis for continuing practice. Finally, I will provide examples of constructivist supervision from a single contemporary model.

DEVELOPMENT OF SUPERVISION MODELS

The study of supervision and training is a relatively new discipline (Holloway & Neufeldt, 1995). Models, however, have proliferated in the past 20 years. Some approach supervision from a modernist viewpoint; others, from a constructivist view; and still others combine both perspectives.

Modernist Approaches to Supervision

The academic researcher sees the task of supervision as the transmission of scientific knowledge from expert supervisors to novice practitioners. Lambert (Lambert & Arnold, 1987; Lambert & Ogles, 1988) has argued that supervision's effectiveness is dependent on the state of scientific knowledge of effective psychotherapy. To the degree that effective approaches have been devised and applied to large samples in controlled experiments, we can assume that we know what counselors and therapists should be doing. Supervision, then, is a matter of teaching them to carry out these validated procedures. Expert authorities transmit knowledge to uninformed counselors, in what Freire (1993) has called the banking concept of education, in which, in this case, supervisees are receptacles and supervisors make deposits.

Ivey and his colleagues (Ivey, 1971; Ivey, Normington, Miller, Merrill, & Haase, 1968) developed a widely used approach to pre-practicum training in which counselors learned distinct listening and responding skills. In an extension of this concept, experts in various approaches have developed training manuals, initially to teach experienced therapists in large research projects to carry out particular therapeutic procedures (Beutler, Machado, & Neufeldt, 1994; Lambert & Arnold, 1987). In all of these cases, supervisors have monitored the counselors' conformity to the prescribed behavior. In their discussion of training at the Vanderbilt project, Henry, Strupp, and their colleagues (Henry, Strupp, Butler, Schacht, & Binder, 1993) reported that indeed, manualized training increased therapists' proficiency with and use of the time-limited dynamic therapy skills delineated in the manual. They further stated that the supervisor who was most effective stopped the videotapes regularly and delivered feedback on performance of specific skills (Henry et al., 1993). This is consistent with the expert authority model. However, they also found that those therapists who conformed most closely to the manuals were less warm and more hostile with clients than they had been prior to training (Henry et al., 1993). Manuals are currently used not just with experienced therapists but in academic training programs (Lambert & Ogles, 1988) as a means of transmitting empirically based counseling methods, and supervision consists of ensuring counselors accurate demonstration of the specified techniques at an appropriate pace.

Research on supervision, while not always supportive of the manualized training approaches, nonetheless confirms that most supervision is currently conducted in a top-down fashion. In analyses of interaction between supervision participants, Holloway and her colleagues (Holloway, 1982; Holloway, Freund, Gardner, Nelson, & Walker, 1989; Holloway & Wolleat, 1981; Nelson & Holloway, 1990) demonstrated that the supervisor maintains relational control. This emphasizes the role of the supervisor as expert. A significant problem with the idea of supervisor as expert, however, arises in the context of both supervisee and client differences from the European-American population on which most research is based (Bernard & Goodyear, 1992; Brown & Landrum-Brown, in press). How can the supervisor be an expert with all clients and all therapists within our diverse, multicultural society?

Constructivist Approaches to Supervision

Holloway (1995) acknowledged that each supervisory interaction involves a relationship among the client's, the counselor's, and the supervisor's personal and cultural characteristics and perceptions. Because of the uniqueness inherent in each relationship, practice-based models of supervision have developed. While the supervisor continues to hold the relational control for the most part, the supervisee's own experience — that is, her construction of the events in an individual session — becomes the focus for interaction.

Kagan's (1980, 1983) model, Interpersonal Process Recall, initially an approach to psychotherapy, developed into a collaborative supervision approach. Kagan identified participants as the best authority on their own dynamics and the best interpreter of their own experience (1980, pp. 279–280). After a counseling session, supervisors immediately met with counselors, who described their own intentions and experiences in the session. Discussion of the session proceeded on that basis, with the counselors' own exploration and examination of their work encouraged by their supervisors.

A second thread of practice-based supervision developed out of the psychoanalytic model. Parallel process, what Schön (1983, 1987) called the hall of mirrors, describes the reenactment of the therapy session within the supervision session. Documented in a case study by Friedlander, Siegel, and Brenock (1989), parallel-process supervision allows the supervisor and counselor to reconstruct the dynamics of the counseling session by examining and interpreting their own interaction (Ekstein & Wallerstein, 1972).

Skovholt and Rønnestad (1992a, 1992b), in a 6-year qualitative study of counselors and therapists, described the evolution of practitioner thinking throughout the professional lifespan. As Polkinghorne (1992) predicted, these practitioners reflected continuously on their personal and clinical experiences in order to develop a unique approach to each client. Those who did not reflect, who tried instead to base their practice entirely on a single, well-researched method, tended to grow discouraged and sometimes left the profession altogether. With that knowledge in mind, Rønnestad and Skovholt (1993) recommended that supervisors resist the temptation to tell beginning counselors what to do. Instead, they suggested, the supervisors' task is to support the therapists' reflections on their new experiences with clients.

In a further elaboration of this idea, Neufeldt, Iversen, and Juntunen (1995) proposed a model for supervision that incorporated the ideas of Schön (1987) for the education of the reflective practitioner. Supervisors, in this model, encourage supervisees to develop hypotheses about their clients, based on interaction with the particular client as well as prior knowledge and clinical experience. They test these with moment-by-moment interventions in sessions. Each client's response to an intervention is examined in light of the counselor's hypotheses. Supervision facilitates an analysis of the events in session that gradually constructs both a picture of the client and an effective means of working with the client.

Approaches Combining Modernist and Constructivist Principles

Several important and influential models incorporate both modernist and constructivist principles. It was initially assumed that a supervisee's personal experience with counseling would enable him or her to construct a means of interacting effectively with clients. To that end, counselors in training were required to participate either in individual therapy (as in psychoanalysis) or in the personal encounter groups (in humanistic approaches) that often served as supervision groups in the late 1960s and early 1970s (Bernard & Goodyear, 1992). While this model was constructivist in its provision of experiences, it was authoritarian in its assumption that a single approach, such as psychoanalysis or Gestalt therapy, was appropriate for all clients.

Several supervisory approaches developed with a cross-theoretical emphasis. The developmental approaches, described by Stoltenberg (1981), Loganbill, Hardy, and Delworth (1982), Blocher (1983), and Stoltenberg and Delworth (1987) have dominated thinking about supervision of counselors in trainng for the past 15 years. In a constructivist fashion, they rejected the idea that one supervisory strategy would be effective with all trainees. In this model, supervisors were expected to assess each trainee and deliberately match supervision strategies to the counselors' developmental level during training (Holloway, 1992; Stoltenberg & Delworth, 1987). In a modernist fashion, however, assessment relied almost entirely on the idea that year of training dictated level of development and was supported by research on the preferences (Heppner & Roehlke, 1984; Worthington, 1987) and case conceptualization skills (Borders, 1989) of beginners. The notion that group norms can suggest how to work with individuals is in opposition to social constructivism (Polkinghorne, 1992).

Holloway (1995) recently presented a systems approach to supervision that incorporates both constructivist and modernist assumptions. She attends to the unique supervisory relationship in constructivist fashion with an emphasis on contextual factors. Among the contexts she defines are the institution in which supervision is taking place and the personal characteristics and coping styles of the client, counselor, and supervisor. At the same time, consistent with her own research, she places the supervisor in firm control of the relationship and defines the supervisor as the translator of theory and research to practice (p. 2).

PRINCIPLES OF SOCIAL CONSTRUCTIVIST SUPERVISION

Each of these models has illustrated elements of social constructivism. As yet, however, no one has articulated the social constructivist approach to supervision. Here I explain its basic principles.

Principle 1
Supervision Changes in Each Context

Like all interpersonal events, supervision takes place within a context. The large context is the view of psychotherapy within the society as a whole and the changing nature of service delivery, for example, the growth of managed care. In addition, the social context within which supervision occurs is the culture of its participants. Holloway (1995) explicitly describes supervision as a relationship that differs across individual counselors (supervisees), supervisors, clients, and training institutions or agencies. By its very nature, the context dictates the nature and rules of supervision.

Recognition of cultural differences within European and American societies has contributed substantially to the development of social constructivist approaches to knowledge within psychology. This is particularly evident when a supervisor, counselor, and client differ in terms of race, ethnicity, gender, sexual orientation, and/or religious beliefs. When a male African American supervisor with a fundamentalist Christian background, for instance, is assigned to supervise an Asian American woman for couples counseling of Jewish male homosexuals in a committed relationship, the situation is very difficult. In that instance, the constructivist might encourage case assignment to another supervisor. Cross-cultural supervision relationships with less vivid value conflicts occur frequently and can be handled effectively if each participant attends to the cultural context. The same African American supervisor, for instance, could be an enormous resource for the same Asian American as she works with a struggling European American teacher in a Christian school for young male African Americans. In that instance, cultural differences within the supervisor-counselor-client triad enable more effective cross-cultural counseling.

The training program or agency provides the general context within which supervision occurs. Rønnestad (personal communication, September 22, 1994) stated that the "total learning environment" is important to the supervision process in various ways. He commented that the "atmosphere, the setting in which the learning will occur, the culture of the institution, is highly impactful in terms of allowing the process to evolve uninterruptedly." He added, "Tom and I were struck by high levels of panic, different kinds of requirements that they have which are so pervasive that they carry them with them into the supervisory situation." Training programs differ in both theoretical approach and the degree to which research and practice are valued. Supervision sometimes occurs, for instance, in research-oriented academic institutions where clinical interests are not valued (Bernstein & Kerr, 1993) and clinical work and clinical supervisors are seen as secondary to research and researchers (Neufeldt, 1993). Agencies, on the other hand, differ in terms of funding, number of sessions allowed, and clientele served. Supervision may occur in a hospital or community agency where the requirements of the agency clientele, organizational structure and climate, and professional ethics and standards may conflict (Holloway, 1995).

In turn, supervisors' age, training, life experience, and professional experience as therapists and as supervisors influence their response to trainees. Likewise, the client's problem and the counselor's experience influence the interaction. If the client is in crisis, for example, the trainees' desire for directive supervision intensifies (Tracey, Ellickson, & Sherry, 1989).

The characteristics, personal values, and personal style of the individual client, the individual therapist, and the individual supervisor, as well as current events in the personal life of each, provide the particular context in which supervision occurs (Holloway, 1995; Neufeldt et al., 1995). Among these characteristics, the age, training, and professional and life experience of supervisees (Skovholt & Rønnestad, 1992a) influence their willingness to take direction and think through dilemmas and their ability to understand their clients experiences. Numerous models (e.g., Hogan, 1964; Loganbill et al., 1982; Rønnestad & Skovholt, 1993; Stoltenberg, 1981; Stoltenberg & Delworth, 1987) have focused on the developmental level of the counselor, particularly the individual in early training. In a study of a particular form of cognitive development among counselors, Holloway and Wampold (1986) differentiated counselors' abilities to conceptualize cases on the basis of cognitive complexity. Without attention to these differences, the constructivist supervisor is ineffective.

In discussing the process in which the therapist and supervisor engage, Rønnestad (personal communication, September 22, 1994) stated that it is "likely that there is a strong impact of personality upon actors engaged in this process and the level of intensity and profoundness. I can certainly imagine that there are things detrimental to this process." Certainly an authoritarian, didactic supervisor differs from a collegial, permissive one, and each interacts differently with an anxious, dependent trainee and a relaxed, self-motivated one to construct knowledge of the therapeutic process. A reactant supervisee, for instance, may resent or resist the directive supervisor who provides highly structured supervision (Tracey, Ellickson, & Sherry, 1989). Analyses of supervisor style (Friedlander & Ward, 1984) and power and involvement (Holloway et al., 1989) show variations across supervisors of different theoretical persuasions, and these, in turn, vary with supervisees of different genders (Nelson & Holloway, 1990).

The client, of course, is the third participant in the supervision process (Holloway, 1995). The difficulty of the particular case and the level of client improvement affect the supervisor's response to the trainee (Rounsaville, O'Malley, Foley, & Weissman, 1988; Strupp, Butler, & Rosser, 1988; Ward, Friedlander, Schoen, & Klein, 1985). A client in crisis precipitates directive supervision sessions (Tracey et al., 1989). Clearly, clients whose problems and experiences touch on those of either the therapist or the supervisor affect supervision. As a young therapist, I did co-therapy with a couple. The wife's emotional report that her mother had recently killed herself occurred within a month of my own father's suicide. My reaction to the counseling session established a client and therapist context, from which my supervisor worked to help me to construct an understanding of the session. He responded empathically to me, and when I was ready, he helped me to examine how my feelings interacted with the client's very different feelings in the session.

Perhaps the quintessential theory that attends to the elements contributed by counselor, client, and supervisor is the theory of parallel process. In that model, the relationship between client and counselor provides the context in which supervision occurs. In supervision the counselor imitates the client's earlier behavior, and together, the counselor and supervisor construct a session that resembles the one constructed earlier by the client and counselor (Bernard & Goodyear, 1992; Friedlander et al., 1989). In this way knowledge of client dynamics is not described by one to the other but is developed together.

It follows that constructivist supervision should be grounded in a context and consistent with previous knowledge. The constructivist supervisor values trainees' previous work and personal experience, grasp of knowledge of psychotherapy theory, ideas and hypotheses, current understanding of the client, and the meaning they attach to therapeutic events.

Principle 2
Knowledge Is Co-constructed with the Supervisee

A constructivist view opposes the idea of the banking concept of education in which students are receptacles and teachers make deposits (Freire, 1993).

Instead, trainees and supervisors engage as collaborators in learning and teaching rather than as novices with a knowledgeable authority. They aim together to develop the therapist's ability to make sense of therapeutic events based on his or her own experience as well as that of others, to predict the consequences of therapeutic actions, and to devise new actions when the results do not match those predictions.

Constructivist supervisors must be able to tolerate the particular initial frustration of beginners who want to be given structure (Stoltenberg & Delworth, 1987; Worthington, 1987) and told how to counsel. Otherwise, they only encourage trainees' well-learned mechanistic (Pepper, 1961; Steenbarger, 1994) view of the counseling process and reinforce their reliance on universal categories (e.g., diagnoses) and external authority (i.e., expert formulas) to assess their plans and progress (Rønnestad & Skovholt, 1993). The supervisor assumes that what counselors, novices, and experienced professionals alike need is a way to think through the puzzle presented by clients (Rønnestad & Skovholt, 1993).

Principle 3
Knowledge Is Based on Personal and Professional Experience

The constructivist supervisor and counselor, while knowledgeable about theories and research in the field, collaborate and build practice knowledge on the basis of experience with individual cases. Skovholt and Rønnestad (1992a) stated that experienced therapists used both their personal and clinical experiences as the basis for practice. Particularly in cases of painful personal experiences, such as divorce, aging, illness, and the death of family members, counselors poignantly described how they reconstructed their views of human life and clinical work. As the parent of an adolescent, for instance, I have become considerably more humble about how much parents can protect their children from devastating personal experiences. In turn, that influences the way that I work with both parents and children in clinical practice.

Together counselors and supervisors examine individual counseling sessions and think through cases. In the model described by Neufeldt and colleagues (1995), each supervisor encourages supervisees to construct hypotheses, plan interventions, and use the results of their experiences with clients to make new hypotheses. In short, the supervisor teaches the reflective process (Neufeldt, Karno, & Nelson, 1996; Schön, 1983) so necessary to therapists' professional development both during training and beyond (Skovholt & Rønnestad, 1992a, 1992b).

Neufeldt and colleagues (1996) interviewed Schön, Skovholt, Rønnestad, Holloway, and Copeland, all experts on reflectivity and how it might appear in supervision. The experts indicated that reflectivity is a stance rather than an action. In a reflective stance, the therapist and supervisor examine therapist actions, emotions, and thoughts, as well as the interactions between the client and counselor. The process can be a superficial exploration or one that is profound and meaningful for the counselor.

Principle 4
The Test of Knowledge Is Pragmatic and the Result Is Clinical Wisdom

In a constructivist view, hypotheses are not tested by statistical means. They are, instead, tested in a practical situation. A hypothesis is verified when it predicts results that can be used. In Polkinghorne's (1992) words, "The kind of knowledge essential to the psychology of practice is knowledge of how to produce beneficial therapeutic results" (p. 161). Supervisors aid counselors to develop practice knowledge when they encourage them to evaluate the results of their interventions in session. Like the effective supervisor of manualized therapy, the constructivist supervisor stops the videotape or the narrative report of the counseling session to examine what has transpired. Instead of commenting on how the therapist has conformed to specified therapeutic procedures, however, the supervisor inquires about the therapist's intentions and expectations. How did the counselor decide to make that intervention then and what did he or she imagine the client would do in response? Such questions require counselors to reflect on their understanding of the client as well as the results of their own actions. Whatever the result, whether or not it was predicted, this allows learning.

Schön (1987) points out that the unexpected result, the surprise, is the occasion for new learning. Skovholt and Rønnestad's (1992a) therapists cited their failures with clients, their mistakes, as critical in the evolution of their practice knowledge. It is the surprise that causes one to reexamine one's assumptions and change course. The supervisor facilitates this. By treating unexpected results not as mistakes but as opportunities for learning something new about either the client or the counseling process, the supervisor provokes not fear of error but curiosity. In this way, the supervisor teaches the counselor not so much to perform in session as to develop a manner of thinking about work with clients.

While counselors may initially reflect on practice (Schön, 1983) in supervision, they soon learn to reflect in practice, that is, consider results and revise their strategies during the session. Or, in Polkinghorne's (1992) words, "learning to do therapy is accomplished through the successes and failures that follow actual performance" (p. 162).

Neufeldt and colleagues' (1996) experts described the results of reflection. In the short term, supervisees were expected to change both their perceptions of events and their behavior in counseling. The long-term possibilities, however, are perhaps the most interesting. Development occurs, these experts said, as reflective practitioners are increasingly able to make meaning from their experiences. Similarly, Cohn (1989) predicted a growth in clinical wisdom as a result of practice. In fact, experienced clinicians demonstrate the qualities thought to make up wisdom to a much greater degree than the general population of adults (Smith, Staudinger, & Baltes, 1994). Stone (1988) noted that supervision provides a domain involving such nontrivial factors as human context, affective experience, and personal beliefs.

The supervisor, then, responds to each counselor and each counseling event in a unique and even artful (Holloway, 1992) fashion. Supervisory success is measured pragmatically, not by the counselor's faithful demonstration of prescribed techniques but by the supervisee's growth in the ability to think clinically. Like counselors, constructivist supervisors examine the effects of their interventions on their supervisees and learn most from the unexpected.

Specific practical applications from the perspective of the model proposed by Neufeldt and colleagues (1995) are described in the next section, and each is followed by a vignette that illustrates the application with trainees. In the spirit of constructivism, I suggest these as possible examples and do not issue them as prescriptions. I assume each supervisor will develop his or her own methods of inquiry with each unique supervisee.

PRACTICAL APPLICATIONS

All work with supervisees is based on an assumption that they bring important knowledge and experience as well as personal values and characteristics to training. The initial supervision session highlights these attributes in both the supervisee and the supervisor.

Exploration of Trainee Background

Careful inquiry can elicit descriptions of trainees' personal history, racial and ethnic heritage and its role in their social experience, and beliefs and values they learned growing up and have developed since. Previous training and professional experience, how they decided to enter the field of counseling, and what strengths they believe they have to offer in their role as counselors are additional relevant factors. Exploration of some aspects of a supervisee's background might sound like this:

> SUPERVISOR: So now that I understand that you are a returning student with a background as a teacher, what else do I need to know about you that will help me as your supervisor?
>
> TRAINEE: Well, I have two school-age children, a boy and a girl. I've

been divorced for three years and I'm raising the children on my own.

SUPERVISOR: So that certainly has an impact on your priorities in training. In addition, it gives you some empathy with others in similar situations.

TRAINEE: Yes, I think so. I had a lot of therapy during that divorce, and I think that's what finally made me decide to become a counselor myself.

SUPERVISOR: So your counseling experience was a positive one?

TRAINEE: Well, the first one wasn't. But when I decided to leave the first therapist and go to a woman about my age, that made a difference. I could see how the first therapist never understood me and yet kept telling me what I should do. The second one appeared to understand me much better, and yet she encouraged me to figure out things myself. And she was a model for me and I thought I could be good at this work. Even a year after I had finished therapy, I still wanted to do it, so I went for it.

SUPERVISOR: What do you see as strengths you have that fit you for this kind of work?

TRAINEE: Well, I've been to hell and back!

SUPERVISOR: Yes.

TRAINEE: Also I must be a good listener. I'm the person all my friends come to when they want to talk over their problems.

SUPERVISOR: That's a good observation.

In this example, the supervisor explored what the trainee brought to the process of learning to be a therapist and in so doing validated the importance of previous experiences.

Encouragement of Hypothesis Development

Because supervisors supply at least as many questions as answers, they need to warn supervisees of the frustration they may experience in the process. Supervisors explain, as a third and central element of constructivist supervision, that their goal is to help counselors learn to think about clients and their work with them, not to provide specific directives about particular clients or events in therapy.

With an experienced therapist, this process can draw on hypotheses developed over years and tested in the current situation. An example of case planning with an experienced counselor follows. In this instance, the counselor is designing a treatment strategy for time-limited therapy based on his experiences with similar clients. This example is particularly pertinent to the current managed-care environment in which much counseling takes place. The counselor's hypotheses in this vignette are constructed from the client-treatment matching ideas of Larry Beutler (Beutler & Clarkin, 1990; Beutler & Gaw, 1995).

SUPERVISOR: So, Rick, you have a new case and you've seen her once?

RICK: Yes. She's a 35-year-old depressed woman but she's not showing enough sleep or appetite disturbance to make me think I should refer her for medication.

SUPERVISOR: So your first hypothesis is that you can work with her strictly in a counseling mode. Tell me your other hypotheses.

RICK: Well, in the first session I got the impression that she is very bright, rather introspective, and that she is willing to cooperate with me in whatever I suggest. She has some social support from family and friends, but she seems to be a perfectionist about work and very critical of her own performance there. Based on other perfectionists I've worked with, I think that's the area we should focus on.

SUPERVISOR: Okay. So what do you imagine might work well with her, given the constraints of the six to nine visits she's allowed?

RICK: Well, I've worked with a lot of perfectionists, and I've found it helpful to help them develop some more realistic expectations of their performance. I think we need to talk about her expectations of herself. How did she get those ideas? What use have they been to her up till now?

SUPERVISOR: Yeah, that makes sense, but of course you don't have much time to delve into her history.

RICK: No. But she seems to want to understand herself, and I don't think we will move forward until she sees where she learned such demanding standards.

SUPERVISOR: Okay. So you think you have to get a sense of how she's constructed her expectations. Then what?

RICK: Then I think we can look at the events in her current life that trigger her self-criticism and construct together some realistic responses. Because she is so hard-working and cooperative, I think she'd be willing to do that and to try out some new ways of thinking about herself at work.

SUPERVISOR: All right. So this is your own experimental research project. What happens if she refuses to consider your ideas?

RICK: Then I have to revise my idea and assume she is reactant. And that means I have to elicit more of her ideas about how to proceed.

SUPERVISOR: So in this research project, whatever the result of your hypotheses, you'll know more about how to proceed.

In this segment, the supervisor defines the counselor's case conceptualization as a series of hypotheses. By calling it a research project, the supervisor highlights the experimental nature of what the counselor is doing and defines the results as useful, whatever they are.

Interventions as Action Research

In order to carry the reflective process one step further into a model of action research (Argyris & Schön, 1974), the supervisor collaborates with the trainee to test specific hypotheses about clients. Action research in counseling is the test of the counselor's hypotheses in the actual counseling session.

To teach counselors to test hypotheses in session is at the core of constructivist supervision. If counselors can learn that all interventions are based on hypotheses about the client and the therapeutic interaction, they can regard everything that happens in session with curiosity. This is a critical shift from the anxiety-laden approach of "Did I do this right?" Rather, the question becomes "What did I learn when I said or did that?" "Was my hypothesis confirmed?" or "Do I have new information that will allows me to make a new hypothesis?"

This is a complex task for the supervisor and takes a considerable amount of time. It is not easy to convince students that we are just inquisitive, particularly in a graduate program where students are constantly evaluated in various arenas. In my early enthusiasm for this approach, I learned just how difficult it is. A novice counselor showed a videotape in class and criticized herself because she had not gotten the client to express any feelings. Hoping to deflect the student's self-criticism and turn it to reflective reasoning, I asked, "How did you decide that she needed to express her feelings?" The student came to my office afterward, burst into tears, and expressed a deep sense of failure. I recounted this incident with some puzzlement to Donald Schön, who asked me (personal communication, February 16, 1994) how she understood my questions. I said that she felt criticized. He began to ask my ideas about when someone should express feelings in therapy, and so I put out several ideas, which he then summarized as four theories. He pointed out that while I had these theories as I asked my questions, the student didn't know about them. He added that the student was correct in believing that she was being criticized, because I was challenging her assumption that expression of feelings was always a desirable goal. This was a surprising revelation for me — new information and the basis for new hypotheses about constructivist, or reflective, supervision.

At this point, my hypotheses about constructivist supervision include the following:

1. Supervisors and instructors should explain the model from the very beginning. While supervisees find it difficult to integrate this into their picture of counseling and believe that the supervisor means it, the explanation lays the groundwork for subsequent discussion of all interventions as efforts to test hypotheses.
2. Before counselors present videotapes, supervisors ask them to describe what they understand about the client's history and what their further hypotheses about the client are.
3. Counselors then describe their intentions and the particular hypotheses they were pursuing in the segment they are about to show.
4. After showing the videotape, supervisors ask what trainees learned from that experience. They include the counselor's feelings during and after the session as information learned. Then they ask what counselors would like from the supervisor and peers at this point. This process, over time, can facilitate the trainees' perception of counseling as action research about what facilitates client growth in general and this client's growth in particular.

Constructivist supervisors use their clinical knowledge to offer observations after observing a session or hearing a counselor's description. But they wait until trainees have begun to develop their own hypotheses and then add ideas as part of the search for understanding as well as future planning. In this way, they support the trainees' exploration and contribute what they know from their training and experience as an additional challenge. This is particularly effective with a group of trainees, and an example of group discussion follows:

> SUPERVISOR: Now that you've seen yourself on videotape, Jane, tell us what you were thinking and feeling during that part of the session.
> JANE: I was frustrated. I couldn't seem to get her to talk about her feelings, and yet I felt there were a lot there.
> SUPERVISOR: What made you think so?
> JANE: I don't know. Well, she just seemed so together. Here she is, an African American student on a predominantly white campus where blonde is beautiful and the beach bunny image predominates. How can she not have any feelings?
> SUPERVISOR: So it wasn't so much that you felt tension but that what she said didn't fit your hypotheses.
> JANE: Yeah, I guess so.
> SUPERVISOR: What hypotheses do the rest of you have about this?
> RICK: Well, you know, maybe she is so used to covering up her feelings

that she really doesn't know how to start. Maybe you have to
model feelings somehow.

SUPERVISOR: That's one idea. Are there others?

MARY: Maybe she really has no anxiety about the things you're talking
about like her career plans and her schoolwork. Maybe she came in
about something else and she hasn't told you why yet. What did
she say at first?

JANE: She said something about having trouble with her roommate,
but then she didn't talk about that.

BILLY: You know, one of the things that might be going on is that you
are Korean American and she is African American. Perhaps she
doesn't know whether to trust you.

JANE: You know, that's a good point. I didn't think of that. And she's
from the part of Los Angeles where the uprising took place, and
there was a lot of hostility expressed toward the Korean merchants.

SUPERVISOR: It sounds as if you have a lot of hypotheses, and they are
worth exploring.

Before you go further, you may want some additional information, for instance, a sense of her cultural identity development.
Most models suggest that some clients are at a stage where they really don't see differences and, instead, identify with the majority culture; others identify so strongly with their own racial or ethnic
group that they don't want to deal with any counselor who is not
African American and identifies as such, and still others recognize
and value the differences. Getting some sense of where she is in
these terms could be a prerequisite for further interventions; if she
were at the unaware stage, for instance, bringing up her ethnic identity would probably put her off.

Now what do you make of what we've said, Jane?

In this vignette, the supervisor encouraged the development of hypotheses and was careful to label them as such. She added some important information, and then encouraged the counselor-in-training to consider what had
been discussed in a collaborative fashion.

These applications and vignettes are clearly my constructions, based on
my understanding of research and theory and on my experiences of supervision. To this point, they have been viable strategies to use with trainees and
predictive of trainee growth in the ability to reflect on their work. As Mahoney (1995) has said, all work of educators contributes to a sense of self, which
is central to one's experience of life and to the way one functions within it. In
particular, supervisors' actions can be seen as efforts to facilitate the develop-

ment of counselors' professional selves and to teach them the reflective process to continue that development after supervision ends.

FUTURE DIRECTIONS

The model of supervision presented above must be tested. Several questions present themselves. First, does this approach lead to reflective process on the part of the supervisee? It is rather difficult to say without a means of assessing the occurrence of reflective process. Development of a device to measure reflective process in supervision is a critical next step to follow Neufeldt and colleagues' (1996) exploration of expert definitions. While this is a tricky process in a constructivist framework, we must attempt to describe reflectivity in a fashion that can be recognized and understood by others. Only then can we examine the results, in terms of supervisee reflectivity, of supervisor interventions with supervisees in a given session.

Additional questions can then be asked. What appears to precipitate reflection on the part of supervisees? Does the answer vary dramatically from one supervisee to the next? And then, in turn, how does counselor reflectivity affect the counselor's long-term growth, the counselor's behavior in session, the interaction between the client and the counselor, and the long-term growth of the client? And how is all of that measured? These are critical questions about supervision that are linked closely with research on counseling. Nelson and Poulin's chapter in this volume (Chapter 10) provides some constructivist research strategies and suggests ways to integrate qualitative and quantitative approaches to answer specific kinds of questions.

The importance of research in testing the viability of the model cannot be overemphasized. Constructivist supervisors can use these ideas, in addition to larger-scale projects, to begin action research of their own as they work with each supervisee. What are the supervisors' hypotheses and how do they pan out? This requires us to reflect on our own work with curiosity.

REFERENCES

Argyris, C., & Schön, D. A. (1974). *Theory in practice: Increasing professional effectiveness.* San Francisco: Jossey-Bass.

Bernard, J. M., & Goodyear, R. K. (1992). *Fundamentals of clinical supervision.* Boston: Allyn and Bacon.

Bernstein, B. L., & Kerr, B. (1993). Counseling psychology and the scientist-practitioner model: Implementation and implications. *The Counseling Psychologist, 21,* 136–151.

Beutler, L. E., & Clarkin, J. F. (1990). *Systematic treatment selection: Toward targeted therapeutic interventions.* New York: Brunner/Mazel.

Beutler, L. E., & Gaw, K. F. (1995). Integrating treatment recommendations. In L. E. Beutler & M. R. Berren (Eds.), *Integrative assessment of adult personality* (pp. 280–319). New York: Guilford Press.

Beutler, L. E., Machado, P. P. P., & Neufeldt, S. A. (1994). Therapist variables. In S. L. Garfield & A. E. Bergin (Eds.), *Handbook of psychotherapy and behavior change* (4th ed., pp. 229–269). New York: Wiley.

Beutler, L. E., Williams, R. E., Wakefield, P. J., & Entwistle, S. R. (1995). Bridging scientist and practitioner perspectives in clinical psychology. *American Psychologist, 50,* 984–994.

Blocher, D. H. (1983). Toward a cognitive developmental approach to counselor supervision. *The Counseling Psychologist, 11*(1), 27–34.

Borders, L. D. (1989). Developmental cognitions of first practicum supervisees. *Journal of Counseling Psychology, 36,* 163–169.

Brown, M. T., & Landrum-Brown, J. (in press). Counselor supervision: Cross-cultural perspectives. In J. G. Ponterotto, J. M. Casas, L. A. Suzuki, & C. M. Alexander (Eds.), *Handbook of multicultural counseling.* Newbury Park, CA: Sage.

Cohn, E. S. (1989). Fieldwork education: Shaping a foundation for clinical reasoing. *American Journal of Occupational Therapy, 43,* 240–244.

Ekstein, R., & Wallerstein, R. S. (1972). *The teaching and learning of psychotherapy* (2nd ed.). New York: International Universities Press.

Feixas, G. (1995). Personal constructs in systemic practice. In R. A. Neimeyer & M. J. Mahoney (Eds.), *Constructivism in psychotherapy* (pp. 305–337). Washington, DC: American Psychological Association.

Freire, P. (1993). *Pedagogy of the oppressed* (Rev. ed.) (M. B. Ramos, Trans.). New York: Continuum.

Friedlander, M. L., Siegel, S., & Brenock, K. (1989). Parallel processes in counseling and psychotherapy. *Journal of Counseling Psychology, 32,* 483–501.

Friedlander, M. L., & Ward, L. G. (1984). Development and validation of the supervisory styles inventory. *Journal of Counseling Psychology, 31,* 541–557.

Henry, W. P., et al. (1993). Effects of training in time-limited dynamic psychotherapy: Changes in therapist behavior. *Journal of Consulting and Clinical Psychology, 61,* 434–440.

Heppner, P. P., & Roehlke, H. J. (1984). Differences among supervisees at different levels of training: Implications for a developmental model of supervision. *Journal of Counseling Psychology, 31* (1), 76–90.

Hogan, R. A. (1964). Issues and approaches in supervision. *Psychotherapy: Theory, research, and practice, 1,* 139–141.

Holloway, E. L. (1982). Interactional structure of the supervision interview. *Journal of Counseling Psychology, 29,* 309–317.

Holloway, E. L. (1992). Supervision: A way of teaching and learning. In S. D. Brown & R. W. Lent (Eds.), *Handbook of counseling psychology* (pp. 177–214). New York: Wiley.

Holloway, E. L. (1995). *Clinical supervision: A systems approach.* Thousand Oaks, CA: Sage.

Holloway, E. L., Freund, R. D., Gardner, S. L., Nelson, M. L., & Walker, B. E. (1989). Relation of power and involvement to theoretical orientation in supervision: An analysis of discourse. *Journal of Counseling Psychology, 36,* 88–102.

Holloway, E. L., & Neufeldt, S. A. (1995). Supervision: Its contributions to treatment efficacy. *Journal of Consulting and Clinical Psychology, 63,* 207–213.

Holloway, E. L., & Wampold, B. E. (1986). Relation between conceptual level and counseling-related tasks: A meta-analysis. *Journal of Counseling Psychology, 30,* 227–234.

Holloway, E. L., & Wolleat, P. L. (1981). Style differences of beginning supervisors: An interactional analysis. *Journal of Counseling Psychology, 28,* 373–376.

Hoshmand, L. T. (1994). *Orientation to inquiry in a reflective professional psychology.* Albany: State University of New York Press.

Ivey, A. E. (1971). *Microcounseling: Innovations in interviewing training.* Springfield, IL: Thomas.

Ivey, A. E., Normington, C. J., Miller, D.C., Merrill, W. H., & Haase, R. F. (1968). Microcounseling and attending behavior: An approach to prepracticum counselor training. *Journal of Counseling Psychology, Monograph Supplement, 15,* 1–12.

Kagan, N. (1980). Influencing human interaction — eighteen years with IPR. In A. K. Hess (Ed.), *Psychotherapy supervision: Theory, research, and practice* (pp. 262–286). New York: Wiley.

Kagan, N. (1983). Classroom to client: Issues in supervision. *The Counseling Psychologist, 11*(1), 69–72.

Kelly, G. A. (1955). *The psychology of personal constructs.* New York: Norton.

Kelly, G. A. (1977). The psychology of the unknown. In D. Bannister (Ed.), *New perspectives in personal construct theory* (pp. 1–19). London: Academic Press.

Lambert, M. J., & Arnold, R. C. (1987). Research and the supervisory process. *Professional Psychology: Research and Practice, 18,* 217–224.

Lambert, M. J., & Ogles, B. M. (1988). Treatment manuals: Problems and promise. *Journal of Integrative and Eclectic Psychotherapy, 7,* 187–204.

Loganbill, C., Hardy, E., & Delworth, U. (1982). Supervision: A conceptual model. *The Counseling Psychologist, 10*(1), 3–42.

Mahoney, M. J. (1991). *Human change processes: The scientific foundations of psychotherapy.* New York: Basic Books.

Mahoney, M. J. (1995). Continuing evolution of the cognitive sciences and psychotherapies. In R. A. Neimeyer & M. J. Mahoney (Eds.), *Constructivism in psychotherapy* (pp. 39–48). Washington, DC: American Psychological Association.

Neimeyer, R. A. (1985). *The development of personal construct psychology.* Lincoln: University of Nebraska Press.

Neimeyer, R. A. (1995). Constructivist psychotherapies: Features, foundations, and future directions. In R. A. Neimeyer & M. J. Mahoney (Eds.), *Constructivism in psychotherapy* (pp. 11–38). Washington, DC: American Psychological Association.

Neimeyer, R. A., & Mahoney, M. J. (Eds.). (1995). *Constructivism in psychotherapy.* Washington, DC: American Psychological Association.

Neimeyer, R. A., & Neimeyer, G. J. (Eds.). (1987). *Personal construct therapy case book.* New York: Springer.

Nelson, M. L., & Holloway, E. L. (1990). Relation of gender to power and involvement in supervision. *Journal of Counseling Psychology, 37,* 473–481.

Neufeldt, S. A. (1993, August). *From private practitioner to director of a departmental training clinic: One practitioner-scientist journey.* Paper presented at the annual meeting of the American Psychological Association, Toronto.

Neufeldt, S. A., Iversen, J. N., & Juntunen, C. L. (1995). *Supervision strategies for the first practicum.* Alexandria, VA: American Counseling Association.

Neufeldt, S. A., Karno, M. P., & Nelson, M. L. (1996). A qualitative study of experts conceptualization of supervisee reflectivity. *Journal of Counseling Psychology, 43,* 3–9.

Pepper, S. C. (1961). *World hypotheses: A study in evidence.* Berkeley and Los Angeles: University of California Press.

Polkinghorne, D. E. (1992). Postmodern epistemology of practice. In S. Kvale (Ed.), *Psychology and postmodernism* (pp. 146–165). London: Sage.

Rønnestad, M. H., & Skovholt, T. M. (1993). Supervision of beginning and advanced graduate students of counseling and psychotherapy. *Journal of Counseling & Development, 71,* 396–405.

Rounsaville, B. J., O'Malley, S. S., Foley, S., & Weissman, M. M. (1988). Role of manual-guided training in the conduct and efficacy of interpersonal psychotherapy for depression. *Journal of Consulting and Clinical Psychology, 56,* 681–688.

Schön, D. A. (1983). *The reflective practitioner.* New York: Basic Books.

Schön, D. A. (1987). *Educating the reflective practitioner.* San Francisco: Jossey-Bass.

Skovholt, T. M., & Rønnestad, M. H. (1992a). *The evolving professional self: Stages and themes in therapist and counselor development.* Chichester: Wiley.

Skovholt, T. M., & Rønnestad, M. H. (1992b). Themes in therapist and counselor development. *Journal of Counseling & Development, 70,* 505–515.

Smith, J., Staudinger, U. M., & Baltes, P. B. (1994). Occupational settings facilitating wisdom-related knowledge: The sample case of clinical psychologists. *Journal of Consulting and Clinical Psychology, 62,* 989–999.

Steenbarger, B. N. (1994, April). *Context, construction, and complexity: Paradigmatic challenges to the counseling profession.* Paper presented at the annual meeting of the American Counseling Association, Minneapolis.

Stoltenberg, C. (1981). Approaching supervision from a developmental perspective: The counselor complexity model. *Journal of Counseling Psychology, 28,* 59–65.

Stoltenberg, C. D., & Delworth, U. (1987). *Supervising counselors and therapists.* San Francisco: Jossey-Bass.

Stone, G. L. (1988, August). *Clinical supervision: An occasion for cognitive research.* Paper presented at the annual meeting of the American Psychological Association, Atlanta.

Strupp, H. H., Butler, S. F., & Rosser, C. L. (1988). Training in psychodynamic therapy. *Journal of Consulting and Clinical Psychology, 56,* 689–695.

Tracey, T. J., Ellickson, J. L., & Sherry, P. (1989). Reactance in relation to different supervisory environments and counselor development. *Journal of Counseling Psychology, 36,* 336–344.

Ward, L. G., Friedlander, M. L., Schoen, L. B., & Klein, J. G. (1985). Strategic self-presentation in supervision. *Journal of Counseling Psychology, 32,* 111–118.

Worthington, E. L. (1987). Changes in supervision as counselors and supervisors gain experience: A review. *Professional Psychology: Research and Practice, 18*(3), 189–208.

CHAPTER 13

Principles of Constructivist Training and Education

Chris Lovell and Garrett J. McAuliffe

Constructivist counseling is at the core an "epistemic endeavor" (Mahoney, 1991, p. 115). Thus, its practitioners tend to make "epistemological commitments" that entail movement away from conventional, "objectivist" ways of thinking about and doing the work of the counselor toward both a new set of constructivist assumptions concerning the nature of knowledge, truth, and meaning and a new array of constructivist clinical preferences (Neimeyer, 1995). Chief among the new assumptive and practice changes to be found in this postmodern turn in counseling are a shift in emphasis "from the object of knowledge to its representation," an "abnegation" of counselor authority, a relativizing of truth (especially to social contexts), and a sense that therapeutic meaning is a "jointly constructed reality" (Gergen & Kaye, 1992, pp. 173–175).

If constructivist counseling does involve its practitioners in such (often radical) philosophical change, these questions might be asked: "How did constructivist counselors get there? How is such a new epistemology attained?" The purpose of this chapter is to discuss these questions within the dual frameworks of (1) emerging adult development theory of epistemological change and (2) the cognitive developmental approach to counselor education. (Thus, our title implicates both the education of constructivist counselors and a philosophy of education that is itself constructivist.) In the discussion, we will summarize our recent research on counselor epistemological development, a study that supplies empirical grounds for our own (tentative) paradigm of "how constructivist counselors get there."

Though writers on constructivist counseling are increasingly clear that the work demands a new epistemology, there is considerably less clarity on how such a new outlook is attained. Hoyt (1994) playfully entertains the possibility that therapists might change overnight to the new way of helping;

Mahoney (1995) suggests "lessons get learned" and an "epistemological conscience" develops; and Efran and Fauber (1995) see that many practitioners have "bumped" into constructivism, but have difficulty putting it into practice because they do not have "sophisticated" epistemologies.

Counselor difficulties with constructivism arise because "many therapists . . . are in a transitional phase" in their movement toward an "epistemological perspective," posits Fruggeri (1992, p. 41) without detailing the phasic movement. Andersen (1993), however, is somewhat more specific in his account of his own personal transformation, as he interweaves his story with a description of the changing therapeutic zeitgeist. The movement, both in historical era and in his own epistemology, was away from a romantic view of the self, which "is governed by the heart and is characterized by deep commitment to relationships, friendships, and life purposes" (p. 104). In its place came another perspective, a modernist one, where rational thought process was thought to constitute the self.

Freud, Andersen (1993) shows, started with the romantic view but finished with the thoroughly modernist assumption that the therapist's role is to help clients in their search for rational explanations and to stimulate the acquisition of a new self. Family therapists, likewise, assume "that they, through their expert understanding of a person's position in an objectively identifiable system, can intervene and change the system and the person" (Andersen, 1993, p. 305).

Moving from these and other examples of therapists who are imbued with modernism, Andersen (1993) next accounts for those nascent constructivists who bridge the modern and postmodern views. These helpers see, in a client's ability to shift old understanding of the presenting problem to new understanding, much the same dynamic inherent in a client's ability to shift selves. Thus, the goal of therapy is to help in the search "for a more useful description and understanding of a problem than what the client had before coming to therapy," a process that is nonetheless "a result of an individual cognitive act" (p. 305).

Finally, Andersen (1993) provides a snapshot of the relativistic, full constructivist view:

> A rather small proportion of contemporary psychotherapists, who hesitate to call themselves therapists, have a postmodern view of Self, in which the Self is basically seen as constituted through language and conversations. (Actually, whatever one comes to understand is, by and large, a result of the language and conversations one is *in*.) These "therapists" offer their presence and attention so that, hopefully, a new context is created. In this new context the client will talk and think about what she or he is trying to understand differently, and a more useful understanding will emerge. The client and the "therapist" are talking *together*. Such "therapists" who are collaborators have only their particular experiences

gathered over time; they are not experts. I see Harold Goolishian's and Harlene Anderson's work as belonging here (Anderson & Goolishian, 1988), as I see my own. I have myself gone through several prejudices before coming to where I am today, and I may yet go through more. (p. 305)

Andersen continues with a description of his personal odyssey and concomitant shifts in therapy orientation (biological to psychological; then, problem solving to systems change to reflecting process to a fully constructivist orientation).

What we find so notable about Andersen's (1993) account is that throughout there is not only a portrayal of historical-theoretical change toward a more accurate understanding of the dynamic properties of the self-in-the-social, but also there is a firm sense of his (and others') personal *development toward* the constructivist perspective. (Though the details of epistemological change are faint in Andersen's story, the "prejudices" he describes show striking isomorphism to stages described by cognitive developmental theory.) That therapists might move through "several prejudices" on the way to an embrace of constructivism is only implicit in other major contemporary statements on the impact the new epistemology is having on counseling and psychotherapy. Mahoney, for example, expresses convictions about the personal "conceptual/practical perturbation" that will be entailed if practitioners and policymakers are to revise provision of psychological services in the face of "constructive metatheory" (1991, p. 117).

Lyddon (1990) speculates that counselors can move more surely to the constructivist philosophy after exploring their own assumptions about the nature of human change, and Lyddon and Adamson (1992) suggest that movement to such a philosophy may be related to adult cognitive development. For Gergen (1994), the requirements of the postmodern turn will demand a "new psychologist," one who is sensitive to the relational and to the constructed nature of reality. The recurrent encounter with the pragmatics of "what really works" is what finally moves the therapist away from rigid orthodoxy toward constructivism, say DeShazer and Weakland (Hoyt, 1994). The list could go on, of course, but we rest by restating our point: Though hinted at throughout, almost nowhere in the emerging literature on the new constructivism in counseling and psychotherapy do we see an explicit rendering of the epistemological steps taken by a counselor as he or she moves toward the constructivist habit of mind.

This omission is surprising in view of the abundant literature — dating to the early sixties — on adult cognitive development, a literature that includes in many instances descriptions of a developmental end point where persons assume a philosophical stance, an epistemology, that sounds remarkably like the "new constructivism." There is an exception to this state of neglect, however, and that is to be found in Rosen's (1991) trenchant application of the cognitive developmental theory of William Perry (1970) to the puzzle of how counselors might come to make a change in epistemology toward the "constructivist perspective." In the next section, we turn to Rosen, Perry, and others who chart developmental movement in epistemology.

ADULT COGNITIVE DEVELOPMENTAL THEORY AND CONSTRUCTIVISM

Mahoney's (1995) poetic sense of the "complexities of developmental processes" (p. 396), where persons in transition are like pilgrims, echoes one (unidentified) psychologist's description of Perry's (1970) developmental scheme as an "'epistemological *Pilgrim's Progress*'" (cited in Perry, 1970). In Perry's scheme of adult development, the "progress" is through epistemological positions from which a person orients himself toward knowing, valuing, and acting. Drawing on Piaget's (Inhelder & Piaget, 1958) genetic epistemology, Perry researched the structural properties of individuals' epistemologies and found patterns that, over time, changed in the direction of increased complexity, differentiation, and adaptiveness. Like Piaget, Perry (1970) assumed the social origins of these developing epistemologies (p. 204); his focus, though, was on the individual's orientation.

Perry's theory is but one of several that offer promising explanations of how counselors might "get to" a constructivist epistemology. Harvey, Hunt, and Schroder (1961), for example, saw that successive stage changes in "conceptual systems" can eventuate in an individual psychological system where a person moves away from an undifferentiating, subjectivist bias and obtains "a more veridical perception" of the diverse social forces influencing how persons construct their standards. Though persons "do not generally exhibit an alacrity for conceptual transformation" (Mahoney, 1991, p. 115), Harvey and colleagues (1961) show how those who do move to "high-concept" reasoning have a deepened sense of the relational and constructed nature of reality.

For Kohlberg (1981), likewise, higher-stage reasoning involves the ability to track and coordinate the viewpoints of each individual in a social situation with a simultaneous ability to understand how the group, or larger social system, has its own meanings, *sui generis,* and how those social meanings influence individual meanings. Kohlberg's social interactionist perspective (grounded in Dewey, Mead, and Piaget) is echoed by Loevinger (1976) when she draws on Adler and Sullivan to emphasize the person interacting with the social environment. In her sequence of stages, it is only after a rather dramatic cognitive change, a "transformation of motives" (1976, p. 418), that the person-in-the-social finally comes, recursively, to know the person-as-the-social.

In Perry's (1970) scheme, the radical epistemological transformation is described as a "reperception of all knowledge as contextual and relativistic" (p. 109). Thus, the self, having undergone such a developmental transformation, perceives both itself and other selves as coupled to social context. Somewhat ironic in the discovery of the socially relativized self, however, is a simultaneous new understanding that people do not have selves that are "givens," but rather (after Dewey) selves are "works in progress." Such selves are (on this transformed view), therefore, amenable to the socially contextualized set of meanings that constructivist therapists see as change-provoking (as in Andersen's [1993] earlier-cited exegesis).

It is the description in Perry's (1970) work of epistemological movement toward relativizing knowledge, self, and the social that Rosen (1991) found useful in describing the development of the constructivist therapist. Drawing on Prochaska's (1984) earlier speculations, Rosen applied Perry's terms ("dualism," "multiplicity," and "relativism") to counselors; it is the relativist therapists, he says, "that have evolved to the point of acknowledging the genuine pluralistic and contextual character of knowledge" (Rosen, 1991, p. 164).

Perry (1970) actually finds the onset of a relativist outlook to occur somewhat earlier than the end point of "contextual" relativism. For certain of his intellectual progeny (Belenky, Clinchy, Goldberger, & Tarule, 1986), this onset of social "connected knowing" can have an epistemological valence of its own, in contrast to "separate knowing." However, according to Belenky and colleagues, it is with the attainment of "constructed knowing" (a state that appears similar to Perry's contextual relativism) that persons are able to coordinate the complex interactions of the social ("connected") with the individual ("separate").

The complex mental operations described by the foregoing several writers on adult cognitive development are also discussed by many other contemporary theorists. For our purposes, however, perhaps no account of adult developmental movement in thought is more apposite than that of another of Perry's successors, Robert Kegan; the movement he depicts is specifically "constructive" development (1982), and the end point is explicitly a "postmodern" achievement (1994). At the ultimate stage, or "order of consciousness," there is a full attainment of the ability to cognize concepts such as "self" or "society" as constructed abstractions (often with ideological overtones), and to apprehend that notions of the self-authoring and self-regulating properties of the self are informed by a "sense of our relationships and connections as prior to and constitutive of the individual self" (1994, p. 351).

Though Kegan's (1994) research finds that very few adults reach the final stage in his model (pp. 191–197), he and his colleagues have determined that on the way from the rigid concreteness and nondiscriminating subjectivism of the lower stages, through the ideologies of modernism, to the final constructivist stance of postmodernism there are measurable, intermediary steps (Lahey, Souvaine, Kegan, Goodman, & Felix, 1988). (Again, we wish to draw attention to the similarity between the empirically derived "evolving self" described by Kegan [1982, 1994] and the movement through "several prejudices" outlined by Andersen [1993].) While with Kegan we would agree it is improbable that any curriculum for adults can stimulate development for all *to* the final, "full" constructivist, orientation, we venture in this chapter that a sound curriculum for counselors can at least prompt movement *toward* constructivism. In the next section, we outline some promising — but not explicitly *developmental* — notions about helping adults toward the constructivist epistemology.

CONVENTIONAL CONSTRUCTIVIST EDUCATION METHODS

To propose a "constructivist counselor education" carries no little irony; seeking to build such on an epistemology that disavows the centrality of any method, that guards against reification of knowledge-process, and that is often engaged in the business of radical doubt, where "givens" of all kinds are deconstructed, is a search that risks yielding a shaky edifice indeed. Though counseling may lately be encountering the constructivist "revolution," the field of education — in both its philosophical musings and in the practical matters of delivering instruction — has largely worked through methodological conflict, and has (over the century since Dewey's initial constructivist insights and subsequent experiments) formulated and tested what seem to be viable approaches.

Duckworth (1986), while acknowledging the irony of "constructivist method," asserts that the constructivist teacher helps people construct their own knowledge by doing two things: First, the teacher provides people with authentic experiences, replicating as closely as possible those phenomena under consideration, and, second, elicits from the students their thinking about these experiences. The teacher asks over and over (and the students learn to ask each other) "What do you mean?", "Why do you think that?", or says "I don't quite get it." Within the constructivist classroom, a culture is created where the students share with the teacher "the responsibility of making sure they understand each other" (p. 489).

Several desirable outcomes are realized in a constructivist classroom, as Duckworth (1986) shows (and has researched): Students learn to think more clearly; the students themselves determine what is important; and they come to depend on themselves. In attaining such outcomes, students need to have "the powerful experience of having their ideas taken seriously, rather than simply screened for correspondence to what the teachers wanted" (p. 487).

Structure promotive of such experience would seem to be a key element in any education for counselors that might be called constructivist. Duckworth captures movement away from what we have come to call an "authority constructing" orientation in students of counseling:

> Learners come to recognize knowledge as a human product, since they have produced their own knowledge and they know that they have. What is written in a book becomes viewed as somebody else's creation, a creation produced just as they created their own. Its origin is not of another order. By contrast, most students — adults and children — believe "knowledge" to be an absolute, which some people have caught on to, and which they, if they are smart enough, will be able to learn from someone who has caught on. (p. 488)

We see achievement of such movement as desirable for our students, but we are cautious about "overchallenge." How easy it is to come across to the authority-constructing student as a teacher who abdicates responsibility by relativizing knowledge!

For Schön (1987), encouraging reflection on another's experience in an effort to understand is key to a constructivist education. However, for Schön second-order "frame reflection" is essential to a constructivist counselor education (he writes of psychoanalytic training, but his discussion of "two psychoanalytic worldmakers" is easily generalized to the education of other helpers):

> In order to come to agreement, they would each have to try to enter into the other's world to discover the things the other has named and constructed there and appreciate the kind of coherence the other had created. Each would have to try to understand the meanings of his own terms in the other's world and identify in his own world the perhaps (odd and unexpected) things and relations that corresponded to the other's terms. In such a process of frame reflection, each might discover how arguments compelling to him seemed utterly inconclusive to the other. (p. 230)

Thus, the object lesson, over and again in the constructivist counselor classroom, is around reflection on process ("frames"), fully as much or even more than it is about the content ("the facts") of the other's position.

Duckworth's (1986) culture of understanding and Schön's (1987) reflective practice are examples of ways constructivist teachers can enhance classroom practice. Though the intent of such constructivist "teacher interventions" is often not overtly developmental, the practices clearly seem likely to stimulate epistemological change in some students.

At this juncture, the reader may well be heard to utter quietly (or loudly!), "But, wait. All of this, listening deeply to the other, making an effort to understand not only the content but the process, and more, all of this sounds like what we do in counselor education anyway!" To this, we would respond, "Yes, we agree." For us, the statement reveals the second irony of any purported "constructivist counselor education": Much of what we already do in our counselor education classrooms is probably "constructivist."

Indeed, an irony of the same kind has probably been uncovered by some readers who have, in encountering the *chef d'oeuvre* of the writing about the ostensible "paradigm shift" represented by constructivist counseling, responded thus: "So what else is new? Joining with the client deeply? Dropping the pretense to expertise toward another's meaning, another's being? Understanding that meanings intertwine? That changes come when one's story is finally heard at a deep level, when meanings are shifted from problem saturation to opportunity orientation? Where have these writers been?" To these reader-colleagues we would offer a reminder that not all of the writers in their professional formation have escaped tutelage in some of the more restrictive and directive approaches; not all have heard well the lessons of Kohutian and Rogerian empathy.

To return to the search for methods that might help shape the constructivist counselor's classroom, a brief definition of such a classroom may well be "a place where the teacher mainly promotes the conversation" (R. Hayes, personal communication, November 4, 1994). In doing this, the constructivist teacher would probably model those same attitudes and behaviors described by White and Daniels (1994) as characteristic of a constructivist counselor's role: "managing conversations rather than managing lives" (p. 110), helping "to broaden and flex perspectives" (p. 109) by changing rigid interpretations through the examination of assumptions and attributions, nurturing multiple perspectives on a problem, and dropping the posture of expert and assuming a position of "not knowing." Indeed, much of what is described in the literature of constructivist counseling practice can be appropriated for, and modeled in, the constructivist counseling classroom. That such instructional methods might actually stimulate epistemological change is only a speculation, however, and the very real possibility exists that students exposed to such instruction might only take away "technique" and not assimilate at the level of "new attitude." In contrast to such speculative efforts, attitude, or assumption, change as a consequence of the *cognitive developmental* approach to counselor education has moved well beyond speculation. In the following section, we briefly: (a) outline the history of the cognitive developmental approach; (b) describe a modest program of research we have undertaken, the aim of which is better to understand the epistemological reasoning of our own students of counseling as they grow toward constructivism; and (c) sketch prototypical epistemic orientations of students of counseling, a sketch that might serve as a conceptual basis for developmental instructional intervention.

COGNITIVE DEVELOPMENTAL COUNSELOR EDUCATION

A major focus of higher education has long been epistemological (Brubacher, 1977), and deliberate efforts toward stimulating the epistemological, or more broadly, cognitive, stage development of college students have been mapped since the 1970s (Pascarella & Terenzini, 1991). In counselor education, early concern for the purposeful psychological development of counselors as part of their professional training prompted some counselor educators to recommend specific opportunities for the trainee to receive psychotherapy as an element of the training program, often as part of supervision (Carkhuff, 1969; McGowan & Schmidt, 1962; Rogers, 1951). Indeed, the counselor trainee's own personal growth was seen by some as more important than the acquisition of particular technical skills (Boyd, 1978; Rogers, 1951, 1975). However, with the arrival of the cognitive developmental way of reckoning "growth," counselors-in-training were now found to undergo *cognitive* structural change, not just (or even) personality or behavioral change (Blocher, 1983; Knefelkamp & Cornfeld, 1977; Logenbill, Hardy, & Delworth, 1982; Stoltenberg, 1981; Stoltenberg & Delworth, 1987).

Applications of cognitive developmental theory to the practice of counselor education, though increasingly widespread during the 1980s, were not immune to criticism. Counselor trainee models of development were seen as lacking sufficient complexity (Miller, 1982), without adequate validity (Holloway, 1987), and inappropriately grounded in empirical research that had taken trainee level of experience as a dominant independent variable, rather than measuring trainee cognitive level (Borders, Fong, & Neimeyer, 1986). Criticism notwithstanding, the decade ended with a consensus statement that empirical evidence does show regular progression in cognitive development in counselor trainees (Gelso & Fassinger, 1990).

Research on the Constructing Counselor

Consider the verbatim responses of two graduate students in a program of counselor education who were asked to give a brief written definition of counseling:

> My professor in Intro said counseling is not just giving advice, it is making sure the person is on the right developmental path. I agree with this but I also think the counselor should be careful not to miss the advising part. (Student 1)

> Counseling is a communicative, committed, focused partnership between individuals aimed at gaining new and better perspectives. It is an endeavor of give and take which strives to assist the client in utilizing

his or her own strengths (however unrecognized they may initially be) in improving upon or coming to terms with a given outcome or situation. (Student 2)

Both students may be seen to be engaged in constructing definitions of counseling. It is only in the constructions of the latter student, however, that one can see outlines of a way of regarding the world of the counselor that in itself might be called "constructivist." With the accent on perspectivism and authorship, even co-authorship (rather than authority), with an air of tentativeness (rather than absoluteness), and with a sense of the socially situated nature of the client (rather than an emphasis on the "problem"), student two exemplifies the counselor who seems grounded in the kind of constructivist epistemology described at places throughout the present volume as a desirable framework for practice.

The student voices cited above—the one a Perry "dualist," the other a "contextual relativist"—are part of a data set we have collected as part of an ongoing qualitative research investigation (at this point cross-sectional in design). The intent of the study is eventually to portray how cognitive structures evolve in the thought of counselor trainees as they confront important issues of counseling practice.

Our method emphasizes "naturalistic generalization" (Stake, 1995). First, we locate students of counseling on both Perry's (1970) scheme and in Kegan's (1982) developmental model. (Assessment is done through use of the Learning Environment Preferences [Moore, 1987], and the Subject/Object Interview [Lahey et al., 1988].) Then, through the use of constant comparative analytic technique (Glaser & Strauss, 1967), we take salient bits of participant reasoning from extreme, or paradigmatic, examples (as in our two voices above) for inductive comparison in an attempt to find any patterns or themes that characterize epistemic thought about counseling at the particular stage.

For example, Student 1, we found, favors an epistemology concerned for regnancy of meaning, for "making sure the person is on the right . . . path," with a bias toward agreeing with authority. These concerns (among others) we find to be generally characteristic (in this student and in others we have assessed at a similar developmental level) of counselors who are oriented to the world through "dualism."

Student 2, our constructivist, was actually found to be somewhat short of full constructivism. Though this student—here (in the present quoted response to the "What is counseling?" question) and elsewhere—does in fact seem to hold "the basic constructivist perspective that humans actively create their own particular reality" (Hayes, this volume), there is still a sense of reality negotiated between individuals, rather than a full embrace of the notion that reality is co-constructed.

Through the method of comparing maximized examples, rudimentary profiles of counselor student "epistemic subjects" (Kitchener, 1986) are now apparent. The "ways of knowing" of these prototypical subjects we label "epistemic orientations." The four orientations, and qualitative themes characteristic of students of counseling at such orientations, were adduced from transcripts of student practice sessions, written responses, semi-structured interviews, and recognition task tests (Lovell & McAuliffe, 1994, 1995; McAuliffe, 1994a, 1994b).

Four Epistemologies

The four orientations are named "authority constructing," "subject constructing," "auto-constructing," and "full" or "dialectical constructing." The orientations, and the corresponding epistemic structures held by the students, were informed by the constructive developmental work of Basseches (1984), Belenky and colleagues (1986), Kegan (1982, 1994), Kohlberg (1971), Loevinger (1976), Mustakova (1995), and Perry (1970). Each way of knowing can be described as "embedded" in a particular set of assumptions about the nature of knowing, a sort of taken-for-granted heuristic that establishes "the way things are known."

From the authors' research with graduate counseling students, a key shift from a "non (or less)-constructivist" to a "constructivist" counseling orientation has been identified. The authority-constructing and subject-constructing orientations seem to be guided by an essentialist search for concrete, objective entities. The one generally holds that counseling is known by experts and the job is to replicate that knowledge (authority constructing); the other (subject constructing) figures that counseling is a multitude of many categories and is done by many persons, with each category and each person holding a kind of subjective "rightness." But a counselor epistemology based on undifferentiated, mutualistic rightness begins to break down in the face of the pragmatics of helping; rightness is seen to be highly contextual, with no context more salient than that of the individual knower's constructions. This epistemological shift toward recognizing the constructed nature of knowledge can be described variously as a "flip" toward "relativistic" (Perry, 1970), "procedural" (Belenky et al., 1986), "system-creating" (Kegan, 1994), and "conscientious" (Loevinger, 1976) knowing.

Following Kegan (1994), this beginning constructivist world view is called "auto-constructing," or "self-authoring," to represent the individual's ability to generate a relatively self-chosen point of view. In its early stages, such an awareness of the constructed nature of knowledge might be called "naive constructivism"; the self-authoring individual tends to believe that he or she is the creator of meaning and that there is a "best" set of procedures for doing the work of counseling. The auto-constructing knower is identified with his or her method to the point where he or she does not recognize the social construction of knowledge and does not seek ongoing dialogue with various texts (persons included) for the purpose of co-construction of reality.

Recognition of the social construction of reality is labeled here the "full constructivist," or "dialectical," orientation. Here, there is growing counselor insight about the social origin of the self where "individual choice" may have some therapeutic operational utility but not much explanatory power; awareness of the "boundedness" of freedom dawns. When a student regularly expresses such a tendency in the intellectual, professional, and interpersonal domains, it might be said that he or she knows in a full constructivist fashion. From the constructive developmental perspective, such a tendency is the culmination of qualitative epistemological changes that require development-enhancing environments.

In adapting adult development theory and research to constructivist counselor education, differences in students' readiness to understand social construction and to practice in a constructivist fashion must be taken into account. Research on counselor development (Benack, 1988; Kegan, 1994; Neukrug & McAuliffe, 1993) indicates that counseling students' readiness for constructivist knowing varies. At one extreme, some students bring a relatively externalized locus and an absolutist frame of reference. This orientation might be called "nonconstructivist." In contrast, some show the tolerance for ambiguity and the interest in co-construction that characterize constructivist counseling.

Models of adult development can guide counselor educators in their assessment of student readiness for constructivist counseling. By having a general sense of a student's constructive tendency, the counselor educator can "match," or provide support for, the current way of knowing. Correspondingly, the educator can trigger "disequilibration" (Piaget, 1965) by "mismatching," that is, by challenging the limits of that way of knowing. Examples of hypothetical, developmentally specific instructional interventions are:

The Authority-Constructing Student. Matching would focus on externality, for example, with behavior modification. Instructor: "Practice the exploration phase of the interview for at least 15 minutes. Let's role-play it now." Mismatching would challenge the student to differentiate his or her own perspective from the client's. Instructor: "How might the client see this? How might she have mixed feelings about this issue? I myself have struggled with balancing my needs and a partner's."

The Subject-Constructing Student. Matching would be nonauthoritarian, multiplistic, and emotionally "close." Instructor: "It seems that there is no right course. Everything seems equally valid. Let's look at the pluses and minuses." Mismatching challenges the subjectivist student to know and act on his or her own, thought-out preferences. Instructor: "Well, it seems that you are inclined to let the client decide among a few options. Will you actually do that?" Student: "What would you do?" Instructor: "Suppose I said, 'Tell the client to join a youth group.' How could you argue against that?"

The Auto-Constructing Student. Matching entails support for a self-derived center of meaning-making and procedure. Instructor: "I hear the firmness in your voice. You've really made a quite rational choice." Mismatching seeks to challenge separateness and autochthonous thought. Instructor: "How might you think of the client's situation developmentally? Psychodynamically? Socioculturally? How are you influenced by your gender assumptions? How might someone from a different culture see this? What other constructions of this situation might there be?" Instructor (in a self-critique): "I feel invested in the cognitive approach, but I've been too closed to the object relations view. I think it's my style to take action, even compulsively. So let's work together on generating alternative perspectives." The instructor takes multiple perspectives, welcomes diversity, considers power in relationships, and encourages the student to do the same.

The Full, Dialectical–Constructing Student. Matching is done through empathic pacing. Instructor: "It seems like you're weighing two opposing ways of handling the situation: the impulse to lash out, and your need to hear and to try to integrate this contradiction to your cherished notion. It seems that you even seek out contradiction. How ironic!"

With such combinations of support and challenge (Sanford, 1962), and with "holding environments" comprising confirmation and contradiction (Kegan, 1982), the developmental counselor educator can occasion epistemological change. While such "holding" seems tailored to supervision and other individual contact, classroom applications are not impossible. Indeed, Bloom's (1956) advice that a teacher, in employing classroom questioning, cycle through lower-order questioning to higher-order questioning might be extended to a more comprehensive vision of a constructivist counselor education classroom where the cycle is through an array of activities (lecture, "buzz groups," individual reports, action projects, etc.) designed to reach learners at all epistemological orientations.

CONCLUSION

Teachers educated in the work of Perry (1970) and Belenky and her associates (1986), can use the idea of different epistemologies or ways of knowing in their own work. Teaching the ways of knowing ought to be part of teacher education programs. (Lyons, 1990, p. 176)

We concur with Lyons and we would move her assertions over into the realm of counselor education, not the least of our motives being a sense that exposure to ideas of "different epistemologies" can itself stimulate development toward constructivism in our students.

We acknowledge that ideas of different epistemologies are already taught in certain programs of counselor preparation (primarily, it appears, in colleges of education). However, as a consequence of the earlier-noted lacunae in most contemporary discussions of how counselors "get to" constructivism, we suspect that adult cognitive development theory is not widely given exposure (credence?) in psychology departments, in psychiatric training, and in social work programs. This is unfortunate; today, when counselors are confronted with the challenge of committing to the "developmentalist/constructivist view" (Byrne, 1995), and when counselor educators are being asked to consider the new "paradigm" (Griffin, 1993) as a basis for their profession, it would seem that any effort directed at a constructivist counselor education should be grounded in part on adult cognitive, or epistemological, developmental theory.

REFERENCES

Andersen, T. (1993). See and hear, and be seen and heard. In S. Friedman (Ed.), *The new language of change: Constructive collaboration in psychotherapy* (pp. 303–322). New York: Guilford Press.

Anderson, H., and Goolishian, H. (1988). Human systems as linguistic systems: Preliminary and evoking ideas about the implications for clinical theory. *Family Process, 27,* 371–394.

Basseches, M. (1984). *Dialectical thinking and adult development.* Norwood, NJ: Ablex.

Belenky, M. F., Clinchy, B. M., Goldberger, N. R., & Tarule, J. M. (1986). *Women's ways of knowing: The development of self, voice, and mind.* New York: Basic Books.

Benack, S. (1988). Relativistic thought: A cognitive basis for empathy in counseling. *Counselor Education and Supervision, 27,* 216–232.

Blocher, D. H. (1983). Toward a cognitive developmental approach to counseling supervision. *Counseling Psychologist, 11*(1), 27–34.

Bloom, B. (Ed.). (1956). *Taxonomy of educational objectives, handbook I: Cognitive domain.* New York: David McKay.

Borders, L. D., Fong, M., & Neimeyer, G. (1986). Counseling students' level of ego development and perceptions of clients. *Counselor Education and Supervision, 30*(1), 36–49.

Boyd, J. (1978). *Counselor supervision.* Muncie, IN: Accelerated Development.

Brubacher, J. S. (1977). *On the philosophy of higher education.* San Francisco: Jossey-Bass.

Byrne, R. H. (1995). *Becoming a master counselor: Introduction to the profession.* Pacific Grove, CA: Brooks/Cole.

Carkhuff, R. R. (1969). *Helping and human relations: A primer for lay and professional helpers* (Vols. 1–2). New York: Holt, Rinehart, and Winston.

Duckworth, E. (1986). Teaching as research. *Harvard Educational Review, 56*(4), 481–495.

Efran, J., & Fauber, R. (1995). Radical constructivism: Questions and answers. In R. A. Neimeyer & M. J. Mahoney (Eds.), *Constructivism in psychotherapy* (pp. 275–304). Washington, DC: American Psychological Association.

Fruggeri, L. (1992). Therapeutic process as the social construction of change. In S. McNamee & K. Gergen (Eds.), *Therapy as social construction* (pp. 40–51). Newbury Park, CA: Sage.

Gelso, C., & Fassinger, R. (1990). Counseling psychology: Theory and research on interventions. *Annual Review of Psychology, 41,* 355–86.

Gergen, K., & Kaye, J. (1992). Beyond narrative in the negotiation of therapeutic meaning. In S. McNamee & K. Gergen (Eds.), *Therapy as social construction* (pp. 166–185). Newbury Park, CA: Sage.

Gergen, K. J. (1994). Exploring the postmodern: Perils or potentials. *American Psychologist, 49,* 412–416.

Glaser, B., & Strauss, A. (1967). *The discovery of grounded theory: Strategies for qualitative research.* Chicago: Aldine.

Griffin, B. (1993). ACES: Promoting professionalism, collaboration, and advocacy. *Counselor Education and Supervision, 33*(1), 2–9.

Harvey, O. J., Hunt, D., & Schroder, H. (1961). *Conceptual systems and personality organization.* New York: Wiley.

Holloway, E. (1987). Developmental models of supervision: Is it development? *Professional Psychology: Research and Practice, 18,* 209–216.

Hoyt, M. F. (1994). On the importance of keeping it simple and taking the patient seriously: A conversation with Steve deShazer and John Weakland. In M. F. Hoyt (Ed.), *Constructive therapies* (pp. 11–40). New York: Guilford Press.

Inhelder, B., & Piaget, J. (1958). *The growth of logical thinking from childhood to adolescence.* New York: Basic Books.

Kegan, R. (1982). *The evolving self: Problem and process in human development.* Cambridge: Harvard University Press.

Kegan, R. (1994). *In over our heads: The mental demands of modern life.* Cambridge: Harvard University Press.

Kitchener, R. F. (1986). *Piaget's theory of knowledge: Genetic epistemology & scientific reason.* New Haven: Yale University Press.

Knefelkamp, L. L., & Cornfeld, J. (1977, March). *Application of student development theory to graduate education: The developmental instruction design of a year-long counselor education curriculum.* Paper presented at the annual meeting of the American College Personnel Association, Denver.

Kohlberg, L. (1971). Stages of moral development. In C. M. Beck, B. S. Critten-den, & E. V. Sullivan (Eds.), *Moral education* (pp. 23–92). Toronto: University of Toronto Press.

Kohlberg, L. (1981). *The philosophy of moral development: Moral stages and the idea of justice.* San Francisco: Harper and Row.

Lahey, L., Souvaine, E., Kegan, R., Goodman, R., & Felix, S. (1988). *A guide to the subject-object interview: Its administration and analysis.* Cambridge, MA: Subject-Object Research Group.

Loevinger, J. (1976). *Ego development: Conceptions and theories.* San Francisco: Jossey-Bass.

Logenbill, C., Hardy, E., & Delworth, U. (1982). Supervision: A conceptual model. *Counseling Psychologist, 10*(1), 3–42.

Lovell, C. W., & McAuliffe, G. J. (1994, June). *Knowing counseling: Stage-related episte-mic structures apparent in counselor trainee discourse.* Paper presented at the annual meeting of the Society for Research in Adult Development, Amherst, MA.

Lovell, C. W., & McAuliffe, G. J. (1995, June). *Knowing counseling, part II: Stage-related epistemic structures apparent in counselor trainee discourse and work samples.* Paper presented at the annual meeting of the Society for Research in Adult Development, Montreal.

Lyddon, W. J. (1990). First- and second-order change: Implications for rationalist and constructivist cognitive therapies. *Journal of Counseling and Development, 69*(2), 122–127.

Lyddon, W. J., & Adamson, L. A. (1992). Worldview and counseling preference: An analogue study. *Journal of Counseling and Development, 71*(1), 41–47.

Lyons, N. (1990). Dilemmas of knowing: Ethical and epistemological dimensions of teacher's work and development. *Harvard Educational Review, 60*(2), 159–180.

Mahoney, M. J. (1991). *Human change processes: The scientific foundations of psychother-apy.* New York: Basic Books.

Mahoney, M. J. (1995). The psychological demands of being a constructive psycho-therapist. In R. A. Neimeyer & M. J. Mahoney (Eds.), *Constructivism in psycho-therapy* (pp. 385–399). Washington, DC: American Psychological Association.

McAuliffe, G. J. (1994a, April). *Exploring counselor trainees' meaning making: Construc-tive development, empathy, and dogmatism.* Poster session presented at the annual meeting of the American Counseling Association, Minneapolis, MN.

McAuliffe, G. J. (1994b, November). *How do they know? Applying adult development to counselor training.* Paper presented at the annual meeting of the Southern Associa-tion for Counselor Education and Supervision, Charlotte, NC.

McGowan, J., & Schmidt, L. (1962). *Counseling: Readings in theory and practice.* New York: Holt, Rinehart, and Winston.

Miller, R. (1982). Commentary-supervision: A conceptual model. *Counseling Psycholo-gist, 10*(1), 47–48.

Moore, W. S. (1987). The learning environment preferences: Establishing preliminary reliability and validity for an objective measure of the Perry scheme of intellectual development. (Doctoral dissertation, University of Maryland, College Park). *Dis-sertation Abstracts International,* 8808586.

Mustakova, E. (1995, June). *Ontogeny of critical consciousness.* Paper presented at the annual meeting of the Society for Research in Adult Development, Montreal, Canada.

Neimeyer, R. A. (1995). Constructivist psychotherapies: Features, foundations, and future directions. In R. A. Neimeyer & M. J. Mahoney (Eds.), *Constructivism in psychotherapy* (pp. 11–38). Washington, DC: American Psychological Association.

Neukrug, E. S., & McAuliffe, G. J. (1993). Cognitive development and human service education. *Human Service Education, 13,* 13–26.

Pascarella, E. T., & Terenzini, P. T. (1991). *How college affects students.* San Francisco: Jossey-Bass.

Perry, W. (1970). *Forms of intellectual and ethical development in the college years.* New York: Holt, Rinehart and Winston.

Piaget, J. (1965). *The moral judgment of the child.* New York: Free Press.

Prochaska, J. O. (1984). *Systems of psychotherapy.* Chicago: Dorsey.

Rogers, C. R. (1951). *Client-centered therapy.* Boston: Houghton Mifflin.

Rogers, C. R. (1975). Empathic: An unappreciated way of being. *The Counseling Psychologist, 5*(2), 2–10.

Rosen, H. (1991). Constructivism: Personality, psychopathology, and psychotherapy. In D. P. Keating & H. Rosen (Eds.), *Constructivist perspectives on developmental psychopathology and atypical development* (pp. 149–171). Hillsdale, NJ: Erlbaum.

Sanford, N. (1962). *The American college: A psychological and social interpretation of the higher learning.* New York: Wiley.

Schön, D. S. (1987). *Educating the reflective practitioner.* San Francisco: Jossey-Bass.

Stake, R. E. (1995). *The art of case study research.* Thousand Oaks, CA: Sage.

Stoltenberg, C. D. (1981). Approaching supervision from a developmental perspective: The counselor complexity model. *Journal of Counseling Psychology, 28,* 59–65.

Stoltenberg, C. D., & Delworth, U. (1987). *Supervising counselors and therapists.* San Francisco: Jossey-Bass.

White, H., & Daniels, L. (1994). Human systems as problem determined linguistic systems: Relevance for training. *Journal of Mental Health Counseling, 10*(1), 105–119.

CHAPTER 14

Sharpening the Critical Edge: A Social Constructionist Approach in Counselor Education

John Winslade, Gerald Monk, and Wendy Drewery

As in most other counselor education programs in New Zealand, the approach to counselor education at Waikato University historically was eclectic. Typically, the students were introduced to seven or eight counseling theories, though usually in a cursory way because of the constraints on time and resources. In the words of a participant in the counseling program in the late eighties, "we were encouraged to select the best aspects of the theories that suited our own way of working." When students were asked to articulate their philosophy of counseling, they would commonly refer to the theories about which they had been instructed, taking bits and pieces from the models that appealed to them. Often they had not thought about the implications for themselves or their clients of the approaches they were espousing.

This relatively uncritical and nonreflexive approach produced counselors who were, in our opinion, unable to consider, for example, the effects of patriarchal attitudes implicit in the counseling orientations they subscribed to and the influence of ethnic and class prejudices on their work.

Over the last few years we have moved deliberately away from an eclectic stance to teaching approaches to counseling. There have been a variety of reasons for this, some of which are signaled here but have been more fully elaborated elsewhere (Monk & Drewery, 1994). Perhaps the most important of these reasons has been the greater challenge to students to articulate the assumptions and beliefs that inform their practice and to critique the assumptions and beliefs that make up the mainstream counseling theories.

We are now focusing specifically on how the assumptions we have as counselors influence how problems and solutions are constructed within the therapeutic relationship. We want our students to think carefully about how power operates within our lives both as counselors and clients and how it can be used with integrity. Rather than teach a variety of counseling approaches in a spirit of comparison that invites students to draw a little from each, we ask them to engage with counseling theory in a deconstructive spirit.

We have found that the theory of social constructionism (Berger & Luckmann, 1966; Gergen, 1985; Harré, 1986), particularly as it has been developed in narrative therapy (White, 1989, 1991, 1995; White & Epston, 1989), affords us opportunities to engage our students with a high degree of reflexivity about their practice. Hence we have moved to concentrate a large amount of the effort in our training program on introducing our students to social constructionist theory and to a compatible narrative approach to counseling. Other approaches to counseling are introduced but not elaborated to the same extent.

THEORETICAL THREADS

Three concepts are central to what we teach our students about counseling theory and practice: discourse, positioning, and deconstruction, all with an awareness of the colonizing influences at work in our country.

Discourse

An understanding of the term *discourse* is a basic starting point in our program. We use the term to refer to the use of language as a form of social practice, following Fairclough (1992). Discourses are interrelated sets of statements or understandings that cohere around common meanings (Gavey, 1992; Hollway, 1983). Such meanings are both a product of social practices and constitutive of such practices. Discourses position individuals in power relations with one another. This use of the term *discourse* draws on the performative aspects of language. It treats discourses both as ways in which people act on the world, and as ways in which the world acts on, or constitutes, persons as individuals. Our intention is to emphasize the dynamic character of instances of language usage, and the creative potential of such activities in the shaping and *performance* of lives. After all, the shaping and performance of lives is the territory that counseling inhabits.

Social constructionist ideas about discourse are introduced by having students read newspaper articles, children's storybooks, magazines, short stories, and poems; watch videos of interactions or movie clips; share personal anecdotes. They practice the process of discourse analysis in relation to each of these text examples. Our aim is to sensitize students to the ways in which language practices characterize specific contexts. We ask them questions about the implications in a particular text for who can speak, what they can speak about, and whose voice is excluded (Fairclough, 1992; Parker, 1994) or heard only if they speak in terms that are proposed by others (Sampson, 1993).

Students practice identifying subject positions and processes by which people are objectified and marginalized. Together we notice the effects of the modern technologies of power (Foucault, 1980) in recruiting people into self-evaluation and judgment. These discursive practices occur at political, cultural, and interpersonal levels. Sometimes they compete with one another, and indeed, different discourses can offer distinct and even contradictory versions of reality (Davies & Harré, 1990; Weedon, 1987). From time to time, we have students view counseling sessions to practice identifying the dominant discourses and how they position people in relation to themselves and one another.

Positioning

Within any discourse, subjects occupy *positions*. This means that a function of discourse is to offer a particular set of relationships that locate or situate the person in relation to the other phenomena inscribed by the discourse. This usage of positioning is similar to the use of "role" as an explanatory concept in psychology, except that roles tend to be taken as given structures (Davies & Harré, 1990). The ways in which the terms *masculine* and *feminine* are used, for example, usually suggest to us ways in which we are expected to live our lives in relation to our gender (Weedon, 1987). But different discourses offer different subject positions, and frequently these operate together in the same social situations, offering contradictory positionings.

Everyday living is fraught with possibilities for conflict between discursive positionings, and each one of us must continually struggle for coherence as we constantly occupy mutually contradictory positions at one and the same time. To work as counselors, our students need, we believe, to develop a sharp political awareness of how these conflicts evolve at the local level. This evolution is continuous and never complete. We are always offering each other discursive positions and, often without much thought, taking them up. However, while it is obviously important to "locate" oneself, to take positions, it is useful for us to recognize that subject positions are temporary and conditional rather than constant and absolute. Conceiving of positioning in this fluid way opens up possibilities of change of both a personal and a social nature.

Deconstruction

Deconstruction is another concept that we want our students to become familiar with. The objective of working with deconstruction is to upend the usual privilege given to dominant knowledges, and, in so doing, not only to understand but also to subvert the ways in which such systems constitute everyday social practices.

In White's (1991) approach, which we teach our students, this process of subversion is achieved by "rendering strange" and "objectifying" these familiar and everyday practices. We shall return later to look further at his methods of achieving this purpose.

Colonizing Influences

In New Zealand, deconstruction of counseling knowledge must take account of the processes of cultural colonization of Maori by Pakeha and query counseling approaches that might collude with this ongoing process, often in subtle ways. An important way in which we give students an opportunity to experience cultural difference is through taking them as a group to live in a Maori context and observe Maori protocol and interact with each other and with local Maori people from discursive positions that may not be familiar to them. As well as leading to greater cultural awareness, this experience contributes to a process of deconstructing cultural privilege.

THE SOCIAL CONSTRUCTION OF COUNSELING KNOWLEDGE

As Foucault (1980) has shown, knowledge itself exists within discourse. Because discourse shapes the terms and categories available to us, it is only within discursive frameworks that it is possible to make claims to know. Thus the meanings of statements about counseling theory, as with other canons of knowledge, are both constrained and made possible by the cultural milieu of their utterance. Therefore we seek to teach the ideas that constitute counseling theory in relation to their cultural location.

Humanism and Counselor Education

In our view, counselor education has been dominated from its inception by humanistic discourse (Durie, 1989; Waldegrave, 1990). Humanism, in psychology, historically has had a tendency to locate human problems within individuals as distinct and separate from social, cultural, and political contexts in which people live. The dislocation of the problem from the social context has tended to obscure the impact of Western individualistic ideology on those who identify with indigenous collective ideologies and to underestimate the effects of patriarchy on counselor educators, counselors, and clients alike. In addition, rarely do humanistic theories address the marginalizing effects of middle-class values on class groups that do not embrace the same language practices.

To illuminate these issues, our students are asked to present seminars on mainstream counseling theories in ways that bring to the fore the cultural assumptions inherent in them. Skills practiced earlier in deconstructing text are applied in order to identify common, taken-for-granted assumptions about clienthood, change, personal growth, and other concepts in counseling. We encourage students to ask questions about the "truth value" of theory in relation to such cultural context rather than in relation to universal precepts. For example, notions of "self-actualization" (often presented as universal truths in humanistic psychology), which assume an individualistic or patriarchal view of what one is striving for in life, are subjected to scrutiny. Also, dominant counseling discourses might be questioned about their tendency to invite both clients and counselors to adhere to essentialist descriptions of the self. Questions are asked of each theory as to how it positions clients and counselors in relation to issues of class and gender.

Discourse and the Production of Client Concerns

Discourses are also at work in the production of the kinds of concerns about which people consult counselors. Personal problems are produced in social contexts. From a constructionist perspective, personal meaning can be produced only within social contexts, and neither originates with individuals nor exists somewhere "out there" to be discovered (Harré, 1986; Olssen, 1991; Wittgenstein, 1953). In other words, meaning is related directly to the agendas and common purposes of actors in social contexts. It is in this sense that it is possible to say that the individual is always-already social. We cannot think of individuals as surrounded by a social world, or entering into one. The social world is implicated in their sense of being an individual. Poststructuralists use the term "production of subjectivity" where psychologists might use the term "identity formation" (Henriques, Hollway, Urwin, Venn, & Walkerdine, 1984). Foucault (1977, 1981) suggests that individual subjectivity is inscribed by discourse. This idea implies that the possibilities for self-description, indeed, for formation of the self as an identity, are bounded by the discursive opportunities available (Davies, 1991).

The problems we bring to counseling can be produced, experienced, and named only within such discursive frameworks. In a very important sense, "reality" is what we say it is, for there is no way in which we can know it directly. Thus, a poststructural view calls into question the existence of any such entity as the "essential self" (Parker, 1994). Personal identity becomes a complex phenomenon involving multiple positionings, many of which may be contradictory (Weedon, 1987).

A social constructionist approach to counselor education requires us to engage our students in theorizing both personal and social change in ways that acknowledge issues of power. It also encourages us and our students to notice possibilities for changes in power relations happening before our eyes in the counseling interview.

Our counseling students also present seminars to each other in which they take frequently encountered client concerns (such as sexual abuse, grief, eating disorders, alcohol abuse, depression, violence, etc.), examine the social contexts in which such problems become descriptive of people's lives, and outline approaches counselors might take to help clients with these concerns.

Discourse and the Person of the Counselor

We also want our students to ground these understandings in their own lives and to understand that discourses are as constitutive of the counselor as a person as they are of the client. Therefore, we ask them to write a personal autobiography that focuses on the impact of the various discourses they have encountered on the sense of self that they have assumed as their own. Specifically they are asked to identify their positioning in dominant discourses that relate to gender, class, sexual orientation, and ethnicity. We then workshop the biographies and draw out the common themes that are present across individuals' experience. This is often experienced as a wrenching exercise that sheds much light on taken-for-granted aspects of ordinary experience and increases students' sensitivity to the constitutive aspects of discourse in the lives of the people who seek their help.

In other classes students are given opportunities to experience the impact of counseling conversations from the perspective of the client and in this way to explore the ongoing effects of the discourses that impact on their experience. During one of these small-group discussions, one student, in the role of the client, was able to identify the effects on her of the dominant discourses' occurring in a hospital and medical setting in her role as a nurse educator. She became aware of how the medical discourses shaped which knowledge was to be taught as it pertained to mental health and healing and how she increasingly found herself placed outside of these dominant discourses. Her repositioning within discourse meant that she would be leaving the setting where these dominant medical discourses were most prevalent. She decided to opt for a community setting where other, more favored discourses prevailed in relation to alternative approaches to healing.

In line with our desire to break from the influence of individualistic discourses, we do not regard the development of a counselor as occurring primarily within the context of a private relationship between a lecturer and a student. Rather, we seek to establish with our students a learning context in which there is an increasing complexity of audiences to the ideas we are wanting to promote and to students' engagement with these ideas. A narrative approach to counseling is most likely to flourish in a culture that supports its growth. To this end we ask our students early in their training to become used to showing their work to others, seeking feedback, and then reflecting on this feedback. Feedback might be sought on different occasions from a variety of sources: counselor education program staff, peers, other students from previous years, field supervisors, professional colleagues, and, perhaps most importantly, clients. Written tasks require them to reflect on and interpret the feedback they receive, storying their development as counselors.

In addition, students keep a journal in which they are free to write in an informal, provisional way of the thoughts they are having about their work and the connections they are building between practice and theory.

We also set up a series of professional development interviews in which students develop narrative accounts of their professional progress. In these interviews, which take place with the program staff, with fellow students, and with their placement supervisors, we seek to foster a spirit of curiosity about the stories of their evolution as counselors. They might be asked to identify the restraints they are experiencing in their professional development and to notice the alternative stories of competence as they emerge. Opportunities frequently open through this process for the development of meaning around a story of a professional identity and an ethical integrity in practice.

We view the process of learning to be a counselor as parallel to the process by which clients make changes in their lives. We seek to engage with students in the development of a professional identity and a repertoire of professional practices that embody the commitments we define together in all of the above experiences. White's (1991) use of the phrases "landscape of action" and "landscape of consciousness" provides a useful reference point for staff and students in this process of professional education. The realm of action is the realm of events in which people take part. The realm of consciousness is the realm of meaning-making, of storying events into sequences and plots, of thematic development.

For student counselors, the instances of trying out new skills and responding to particular client needs all occur on the landscape of action. In the classroom, in interviews, in supervision, and in written work, they are constantly involved in making meaning around these events on the landscape of consciousness. As they build connections between the two landscapes, the meanings are more likely to become embodied in further intentional action and the actions are likely to be interpreted in evolving systems of meaning.

Our job as counselor educators is to provide the conditions, suggest the readings, offer the feedback, and ask the questions that will facilitate the connections between the two landscapes. Gradually, when we are successful in establishing these conditions, knowledge about counseling theory and practice develops alongside a professional identity as a counselor.

At the end of the first year of training this process culminates in the writing of a retrospective report on the learning they have noticed in their training so far and a professional development plan in which they give an account of their counseling approach and its current state of development as well as their hopes and plans for its future progress.

THE COUNSELING PROCESS

The model of counseling we have been teaching has three main emphases: (1) engagement; (2) deconstruction of subjected positions in problem stories; and (3) the development of a subject*ive* position in alternative (or preferred) stories. These emphases tend to be somewhat sequential in nature but seldom fit neatly into a linear time frame. All are present to some degree at every stage of a counseling process. The distinction between the subjected and the subjective position in relation to a problem story is, we believe, crucial. It relates to the alternative, but connected, uses of the term *subject* that Foucault (1980) referred to. A position within a discourse that is problematic and painful may involve a sense of being subject*ed* or ruled by the discourse. It is quite a different thing to take up a subject*ive* position in relation to a problematic issue. This is a position of agency in relation to the problem. As a metaphor, it draws on a different meaning of the word *subject*. This meaning is the one we use in reference to the grammar of a sentence. The subject of a sentence provides the impetus for the verb and the predicate. The subject is regarded as the author of the action rather than the object of it. We teach our students that clients often come to us experiencing themselves as subjected and unable to identify possibilities for agency in their own lives. The counselor's task is to engage them in a conversation and a relationship that trace the effects of discourses that have subjected them and that also builds a sense of agency around a subjective position that may be located in alternative stories. Let us now focus on each of these emphases in turn.

Engagement

In teaching our students the skills of engagement with clients, we find that writers about narrative approaches to counseling have concentrated more on mapping out overarching templates for the direction of a counseling process and on types of questions that may be asked than they have attended to the detail of how the counselor might interact with the client on a moment-by-moment basis. (Note that this is a reference to published writings rather than to practice.)

Hence, it is not surprising to read of the problems noted by Griffith and Griffith (1992) in their psychiatry residents who were applying a narrative approach to their interactions with families. When they paid attention to the failures their students were experiencing, while apparently asking all the "right" questions of the families they were working with, Griffith and Griffith reached the conclusion that the trainees were not learning to adopt a "therapeutic emotional posture" toward their clients. Without a sufficient focus on "relational and dialogical rigor," trainees were inclined to use a "cookbook approach" to asking questions designed to bring about behavioral change, and registering surprise when families did not return for further meetings.

Griffith and Griffith (1992) address this issue by focusing training on adopting relational practices consistent with the epistemological stance embodied in a narrative approach to therapy. We concur and use the term *engagement* to refer to the establishment and maintenance of the kind of dialogue necessary for counseling to have effect. In our counselor education program we draw on some of the microskills traditional in counseling training. But we have found ourselves wanting to look at these in new ways and to teach them differently.

We still believe it is necessary for counselors to be able to establish empathetic, emotionally supportive relationships but we would want to qualify this by making a distinction between rapport-building that remains caught within the discourses in which problems have grown and rapport building that leaves room for deconstruction. It is not enough in our view for a counselor to offer a warranting "acceptance," in the traditional client-centered way, of a client's experience of what has been discursively constructed. If a person's subjective experience has been given to him or her to a substantial degree by the discourses at work in relation to the issue he or she has brought to a counselor, then changes or shifts in consciousness are likely to require some kind of deconstruction of this subjective experience rather than just validation of it through the counselor's accepting responses.

Nor is it enough for counselors to demonstrate their own deconstructive cleverness without building a relationship based on trust and respect with the client, that is, without making it a dialogue. This dialogue must create the conditions for the client to feel safe enough to participate in the deconstructive process.

However, we can see a need for many of the usual ways of thinking about counseling relationships to be recast in a social constructionist framework and elaborated further. To establish a truly collaborative counseling relationship, trainees need to develop "a nose" for how power is constituted in social and professional practices, and a facility for reflexive thinking about their own practice. There is a job to be done to critically examine, with the aid of the social constructionist metaphors, some of the basic building blocks of counseling such as empathy, questioning, immediacy, nonjudgmental attitudes, challenging, and so forth. What we are finding is that inviting students to participate in this critique of traditional counseling practices is stimulating creativity and worthwhile learning, especially in the most intellectually adventurous of them. What follows are some current thoughts about what we seek to teach our counseling students.

At this point let us introduce a case example to illustrate these issues. The case example comes from one of our students, Sonya, working with her client, Jack. She writes about the discourses influencing her engagement with him:

> On first meeting I think Jack would have seen a Pakeha woman of comfortable means, who had the authority of education and the status and power of professional position. How could he, a Maori man, with a history of violence against women, with limited formal education and of subsistence means relate to me? However I think my manner showed me as an empathic woman, offering an egalitarian relationship and demonstrating regard for Jack as a worthwhile person. This was sufficient initially to bridge some of the barriers of apparent difference and was enough for Jack to decide to share his story. In the first session Jack was in a hurry to unload and my first role was in listening and helping Jack to weep and to express his pain and grief for past hurts, loss and abuse, and his remorse for harm done to others. This was an important step in the work that was to follow.

Empathy. Talking about establishing empathy and rapport poses some particular problems because of the strong pull of all the humanistic assumptions in the language we still have available for talking about this issue. We find it fruitful at present to acknowledge this influence and to continue to draw on some of the traditional counseling microskills, such as reflective listening, while at the same time talking about them "in inverted commas" as it were.

Empathy has been argued since Carl Rogers (Rogers, 1951, 1980) as a foundational concept in counseling and as crucial to the opening of possibilities for change for the client. However, the nature of empathy has always been somewhat mysterious. In Rogers's influential formulations, it was described more as an attitude of one person toward another and seemed to be made up of other romanticism-inspired qualities like warmth, positive regard, acceptance, respect.

Since Rogers, empathy has been talked about in ever more modernist terms. Various writers have sought to tie it down by categorizing its components (Brammer, 1988; Carkhuff, 1983; Egan, 1986; Ivey, Ivey, & Simek-Morgan, 1993). In this process the descriptions of it became descriptions of a skill rather than an attitude. It became a set of formulas or patterns of response that could be learned and correctly applied with the appropriate postural lean and fixed smile.

However, the way in which empathy has been described has still retained elements of the romantic vision. There are in fact a handful of metaphors that have been used over and over again with little elaboration. These include statements about "entering another person's world," "seeing the world through another person's eyes," or "walking in their moccasins" (Brammer 1988; Egan, 1986, p. 106; Ivey et al., 1993, p. 21; Nelson-Jones, 1986, p. 96; Rogers, 1980). There has of course been a substantial amount of research into the "effects" of empathy that has been built on such postulates.

But there are several things that look strange about such postulated empathy from a poststructural perspective. First, the assumption that each individual is speaking about a discrete "private perceptual world" (Rogers, 1980) is more problematic when a constructionist approach to identity formation is adopted (e.g., Sampson, 1993). The breaking down of an essentialist, individualistic approach to identity leads to a view of the private perceptual world as populated by fluid, public, social relations. The self and any actuality that might be the assumed goal of Rogers's "self-actualizing tendency" comes to look like a cultural product of conversations or texts mapped onto the person, rather than something arising out of a natural inner core of being. So when we enter another's world, we are entering a socially scripted world. If we can see the power relations that are producing a diminished sense of self in clients, then we may not want to be so accepting and supportive of the "private perceptual world" as a more humanistic account of identity would have us be. In short, the private perceptual world is not assumed to be synonymous with, or the sole property of, the individual person.

Second, the idea that a person is speaking about an inner world that precedes any speaking about it is under challenge from postmodern ideas about the role of language. Words are no longer taken to refer to preexisting thoughts or feelings. A poststructural perspective on language would suggest that it is through speaking in social contexts that we are actually constructing our inner world through conversation rather than simply representing it (Shotter, 1993). This of course includes the kind of speaking that occurs in a counseling session. In the past, great care was exerted by counselor not to insert his or her own attitudes. This was in response to the fear of damaging or interfering with the expression of the client's inner world. However, from a postmodern perspective, a counselor would see more reason to acknowledge both his or her own world and the client's inevitable influence on the production of this world, and would, therefore, invite ways of speaking that assume the client's agency and voice.

At the moment though, we still teach the "reflection of feeling" metaphor, despite its modernist overtones of counselor rationality and objectivity (although we do hedge it with warnings about the cultural bias in this approach to emotion).

We are moving toward teaching an alternative stance to empathy that might be founded on a postmodern or poststructuralist idea of personhood (Gergen, 1991). From this perspective, concepts of self are relational and in an important sense do not preexist the production of the language in which they are talked about. Both counselor and client might be thought of as simultaneously engaged in a process not of discovery but of production of a sense of self. This kind of empathy might be thought of as a positive use of power that positions the client in the counseling session as a person with a voice, and a voice that is being heard by an audience and offered some legitimacy through being heard. Reflection from this perspective might be considered useful, more because it invites a noticing of the process of production of self than because it represents the preexisting feelings that the client is expressing. It invites clients to listen to themselves in a new way, to be an audience to their own production of self.

Audience. We are therefore interested in the concept of audience in relation to empathy and engagement in counseling. If the production of personhood is a social process, as we are suggesting, then counseling can be thought of as a site in which particular, deliberate attention is paid to what is being produced. Counselor education then can be thought of as learning how to be an audience and how to do so in ways that are ethical and invite others also to be an audience to their own production of self.

Curiosity. In addition to an emphasis on empathy, we want our students to value curiosity as an attitude that contributes to the process of deconstruction and reconstruction in therapy. By this we do not mean the kind of curiosity that seeks to *confirm* what we as counselors already know through our training and expertise about the solutions to client problems. Rather, we are referring to the kind of curiosity that seeks genuinely to *learn* about our clients' expert knowledge of their own worlds. To achieve this, trainee counselors often have to shed the effects of years of training in positivistic science and modernist thinking, which might lead them into a search for certainty, predictability, and continuity in understanding client concerns. The cultural influences we are all subject to have encouraged us to privilege certain canons of knowledge as reliable because they have claimed to capture the "essence" of human experience.

The stance of curiosity is described by Anderson and Goolishian (1992) as the "not-knowing position." It requires the adoption of an inquiring but respectful naiveté by the student counselors. In micro-counseling sessions, we ask them to practice asking the kinds of questions that illuminate how things came to be as they are. This includes a curiosity about how pervasive discourses, such as those having to do with gender, class, and ethnicity, have been influential in the production of how things are. Any topic can be a starting point, even some apparently mundane inquiry. To demonstrate this we set students opportunities to be curious about each other in relation to topics such as what one ate for breakfast, or how one came to be a participant in a training course, or what one thought of a recent movie. What we are aiming at is a sense, in our students, that in any counseling interview there may be literally hundreds of lines of inquiry, each with many opportunities to discover how things came to be as they are but, even more importantly, "how things might be otherwise" (White, 1991).

Deconstruction of Subjected Positions in Problem Stories

The communication of empathy and curiosity by counselors opens the way for clients to tell their stories. Since each storying involves a re-authoring of experience, a significant deconstructive process has already taken place. This is especially so if the position the person has been offered in the problem discourse is one that has been isolating or denying a legitimate voice. For example, the invitations to secrecy that often accompany sexual abuse might have trained a person into a very private experience of the story of abuse. The power of this story to continue to isolate the person might begin to be broken down by the act of telling, of bringing it into a more public arena.

Here we find White's approach of "relative influence questioning" useful in advancing the deconstruction (White, 1989). This approach involves asking a series of questions about the effect of the problem story on the person. In these questions care is taken to avoid any internalizing language that might contribute to the person's blaming or judging himself or owning the problem as a personal deficit. Instead, "externalizing language" is used to ensure that the problem is located in the discursive context. For example, the counselor might ask a person suffering from bulimia about the demands bulimia has placed on her life, the effects it has on her view of herself, and the relationships it has recruited her into. In addition, some of the discourses of patriarchy that might be urging her to monitor and discipline her own body through bulimia might be identified and named. Especially with younger children, the problem might be personified and given an exotic name. The "sneaky poo" story about a boy whose life was being controlled by soiling is a well-known example (White, 1989). This naming is a collaborative and vernacular process, undertaken by the counselor and client together. It seeks to avoid the diagnostic labels that position the client as subject to psychiatric or psychological knowledge.

This approach is taught first of all in classroom practice sessions, then in small group micro-counseling practice sessions, then in practice counseling interviews with undergraduate students doing an introductory course in counseling, and then in practicum settings with clients. Along the way we invite our students to find ways to story their own development of competence and to perform meaning for themselves around this.

Let us return to Sonya's work with Jack to illustrate a deconstructive conversation:

> I helped Jack explore the history, the dimensions and the effects of alcohol, abuse and violence in his life and in his relationships as far back as his grandfather and including his peers and his family. I further historicised the story by asking about the origins of such problems in terms of New Zealand history and even spoke a bit about my views of colonial oppression. I think that externalizing the problems in this way and locating them within discourses in our history was a very important step in helping Jack appreciate a new relationship with himself and with other persons in his life. He didn't have to see that just Jack was the problem. He and others before him had been caught up in a discourse that spoke of having no place, no acceptable language and culture, of not being good enough — and had learned to live accordingly.

Development of a Subjective Position in Alternative Stories

While the initial telling of the story is usually saturated with the effects of the problem, as time goes by the narrative counselor and the client begin to identify aspects of experience that stand aside from the problem story. These might be occasions of hope, or minor victories over the problem, or simply parts of one's life that don't get caught up in the problem narrative. White and Epston (1989) have called these exceptions to the problem story "unique outcomes." Because these unique outcomes do not resonate with the problem story they are often bracketed off from people's conscious attention and not incorporated into the stories people tell about themselves.

We teach our students to use the second phase of White's (1989) relative influence questioning at this point. While the earlier process has been one of mapping the influence of the problem onto the life of the person, the next phase reverses the direction of the question. The client is now asked to map his or her influence on the problem. That is, the client is questioned about the unique outcomes to inquire how these might be explained or understood, whether they suggest a different kind of experience or view of self, whether they are preferable experiences to those dominated by the problem story, and so forth. White (1989) has outlined a series of categories of these kinds of questions. Gradually the unique outcomes are elaborated and amplified into a new account, a new history, which opens possibilities for the performance of a different subject position that is subjective (in the grammatical sense referred to above). In the process of examining these possibilities, clients are introduced to a sense of agency in their own lives. They may find a distinctive voice that does not just speak from subjugated positions in dominant discourses but expresses their own preferences for the kind of life they would like to lead. They can also be encouraged to identify audiences to appreciate the performance of the new story of self that is emerging.

> Sonya continues her story of her work with Jack:
> I then began questioning Jack as to how and in what situations temptation [to give into alcohol] might get the better of him. He quickly took up agency in this battle and made a series of small decisions to increase his odds. Most of our sessions became focused on how Jack was making practical changes from week to week; how his relationships with others were changing; what feedback he was getting from others that was helping him revise his opinion of himself; how he perceived the qualities he saw in the new Jack; what effect the changes in his life were having — new friends, activities, interests, renewed health. Then there was a court hearing over the custody of his children. This proved a great opportunity for Jack to re-story himself to others such as lawyers, probation and social welfare officers and the judge, and to incorporate the positive feedback from others into his new sense of personhood. Jack began to discover his power to be agentic in this process. His own re-authoring linked up with a new discourse — that of Maori renaissance — within which he began to position himself. I believe that this repositioning within a wider social context had a very important bearing on why this counseling interaction worked.

We find that this second stage of the relative influence questioning is not easy for our students to master. It requires some confidence to persist because clients are often so caught up in problem stories that they are not attuned to exceptions to them. By their very nature, unique outcomes are usually overlooked. To pay attention to them seems strange. If student counselors are at all unsure, they may easily give up and become caught up in the problem story themselves, defeated like the client by its dominance. Therefore, in training we should give them plenty of opportunity and encouragement and, at times, coaching to persist in their curiosity about the alternative story.

The use of reflecting teams (Anderson, 1987; White, 1995) is useful in this respect. While one student is doing the counseling, others are engaged in listening for the alternative questions that might be asked to elaborate the new story for the client. After the counseling interview, the counselor and the client get to overhear the listeners' having a conversation about what they have heard in which they reflect on the discourses operating on both the client and the counselor and (in a tentative spirit) express their wonderings about how the performance of the alternative story might develop.

CONCLUSION

It is our hope that our counseling students will foster in themselves, as a result of participating in our program, a critical edge and a reflexive dimension to their competence as counselors. The program we have outlined attempts to use the ideas of social constructionism to provide this critical edge and then to develop opportunities for applying these ideas in practice in our lives as counselors and to the lives of the people who consult with us. We have found that narrative therapy is the best way of achieving this at present, so we have sought to take up a position in the world of counselor education based on this approach. In doing so we are hopeful that we and our students can contribute to the development of these ideas in our part of the world.

We would stress in conclusion that what we have asserted here is provisional, unfinished, and historically and culturally loaded. It and we cannot be otherwise. As readers, you will bring your own subjectivity and discursive positioning to the story you make of what we have put forward. Thus, communication is enriched and the dynamic possibilities of consciousness are advanced.

REFERENCES

Anderson, H., & Goolishian, H. (1992). The client is the expert: A not-knowing approach to therapy. In S. McNamee & K. Gergen (Eds.), *Therapy as social construction* (pp. 25–39). London: Sage.

Anderson, T. (1987). The reflecting team: Dialogue & metadialogue in clinical work. *Family Process, 26,* 415–428.

Berger, P., & Luckmann, T. (1966). *The social construction of reality: A treatise in the sociology of knowledge.* London: Penguin.

Brammer, L. M. (1988). *The helping relationship: Process and skills* (4th ed.). London: Prentice-Hall International.

Carkhuff, R. R. (1983). *The art of helping* (5th ed.). Amherst, MA: Human Resource Development Press.

Davies, B. (1991). The concept of agency: a feminist poststructuralist analysis. *Postmodern Critical Theorizing, 30,* 42–53.

Davies, B., & Harré, R. (1990). Positioning: The discursive production of selves. *Journal for the Theory of Social Behaviour, 20*(1), 43–63.

Durie, M. (1989). A move that's well overdue: Shaping counselling to meet the needs of Maori people. *New Zealand Counselling and Guidance Association Journal, 11*(1), 13–23.

Egan, G. (1986). *The skilled helper: A systematic approach to effective helping.* Monterey, CA: Brooks/Cole.

Egan, G. (1994). *The skilled helper.* Pacific Grove, CA: Brooks/Cole.

Fairclough, N. (1992). *Discourse and social change.* Cambridge, England: Polity Press.

Foucault, M. (1977). *Discipline and punish.* London: Allen and Lane.

Foucault, M. (1980). *Power/knowledge: Selected interviews and other writings.* New York: Pantheon Books.

Foucault, M. (1981). *The history of sexuality, Vol. 1: An introduction.* Harmondsworth: Penguin.

Gavey, N. (1992). Technologies and effects of heterosexual coercion. *Feminism and Psychology, 2*(3), 325–351.

Gergen, K. (1985). The social constructionist movement in modern psychology. *American Psychologist, 40*(3), 266–275.

Gergen, K. (1991). *The saturated self.* New York: Basic Books.

Griffith, J., & Griffith, M. (1992). Owning one's epistemological stance in therapy. *Dulwich Centre Newsletter, 1992*(2), 5–11.

Harré, R. (1986). The step to social constructionism. In M. Richards & P. Light (Eds.), *Children of social worlds* (pp. 287–296). Cambridge: Polity Press.

Henriques, J., Hollway, W., Urwin, C., Venn, C., & Walkerdine, V. (1984). *Changing the subject: Psychology, social regulation and subjectivity.* London: Methuen.

Hollway, W. (1983). Heterosexual sex: Power and desire for the other. In S. Cartledge & J. Ryan (Eds.), *Sex and love: New thoughts on old contradictions* (pp. 124–140). London: Women's Press.

Ivey, A. E., Ivey, M. B., & Simek-Morgan, L. (1993). *Counseling and psychotherapy: A multicultural perspective.* Boston: Allyn and Bacon.

Monk, G., & Drewery, W. (1994). The impact of social constructionist thinking on eclecticism in counsellor education: Some personal thoughts. *New Zealand Journal of Counselling, 16*(1), 5–14.

Nelson-Jones, R. (1986). *Human relationship skills.* London: Holt, Rinehart, and Winston.

Olssen, M. (1991). Producing the truth about people. In J. Morss & T. Linzey (Eds.), *Growing up: The politics of human learning* (pp. 188–209). Auckland, Australia: Longman Paul.

Parker, I. (1994, February). *Discourse analysis and material culture.* Workshop at the Discursive Construction of Knowledge International Conference, Adelaide.

Rogers, C. R. (1951). *Client-centered therapy.* Boston: Houghton Mifflin.

Rogers, C. (1980). *A way of being.* Boston: Houghton Mifflin.

Sampson, E. (1993). Identity politics. *American Psychologist, 49*(5), 412–416.

Shotter, J. (1993). *Conversational realities: Constructing life through language.* Thousand Oaks, CA: Sage.

Waldegrave, C. (1990). Just therapy. *Dulwich Centre Newsletter,* (1), 6–45.

Weedon, C. (1987). *Feminist practice and poststructural theory.* Oxford: Basil Blackwell.

White, M. (1989). *Selected papers.* Adelaide, Australia: Dulwich Centre Publications.

White, M. (1991). Deconstruction and therapy. *Dulwich Centre Newsletter, 1991*(3), 21–40.

White, M. (1995). *Re-authoring lives.* Adelaide, Australia: Dulwich Centre Publications.

White M., & Epston, D. (1989). *Literate means to therapeutic ends.* Adelaide, Australia: Dulwich Centre Publications.

Wittgenstein, L. (1953). *Philosophical investigations.* Oxford: Basil Blackwell.

PART V

Implications of a New Paradigm

CHAPTER 15

The Social and Political Nature of Psychological Science: The Challenges, Potentials, and Future of Constructivist Thinking

Thomas L. Sexton and Barbara L. Griffin

The pages of this volume demonstrate the application of constructivist think-ing to the variety of activities that fall within the boundaries of psychological science. As we suspected, when we challenge the current ontological and epis-temological assumptions of professional practice, new conceptual pictures emerge. The approaches defined throughout these chapters illustrate the promises and challenges of adopting a constructivist paradigm in opening up new directions in counseling practice, research, and training.

We have three goals for this final chapter. First, we will tie together the applications presented in earlier chapters into a summary of what the con-structivist alternative has to offer those engaged in the varied practice of psy-chological science. However viable, constructivist ideas must be considered as social processes both within and beyond the profession. Therefore, our second goal is to consider the nature of knowledge and its impact on the viability of professional theories. In this regard, the political nature of profes-sional ideas in developing and maintaining cultural positions of infirmity and social power become important to address. Adopting a constructivist perspec-tive also means that numerous challenges and potentials not specifically ad-dressed in earlier chapters should be considered here. Thus, our final goal is to identify the broad implications that face psychological science as we enter into the dialogue of constructivism.

THE CONSTRUCTIVIST PERSPECTIVE

The constructivist perspective is a broad umbrella of specific dialogues that share a common core and a long philosophical tradition. What is new is that these ideas are now supported by a larger context embodied in postmodernism. Hayes and Oppenheim (Chapter 2) identify six principles that form the core assumptions of constructivism. These principles form a descriptive metatheory that suggests a participatory epistemology of multiple truths in which people actively create their own unique realities and development while dialectically connected to their social context. The constructed meaning and reality are language-based. Evaluation of truth is based on viability rather than validity. It is on these core principles that constructivist models of counseling practice, research, and training are based.

In their analysis, Hayes and Oppenheim note that while constructivists all seem to maintain the central epistemological position of knowing as meaning construction, they differ according to their ontological positions. Critical constructivists argue that we co-create our own personal realities bounded by an unknowable world that imposes constraints on the viability of these realities. Radical constructivicts, on the other hand, argue for ontological idealism in which there is no reality beyond an individual's own experience. Therefore, individuals are entirely self-organizing.

Regardless of the specific ontological position, constructivist thinking is uniquely attuned to a consideration of social setting (Efran & Clarfield, 1993). Culture, for example, is the algorithm of conversation between the social and personal spheres of existence. The cultural context is to personality, behavior, and social meaning as the structure of grammar is to language (Wentworth & Wentworth, Chapter 3). Thus, culture is the link that ties the social realm with the inner workings of the individual. This reciprocal tie is a dialectical rather than a deterministic one. Gender is one of the organizing constructs within that dialectical relationship. Currently gender is a construction in which patriarchy is a dominant discourse that organizes cultural relations. However, in other contexts gender may have different meanings within the cultural dialogue. Thus, the nature and definition of gender are challengeable ideologies situated in time, not in biological imperatives. Along this line, Terry Guyer and Rowell (Chapter 4) suggest that a central element of feminist theory and practice — equity — be redefined as a culture-bound social reality.

Within psychological science, assumptions of development are at the center of determining who is *normal* and, thus, what goals to pursue in practice, research, and education. Models of development have become a metaphoric yardstick to which we compare clients, research participant behavior, and student progress. Rigazio-DiGilio (Chapter 5) suggests that development is a dialectic, reciprocal, and transactional process of meaning-making for families, individuals, and therapists as they move through time. Developmental events are co-constructions that occur between individuals, families, and their wider sociopolitical system. The developmental path is nonlinear, recursive, and adaptive (Basseches, 1984; Hoffman, 1990). Developmental impasses reflect incongruities between world views and contextual demands rather than deficits and problems.

Language plays a central role in the consructivist perspective. Gordon and Efran (Chapter 6) argue that the meanings of language are housed not in the minds of individuals but in the social arrangements and dialogues among people. Language permits recursive layering of abstractions. Unique to humans is that we have the ability to comment on our language, creating progressively complex layers of abstraction. Thus, we can declare something and at the same time disqualify the statement. Emotions, the most common client complaint with which therapists must deal, are intimately intertwined with and embodied in language. Similarly, it is language that permits us to conceptualize past, present, future and distinguish patterns of causality. Therapy, according to Gordon and Efran, is a conversation in which the meanings in language are negotiated between client and counselor. Change is based not on similarity, but on orthogonal interaction (Maturana, 1990) in which the therapist provides something different and unique to the client system. Regardless of the theoretical orientation of the therapist, therapy is an ideal arena for orthogonal interactions.

These notions of change and language apply to various therapeutic settings. Counseling in a multicultural context is based on the common principles of constructivist practice rather than the specific nature of any cultural group. Steenbarger and Pels (Chapter 7) propose that constructivist counseling in multicultural contexts is based on an assessment of the degree to which cultural, ethnic, and racial issues are relevant and salient for clients. The outcome of successful assessment is a co-constructed problem definition that incorporates culture in a way that allows for novel and adaptive solutions. Constructivist principles applied in school settings emphasize the facilitation of students' personal meanings within their diverse personal and cultural contexts. Peavy (Chapter 8) similarly suggests that career counseling must recognize the meaning of the life career histories of clients. Career counseling is based on a constructivist view of self in which central concepts such as career interest and choice are understood as socially constructed meanings that vary depending on the particular social space occupied in society. Thus, career interests no longer have universal meanings, but instead depend on context and meaning. Forster (Chapter 9) suggests that a constructivist orientation focuses attention on facilitation of the personal qualities of flexibility, open-mindedness, self-empowerment, and tolerance for diversity and is therefore well suited as a model for school counseling. The long-range outcome of constructivist school interventions is centered on enhancing the adaptability and survival of students later in life. When based on these alternative principles, school counseling can more aptly be called a guidance process.

Systematic inquiry is the process of professional knowledge-building. It is through formal and informal inquiry that professional explanations of client behavior, the counseling process, and other relevant phenomena develop. Constructivism does not mean the abandonment of a systematic stance for undisciplined subjectivism (Hoshmand & Polkinghorne, 1992). Instead, constructivism refocuses the inquiry process, since, as suggested by Rennie (1994), human experience is complex and meaning-based, and thus not lawful or appropriate for study by logical positivist methods. Constructivist inquiry is an understanding of the meaning of experience within its historical and social context. Since language is the medium of meaning, active negotiation between subject and investigator must take place. The purpose of this dialogue is to ensure that the terminology used adequately represents the experience under study. Nelson and Poulin (Chapter 10) suggest that qualitative research is particularly well suited to this task. Regardless of the specific qualitative approach (e.g., grounded theory or phenomenological analysis), the focus is on the systematic investigation of personal narratives using methods driven by the phenomena under investigation. For example, grounded theory investigations are conducted with systematic data gathering, triangulation of data, and open, axial, and selective coding to distill the patterns of meaning within the personal narratives of a unique phenomenon.

Conceptualizing and measuring therapeutic change is one of the most difficult and elusive research problems for psychological science (Beutler & Hill, 1992; Sexton, 1996). A constructivist approach to this task builds on the notions of therapeutic change as narrative process measured by qualitative research methods. Daniels and White (Chapter 11) illustrate how the principles of second-generation cognitive science lead to defining the conceptual metaphor as a unit of assessing therapeutic change. They propose that conceptual metaphors be measured in terms of their ontological and epistemological characteristics. Measured across the span of a number of counseling sessions, metaphors capture the nature of therapeutic change within the context of therapy.

Professional education is the process of developing various epistemological positions of knowing and acting. Lovell and McAuliffe (Chapter 13) cast the development of professional competence within the framework of adult cognitive development. Teaching occurs through soliciting and eliciting dialogue regarding the thinking and reasoning that students use to explain the phenomena of counseling. Winslade, Monk, and Drewery (Chapter 14) illustrate the integration of the constructivist principles of discourse, positioning, and deconstruction into a systematic counselor education program. Across the curriculum, the processes involved in therapeutic change and narratives of individual, cultural, and personal understanding are of primary interest.

An integral part of professional training is that learning which takes in applied practice under professional supervision. Neufeldt (Chapter 12) proposes that constructivist supervision be based on four principles. Like other interpersonal events, supervision takes place in professional, cultural, and interpersonal contexts that dictate its nature. Within those contexts, supervisee and supervisor are engaged as collaborators in the co-construction of practical knowledge regarding the nature of the therapeutic relationship, successful events of therapy, and change. In a reflective process, the therapist and supervisor examine the actions, emotions, and interactions between therapist and client. The clinical wisdom that is the goal of supervision is based on knowledge of how to produce beneficial therapeutic outcomes (Hoshmand & Polkinghorne, 1992).

THE SOCIAL AND POLITICAL NATURE OF PSYCHOLOGICAL SCIENCE

Constructivist thinking calls attention to the ways in which professional knowledge has an impact on the larger professional, social, and cultural contexts. Modernistic approaches assume an invisible barrier between the knowledge and these contexts. The modernistic goal of knowledge is to develop causal explanations of universal principles that allow for the accurate prediction of future events. Thus, the professional, social, and cultural ramifications of our theoretical models and theories are less important than their truth and validity. As a scientific profession, we are insulated from the responsibility of the pragmatic impact those truths might have on both the profession and the larger social culture.

When one thinks constructively, these barriers fall away. Psychological science is suddenly faced with the realization that the language of psychological science, despite its well-intentioned humanity, simultaneously limits the viability of our work and plays an important role in supporting various social structures and power hierarchies within the culture. Wittgenstein (1953/ 1958) argued that the role of language is at the center of understanding the impact of knowledge. Modernistic psychological science is the language of reification (Gergen & Kaye, 1992). It is a language that treats as real that to which it refers. A constructivist perspective views knowledge as relational. As such, it acquires meaning not from its referential base, but from its social practice. Along this line, Foucault (1977) suggested that knowledge, embodied in language, exists within social discourse. This discourse provides categories and terms that become the basis for understanding the world. Thus, the language is the basis for what is heard, what is not heard, what is said, what is not said (Terry Guyer & Rowell, Chapter 4).

We suggest that the sociopolitical nature of knowledge has implications both within the profession and within the larger culture. We believe these implications become clear when counseling knowledge is viewed as an autopoietic system of conceptual constructs with sociopolitical relevance.

Psychological Science as a Professional Narrative

There are two ways in which the constructivist notions of language and discourse apply to psychological knowledge. For example, the constructivist perspective has led some to suggest that science is governed as much by social dynamics as by the discovery of truth (Gholson, Shadish, Neimeyer, & Houts, 1989). Thus it is the informal social rules within scientific communities that determine what ultimately counts as *fact*. Thus, appropriate scientific questions, answers, and explanations depend *not* on their validity but instead on the degree to which they fit the dominant discourse of the time. Both Latour and Woolgar (1979) and Knorr-Centia (1981) conducted fascinating ethnographic studies of the social process of scientific investigation. In both cases, participant observers within natural science labs observed that what passed as fact depended on an array of social factors embedded in the social interaction among scientists. In a study of the journal referee process, Mahoney (1977) found evidence for a confirmatory bias that supported the prevailing view of theory of the time in the peer review process. It may be that the social processes that are the context of science limit and narrow our understanding of the very phenomena under investigation.

The examples provided by Rigazio-DiGilio (Chapter 5) further illustrate the impact of professional language and discourse. Modernistic attempts to understand clients, families, or counselors create categories that stereotype behavior into that which is "normal" and that which is not. When one reduces the complex phenomena of development to this point, culture, ethnicity, and gender are overlooked. These categories become, as they enter into the professional dialogue, reified into actual states and necessary processes inherent in healthy development.

Professional knowledge can also be viewed as a *system* that has the characteristics of other structurally determined units. Maturana and Varela (1979) proposed that the nature of such systems is autopoietic. Autopoietic activity is a self-generative process in which living systems continually organize and *assimilate* the "perturbations" arising from their interactions with the world. It is the existing structure of that organization that is most influential in the *reality* of the organism. An illustration from their biological research illustrates this point. Maturana and Varela suggested that only 20% of what we see is due to direct impulses from the retina of the eye. The other 80% of what is seen comes from other areas of the brain that prepare us to perceive a selective subset of possible experiences that are similar to events previously experienced. Thus, as biological beings we are better connected to ourselves than to the world. Consequently, what we perceive is more dependent on the nature of the observer than on the object observed.

Mental health professionals operate within an autopoietic system of knowledge. Training and knowledge socialize professionals into the dominant professional narrative. The counseling practitioner enters therapy with a well-developed set of theoretical narratives that carry the seal of professional approval. The theoretical language forms the conceptual system that both limits and promotes what we take to be the world, what we observe, the basis of our professional action, and the justification for professional decisions (Hanson, 1958; Wittgenstein, 1953/1958). Unfortunately, since science is seen as synonymous with truth, we sometimes fail to recognize that we are products of our own language-based narrative, as well as the more prevailing eras of human beliefs that influence all of our culture.

Knowledge systems narrow what we discover and know (Gergen, 1985). For example, in the last 40 years more than 400 different theoretical belief systems were developed (Kazdin, 1994). Each new system arose in response to the perceived inability of the previous ones to explain some certain aspect of the world. While they are seemingly different, each theoretical system posits causal structures located within individuals or their relationships that result in the problematic behavior experienced by clients. However, each of these "new" approaches is epistemological and ontologically the *same* (Cottone, 1992). Theories based on radically different assumptions have had to come from *outside* the traditional academy of psychological professionals. For example, the cybernetic notions that became the foundation of family therapy were developed by anthropologists and engineers (Hoffman, 1990).

Psychological Science as a Cultural Narrative

A number of authors have recognized the role of language and dialogue in establishing, maintaining, and defining assumptions of what is culturally good and bad (Hartmann, 1960; Gergen & Kaye, 1992). The constructivist perspective casts professional distinctions (e.g., gender, ethnicity) as representations of historically situated interchanges rather than as units of truths (Efran & Clarfield, 1993; Gergen, 1985). This line of thinking led White (1991) to argue that politics is an inherent part of any knowledge system.

Like other language systems, professional knowledge has inherent propositions of superiority, inferiority, power, and powerlessness. Accordingly, it is not a matter of whether to bring politics in, but a matter of whether we acknowledge and deal with the implications of reproducing these politics through professional knowledge (White, 1991).

Consider two examples. Gergen and Kaye (1992) among others (Ingelby, 1980; Szasz, 1973) illustrated the manner in which well-intended efforts to understand and elevate the problems of people have resulted in a language of mental disorders that sparked a progressive process of cultural *infirmity*. Since the introduction of the concept of neurosis (sometime in the mid-18th century), the categories of mental disorder have grown geometrically. The current *Diagnostic and Statistical Manual* (American Psychiatric Association, 1994), for example, contains over 200 professionally sanctioned categories of disorders. Once professionally established, these notions of disorder enter the cultural discourse and, as Gergen (1994, pp. 363) pointed out, become "what everybody knows" about human behavior. As part of common language, these reified states are available for each of us to use in the construction of everyday reality. As larger domains of behavior enter the ledger of problems subject to professional treatment, the construction of "infirmity" expands (Gergen & Kaye, 1992). The assumptions that underlie these categories produce explanations that locate people within certain cultural power relations (Fraser, 1989).

The current emphasis on gender and multiculturalism also illustrates the reciprocal connection between professional and cultural narratives. The feminist and multicultural critiques of the last two decades made an important impact on psychological science. Both raised challenges based on the notion that the dominant professional narrative supported certain narrow social positions for both women and members of minority cultures. As such, the profession supported these cultural stereotypes and marginalized these groups. It was the social voice of minority groups and their social agenda that resulted in a surge of professional interest in these issues that ultimately made a place for the dialogues of gender and culture. It is now common to see both ethnicity and gender as areas of professional practice, research, and training.

Curiously, these dialogues have become a new privileged social discourse that shows its own exclusiveness. Feminism and multiculturalism now occupy the position of another professional truth that organizes practice, research, and training around the assumption of specificity (Steenbarger & Pels, Chapter 7). For example, Patterson (1996) suggested that the current multicultural focus on diversity and culture-specific counseling has produced a narrow technique-oriented focus. Similarly, feminism, once a minority professional story, has become the dominant story of gender and as such it is a story that opposes rather than integrates other truths (Terry Guyer & Rowell, Chapter 4).

IMPLICATIONS, CHALLENGES, AND POTENTIALS
OF CONSTRUCTIVIST THINKING

The adoption of constructivist thinking has a number of broad implications. Some of these take the form of challenges while others offer potentials for future development in psychological science. We propose that three of these implications — the challenge of paradigm change, the developing role of advocacy, and the promise of inclusion and integration — are particularly worthy of consideration. The manner in which the professions involved in psychological science respond to these implications may set the future course of constructivist thinking.

The Challenge of Paradigm Change

The dialogue of deconstruction has made the limitations of our current way of thinking increasingly apparent. Maturana and Varela (1979) suggested that as such problems grow the solution lies in moving thinking to a higher logical type. This evolution is of the magnitude of a paradigm shift (Kuhn, 1970). However, a paradigm shift poses a number of professional and personal challenges. As suggested in Chapter 1 of this volume (Sexton), the constructivist paradigm represents a way of thinking that is inherently ambiguous and will require us to *be* different, not just *think* differently. It is a journey not toward new technique but toward ever-expanding epistemological positions. These positions are characterized not by stable knowing, but by ambiguous change that is multifaceted and contextually based (Lovell & McAuliffe, Chapter 13). Gergen (1994) suggested that this shift will demand a *new psychologist* who is sensitive to the relational and constructed nature of reality. Unfortunately, those intimately immersed in the stories rarely initiate such dramatic changes. Thus, the greatest challenge of constructivist thinking is resistance to change (Gergen & Kaye, 1992).

The Developing Role of Advocacy

Constructivist thinkers seek a system of meaning that grants unique insights into the social consequences of knowledge. As an entity, knowledge should be constantly challenged, redefined, and negotiated by all participants. The power that accompanies knowledge need not be viewed either as negative or as a tool of oppression. Instead, power is an inherent element of social dialogue. By considering the role that power plays in shaping consciousness, constructivism offers the potential for a new empathetic understanding of society.

One of our central tasks as constructivist thinkers is to formulate questions that expose the conditions promoting social, political, and educational advantages and disadvantages. In this deconstruction process, the constructivist thinker analyzes how assumptions conceal or distort the social, political, and economic status quo. Constructivists choose strategies that uncover those often-concealed social constructs that promote power differentials. Constructivism calls for us to rethink our current knowledge base and practices with the purpose of understanding our connection with and our professional responsibility to the larger culture. Our advocacy agency will be shaped by this knowledge and will result in a commitment to change.

The writings of this text call for us to become impassioned workers with a new way of knowing that involves passionate participation of the knower in the act of knowing. As constructivist thinkers, we seek insight into how our assumptions and the assumptions of others came to be constructed. We seek to learn about our own thinking. As an internal dialogue, constructivist thinking forces the attention to questions that lead to innovation, new insights, and eventually to new thinking and social justice. As advocates, we are interested in finding ways through which the world can be a more just and equitable place to live. Freedom is a matter of a certain kind of caring about ourselves and for the world, a caring that entails a willingness to expand our beliefs and practices, to shift the boundaries of our thoughts and feelings in order to alleviate the suffering of others. Constructivists can see the importance of moving toward a world where people could work and learn together, a world where inhabitants establish economic and social conditions that make possible individual freedom and social empowerment.

The Promise of Inclusion and Integration

Constructivism is also about the blurring of boundaries between the constructed distinctions in the world. It is about the adoption a complex, inclusive, and integrated epistemological stance. It seems that when we are able to embrace a more inclusive context, elements that previously appeared in opposition can be systematically integrated (Efran & Clarfield, 1993). Mahoney (1991) proposed that constructivist metatheory has emerged as a particularly promising candidate for the exploration and integration of our various and seemingly diverse psychological theories. Constructivist thinking has already begun to pull together areas within psychology such as cognitive, developmental, and linguistic psychology (Agnew & Brown, 1989). The unification potential is probably no more evident than in understanding the process of counseling and behavior change. Lyddon (1993) suggested that constructivist approaches may significantly speed up the recent trend in identifying the fundamental principles of change common to all forms of effective therapy. Hoshmand and Martin (1995) suggest, for example, that it is an increasing pluralism (combination of experimental and qualitative methods) and the flexible use of these methods of discovery and verification that will point the way toward understanding.

CONCLUSION: THE PARADOXICAL NATURE OF CONSTRUCTIVIST THINKING

The nature of constructivist thinking is paradoxical. On the one hand, it is an individually focused, phenomena-driven perspective that acknowledges the unique meaning and reality of the subject under consideration. One the other hand, constructivism is systematic and does not mean the abandonment of a systematic stance for undisciplined subjectivism (Hoshmand & Polkinghorne, 1992).

Equally paradoxical is that while constructivist approaches to practice, research, and education now seem to offer a viable *new* paradigm, they are but one of many perspectives. Considered within their place in the broader landscape of thinking paradigms, it seems that the postmodern critique and the ensuing constructivist paradigm are dialectically related to the eras of thinking that came before (see Chapter 1). Without a modern tradition, constructivism would not have been born. In the future, constructivist thinking is likely to provide the same stimulus for another change. As such, it is likely to be challenged and deconstructed. Along the way another paradigm is likely to come about with a new perspective with which to advance and further our understanding of psychological change, systematic inquiry, and professional training. Constructivist thinkers embrace these transitions as important and natural extensions of the eras of human believing.

REFERENCES

Agnew, N. M., & Brown, J. L. (1989). Foundations for a model of knowing: I. Constructivist reality. *Canadian Psychology, 30,* 152–167.

American Psychiatric Association. (1994). *Diagnostic and statistical manual of mental disorders* (4th ed.). Washington, DC: Author.

Basseches, M. (1984). *Dialectical thinking and adult development.* Norwood, NJ: Ablex.

Beutler, L. E., & Hill, C. E. (1992). Process and outcome research in treatment of adult victims of childhood sexual abuse: Methodological issues. Special Section: Adult survivors of childhood sexual abuse. *Journal of Consulting and Clinical Psychology, 60,* 204–212.

Cottone, R. R. (1992). *Theories and paradigms of counseling and psychotherapy.* Boston: Allyn and Bacon.

Efran, J. S., & Clarfield, L. E. (1993). Context: The fulcrum of constructivist psychotherapy. *Journal of Cognitive Psychotherapy, 7,* 173–182.

Foucault, M. (1977). *Discipline and punish.* London: Allen Lane.

Fraser, N. (1989). *Unruly practices: Power discourse, and gender in contemporary social theory.* Cambridge: Polity Press.

Gergen, K. (1985). The social constructionist movement in modern psychology. *American Psychologist, 40,* 266–273.

Gergen, K. (1994). *Toward transformation in social knowledge* (3rd ed.). Thousand Oaks, CA: Sage.

Gergen, K. J., & Kaye, J. (1992). Beyond narrative in the negotiation of therapeutic meaning. In S. McNamee & K. J. Gergen (Eds.), *Therapy as social construction* (pp. 166–185). Newbury Park, CA: Sage.

Gholson, B., Shadish, W. R., Jr., Neimeyer, R. A., & Houts, A. C. (Eds.). (1989). *Psychology of science: Contributions to metascience.* New York: Cambridge University Press.

Hanson, N. R. (1958). *Patterns of discovery.* London: Cambridge University Press.

Hartmann, H. (1960). *Psychoanalysis and moral values.* New York: International Universities Press.

Hoffman, L. (1990). Constructing realities: An art of lenses. *Family Process, 29*(1), 1–12.

Hoshmand, L. T., & Martin, J. (1995). Concluding comments on therapeutic psychology and the science of practice. In L. T. Hoshmand & J. Martin (Eds.), *Research as praxis* (pp. 235–241). New York: Teachers College Press.

Hoshmand, L. T., & Polkinghorne, D. E. (1992). Redefining the science-practice relationship and professional training. *American Psychologist, 47,* 55–66.

Ingelby, D. (1980). Understanding mental illness. In D. Ingelby (Ed.), *Critical Psychiatry.* New York: Random House.

Kazdin, A. E. (1994). Methodology, design, and evaluation in psychotherapy research. In A. E. Bergin & S. L. Garfield (Eds.), *Handbook of psychotherapy and behavior change* (pp. 19–71). New York: Wiley.

Knorr-Centia, K. D. (1981). *The manufacture of knowledge: An essay on the constructivist and contextual nature of science.* Oxford: Pergamon Press.

Kuhn T. S. (1970). *The structure of scientific revolutions.* Chicago: University of Chicago Press.

Latour, B., & Woolgar, S. (1979). *Laboratory life: The social construction of scientific facts.* Beverly Hills, CA: Sage.

Lyddon, W. J. (1993). Developmental constructivism: An integrative framework for psychotherapy practice. *Journal of Cognitive Psychotherapy, 7*(3), 217–224.

Mahoney, M. J. (1977). Publication prejudices: An experimental study of confirmatory bias in the peer review system. *Cognitive Therapy and Research, 1,* 161–175.

Mahoney, M. J. (1991). *Human change processes: The scientific foundations of psychotherapy.* New York: Basic Books.

Maturana, H. R. (1990). Science and daily life: The ontology of scientific explanations. In W. Krohn, G. Kuppers, & H. Nowotny (Eds.), *Self organization: Portrait of a scientific revolution* (pp. 12–35). Boston: Kluner.

Maturana, H. R., & Varela, F. J. (1979). *The tree of knowledge: The biological roots of human understanding.* Boston: New Science Library.

Patterson, C. H. (1996). Multicultural counseling: From diversity to universality. *Journal of Counseling and Development, 74,* 227–231.

Rennie, D. L. (1994). Clients' deference in psychotherapy. *Journal of Counseling Psychology, 41,* 427–437.

Szasz, T. S. (1973). *The second sin.* New York: Anchor Press/Doubleday.

Sexton, T. L. (1996). The relevance of counseling outcome research: Current trends and practical implications. *Journal of Counseling and Development, 74,* 590–600.

White, M. (1991). Deconstruction and therapy. *Dulwich Centre Newsletter,* 21–40.

Wittgenstein, L. (1958). *Philosophical investigations* (3rd ed.) (G. Anscombe, Trans.). New York: Macmillan. (Original work published 1953)

About the Editors and the Contributors

THE EDITORS

Barbara L. Griffin is Professor of Counseling and Educational Leadership at Clemson University, where she coordinates the Student Affairs major. She received her doctoral training at Florida State University. She teaches counseling theory, techniques, and student development in higher education. Her research interests lie in the areas of gender equity and student developmental theory.

Thomas L. Sexton is Associate Professor in the Department of Counseling and Educational Psychology at the University of Nevada, Las Vegas. He received his doctoral degree from Florida State University in counseling psychology. He is a licensed psychologist and teaches in the Marriage and Family Counseling Program. His research interests focus on the efficacy of counseling and the interactional nature of the counseling relationship. He serves on the editoral board of both *Counselor Education and Supervision* and the Counseling and Development series of Teachers College Press.

THE CONTRIBUTORS

M. Harry Daniels is Professor and Chair, Department of Counselor Education, University of Florida, Gainesville, FL.

Wendy Drewery is Senior Lecturer in Education Studies at the University of Waikato in Hamilton, New Zealand, where she teaches in the Counseling and Health Development Programs at the graduate level, and Human Development at the undergraduate level. Her first degrees were in philosophy and her Ph.D. dissertation was on women's decision making at mid-life. Her research and writing span several areas, including social constructionism in counseling and ethical decision making, feminist theory, aging, and public health.

Jay S. Efran is Professor of Psychology and Director of the Psychological Services Center at Temple University, in Philadelphia, where he has also served as Director of Clinical Training. He received his Ph.D. (1963) in clinical psychology from Ohio State University. He is the co-author of *Language,*

Structure and Change: Frameworks of Meaning in Psychotherapy (with M. D. Lukens and R. J. Lukens, 1990), and he has written extensively on issues of contextualism and constructivism.

Jerald R. Forster is Professor in Educational Psychology at the University of Washington in Seattle. He is the coordinator of Counselor Education Programs and he also directs the Dependable Strengths Project. He received his doctoral degree in counseling psychology from the University of Minnesota. Currently he trains school counselors and the supervisors of counselors. His primary research focus is on the facilitation of personal development. He is currently developing a rationale and framework for facilitating adaptability in postmodern society.

Don E. Gordon is a research assistant at the Center for Research in Human Development and Education at Temple University.

Linda Terry Guyer is Associate Professor and Program Director of the Marriage, Family and Child Counseling Program at San Diego State University, Department of Counseling and School Psychology. Her doctorate was in education.

Richard L. Hayes is Professor of Counseling and Human Development at the University of Georgia, Athens. He is a Harvard College graduate and received his master's and doctorate in counseling psychology from Boston University. His teaching and research are focused on the application of developmental psychology to counseling practice and the creation of collaborative social organizations in the promotion of human development. He has published more than 50 articles and/or book chapters on counseling and human development.

Chris Lovell is Assistant Professor in the Department of Counseling and Educational Leadership at Old Dominion University. He received his Ed.D. from the American University. He is a member of the board of directors of the Society for Research in Adult Development. His research interests are in the area of counselor development and empathy.

Garrett J. McAuliffe is Associate Professor in the Department of Counseling and Educational Leadership at Old Dominion University. He received his Ed.D. from the University of Massachusetts. His research interests are in the areas of cognitive development in adults, multicultural awareness, career decision making in adulthood, and counseling student development.

Gerald Monk is Senior Lecturer and Director of the Counselor Education Program at the University of Waikato, New Zealand. He gained a master's degree and postgraduate diploma in educational psychology at the University of Otango, New Zealand. He introduced narrative therapy into the master's program at Waikato in 1993 and this has now become the primary modality in counselor training. He continues to work in private practice and to engage in both narrative mediation and narrative counseling.

Mary Lee Nelson is Assistant Professor in the Educational Psychology Department at the University of Washington in Seattle. She received her doctorate from the University or Oregon. She has published numerous articles on counseling supervision and the nature of the supervision process. Her work has led naturally to the study of reflectivity in supervision and participants' phenomenological experiences of supervision.

Susan Allstetter Neufeldt is Lecturer and Director of the Ray E. Hosford Clinic in the Counseling/Clinical/School Psychology Program within the Graduate School of Education at the University of California, Santa Barbara. She has written numerous articles and one text on supervision practice. She teaches a seminar and practicum for doctoral-level supervisors each year according to the social constructivist principles described in this chapter.

Ramona Oppenheim is a doctoral student in the Department of Counseling and Human Services at the University of Georgia in Athens, GA.

R. Vance Peavy is Professor Emeritus at the University of Victoria. He is now a resident scholar at NorthStar Research in Victoria, BC, Canada, where he is a writer-researcher and mentor in counseling theory, research, and practice.

Laurie C. Pels is a graduate student in the Department of Counseling and Human Services at Syracuse University.

Karen Poulin is a staff psychologist at the University of Missouri in Columbia. Her background in symbolic interactionism and dimensional analysis prepared her to conduct a qualitative study of supervision participants' perceptions of their supervision experiences. She continues to conduct qualitative inquiry and serves as a consultant to qualitative researchers at the University of Missouri.

Sandra A. Rigazio-DiGilio is Associate Professor in the COAMFTE-accredited master's and doctoral marriage and family therapy programs at the University of Connecticut, Storrs. Additionally, she holds a joint appointment in the Department of Psychiatry. She received her doctoral degree from the Counseling Psychology Program at the University of Massachusetts. She is a licensed psychologist, a licensed marriage and family therapist, and an AAMFT approved supervisor. She is currently an associate editor for the *Journal of Mental Health Counseling*. Her research interests focus on the integration of human and systemic development theories into mainstream individual, family, and network therapy, supervision, and training.

Lonnie L. Rowell is Assistant Professor in the Counseling Program in the School of Education at the University of San Diego. He received his doctoral training at the University of Southern California. He co-facilitated men's consciousness-raising groups in the 1970s and 1980s and is currently a group leader for men's domestic violence groups.

Brett N. Steenbarger is Assistant Professor of Psychiatry and Director of Student Counseling at the SUNY Health Science Center in Syracuse. He is also Assistant Adjunct Professor of Counseling and Human Services at Syracuse University. He teaches coursework in brief therapy, multicultural counseling, human development, and mental health counseling at both institutions and has served as practice manager for a multispecialty behavioral group practice at the Health Science Center.

Carlene M. Wentworth is a licensed professional counselor in private practice, with a specialty in children and adolescents. She holds an adjunct professorship at Clemson University, where she received her M.Ed. in 1992. Her background is in anthropology and sociology. A musician, she is developing therapeutic metaphors for children that combine story and music. She is currently completing an Ed.S. in counseling at the University of South Carolina.

William M. Wentworth is Professor of Sociology at Clemson University. He received his Ph.D. from the University of Virginia in 1978. He has written numerous articles and books, primarily from a social constructionist perspective. His interests include the sociology of religion, human emotions, and theory.

Lyle J. White is Associate Professor and Coordinator of the Counselor Education Program, Department of Educational Psychology and Special Education, Southern Illinois University at Carbondale.

John Winslade is Senior Lecturer in Education Studies at the University of Waikato in Hamilton, New Zealand, where he teaches in the Counseling and Health Development Programs.

Index

Freud and the Politics of Psychoanalysis